Psychological Aspects of Functioning, Disability, and Health

David B. Peterson, PhD, is a licensed Clinical Psychologist, Certified Rehabilitation Counselor, and Rehabilitation Psychologist with expertise in adjustment to the emotional and physical consequences of disability, and coping with and confronting environmental and attitudinal barriers, stress, and related social adjustment. His evaluation expertise includes comprehensive assessment of biopsychosocial functioning, activity limitations, participation restrictions, and environmental barriers and facilitators to functioning. For two decades, he has provided various aspects of psychiatric rehabilitation services and currently serves as a medical expert for the Social Security disability adjudication and review process.

Dr. Peterson has been affiliated with several of our nation's top graduate programs in rehabilitation counseling and psychology, and has provided significant university, national, and international service to the rehabilitation counseling and psychology communities. His research interests include the clinical implementation of the *International Classification of Functioning, Disability and Health* (*ICF*) and computer-based training in clinical problem solving and ethical decision-making. He has contributed to 45 scholarly products and 43 state and national presentations at professional conferences, has directed six research/training grants totaling over $1.7 million, and is currently a member of four editorial boards for peer-reviewed journals.

Psychological Aspects of Functioning, Disability, and Health

DAVID B. PETERSON, PhD

SPRINGER PUBLISHING COMPANY

NEW YORK

Springer Publishing Company, LLC
11 West 42nd Street
New York, NY 10036
www.springerpub.com

Acquisitions Editor: Sheri W. Sussman
Senior Editor: Rose Mary Piscitelli
Project Manager: Ragavia Ramakrishnan
Cover design: Mimi Flow
Composition: S4Carlisle Publishing Services

ISBN: 978-0-8261-2344-2
E-book ISBN: 978-0-8261-2346-6

10 11 12 13/ 5 4 3 2 1

The author and the publisher of this Work have made every effort to use sources believed to be reliable to provide information that is accurate and compatible with the standards generally accepted at the time of publication. The author and publisher shall not be liable for any special, consequential, or exemplary damages resulting, in whole or in part, from the readers' use of, or reliance on, the information contained in this book. The publisher has no responsibility for the persistence or accuracy of URLs for external or third-party Internet Web sites referred to in this publication and does not guarantee that any content on such Web sites is, or will remain, accurate or appropriate.

Library of Congress Cataloging-in-Publication Data
Peterson, David B.
   Psychological aspects of functioning, disability, and health / David B. Peterson.
      p. cm.
   ISBN   978-0-8261-2344-2
   1. Clinical health psychology. 2. International classification of functioning, disability and health. 3. Diagnostic and statistical manual of mental disorders. I. Title.
   R726.7.P48 2010
   616.001'9—dc22
                                                                              2010021857

Printed in the United States of America by Hamilton Printing

*T*o my mother, June Peterson, for her unconditional support and love; to Nancy Sanders for creating opportunities and for a lifetime of friendship and inspiration; to Maxine Pritchard Miller for love and support during the lean college years; to Peter Nathan for encouraging me to find my own voice in scholarship; to my colleagues at the University of Wisconsin-Madison, the University of Iowa, New York University, Illinois Institute of Technology, and California State University, Los Angeles, for affording me time and treasure for my work to grow; and to Oscar Ramon Villasmil for 10 years of love, support, and a most valuable friendship.

Contents

Prologue

I first learned about the *International Classification of Functioning, Disability and Health* (*ICF*; WHO, 2001) during the last academic year of my tenure at the University of Iowa in 1998, where I began my academic career as an assistant professor in rehabilitation education. At that time, the *ICF* was called the *International Classification System of Functioning and Disability; Beta-2 draft* (*ICIDH-2*; WHO, 1999). The *ICIDH-2* held great interest for me as I learned of its progressive conceptualization of disability within the context of health and functioning. The *ICF*'s conceptualization of disability was similar to that presented in much of the rehabilitation literature that I consumed up to that point in my reading and was consistent with my identity as a Certified Rehabilitation Counselor (credentialed in 1993), Licensed Mental Health Counselor (1997), and licensed clinical rehabilitation psychologist (1999). Because of the *ICF*'s developmental history, its concepts and assumptions reflect the holistic values and philosophies espoused in rehabilitation education: the dignity and worth of all people, and the inclusion of people with illness and disabilities in society to the fullest extent possible (Frank & Elliott, 2000; Frank, Rosenthal, & Caplan, 2009; Peterson & Rosenthal, 2005a; Riggar & Maki, 2004; Scherer et al., 2004).

As I embarked on my career as a student of psychology in 1988, I was quite unaware that 8 years prior, the original version of the *ICF* was first published as the *International Classification of Impairments, Disabilities, and Handicaps* (*ICIDH*; WHO, 1980). It was during the late 1970s that the World Health Organization (WHO) first endeavored to create a functional classification complement to their diagnostic classification system, the *International Statistical Classification of Diseases and Related Health Problems*, currently in its Tenth Revision (*ICD-10*; WHO, 1992). The *ICIDH* and later *ICF* were designed to be used with the *ICD* to create a more complete classificatory picture of an individual's health and functioning.

Subsequent to learning about the *ICIDH-2*, in 1999 I attended a training session for psychologists interested in participating in the field trials for the beta version of the *ICF*'s predecessor, the *ICIDH-2*. As a result, I had the good fortune of being a U.S. participant in the revision process for the *ICF*, among participants from 65 countries (WHO, 2001, p. 263). In addition to applying the *ICIDH-2* to clinical practice, participants also contributed, through their responses to critical survey questions, to the consensus data used in addressing key conceptual issues at that point in the *ICF*'s development.

During my tenure as director of the Rehabilitation Education Graduate Programs at New York University, the current version of the *ICF* was published in 2001. In association with its release, I was invited by the Practice Directorate of the American Psychological Association to participate in the alpha drafting efforts for the *Procedural Manual and Guide for a Standardized Application* of the *ICF*, a joint effort between the American Psychological Association (APA) and the World Health Organization (WHO). It was during this effort that my familiarity with the nuances of the *ICIDH-2* increased exponentially, and along with it my interest in seeing the *ICF* become widely adopted in international health care endeavors.

In an attempt to share my enthusiasm for what the *ICF* was and its prospects for improving health and health-related care for people with disabilities, during my tenure as associate professor in the Institute of Psychology within the Illinois Institute of Technology, I contributed to the publication of several conceptual overviews of the *ICF* for two rehabilitation-related journals (special issues referenced below). I also contributed to several chapters in seminal reference texts (also noted below). I presented some of this work at peer-reviewed and invited national and international professional meetings in counseling and psychology. Consequently, the idea of writing this text seemed a natural extension of my previous work to promote the clinical implementation of the *ICF*.

During my training in psychology and rehabilitation, I benefited from significant clinical experience in acute-care psychiatric hospitals in a Midwest urban center. I learned about mental illness and its treatment under the supervision of psychiatrists, psychologists, psychiatric nurses, social workers, and mental health counselors. My internship experience as a rehabilitation counselor provided experience in counseling people who were deaf. My practicum and internship experiences in psychology provided me with experience in a subacute and postacute rehabilitation hospital and care network, which provided me with a very broad exposure to physical and psychiatric rehabilitation. Finally, my residency as a psychologist resident focused on working with people with a combination of developmental, physical, and psychiatric disabilities. In the end, psychiatric rehabilitation occupied the majority of my clinical experience.

This text therefore focuses on mental disorders specifically, rather than disability in general, and the use of the *ICF* in working with people who have psychiatric diagnoses. The text serves as a useful overview of the *ICF* in the context of the *Diagnostic and Statistical Manual of Mental Disorders, Fourth Edition, Text Revision (DSM-IV-TR*; American Psychiatric Association, 2000).

I have been most fortunate in my career to have had remarkable opportunities that contributed to the prospects for my writing this text. Having been an assistant and associate professor in four nationally ranked programs in rehabilitation, I have worked with and been mentored by remarkable scholars in rehabilitation and psychologist education, and learned a great deal from the remarkable students attracted to these academies. Three of my university appointments were in the largest urban centers in the United States (New York City, Los Angeles, and Chicago), and so as a licensed clinical psychologist specializing in disability and function, I worked with remarkably diverse individuals from all walks of life and with all manner of life challenges.

Over 20 years of clinical work with people with disabilities, and 16 years of research experience as a rehabilitation counselor and psychologist educator, have afforded me the privilege of serving as a clinical psychologist medical expert for the Office of Disability Adjudication and Review (ODAR) for the Social Security Administration. Reviewing hundreds of psychological case files has given me a very unique opportunity to reflect on the work of others' in psychology and psychiatry and to apply the conceptual framework of the *ICF* in formulating my opinions that inform the ODAR adjudication process. Specifically, my opinions were informed by the *DSM-IV-TR* and the *ICF*'s conceptual framework. For hundreds of cases I have reviewed to date, both diagnostic and functional data were considered within the environmental context. I believe that these data and their reciprocal relationships are critical to consider in order to understand the impact of activity limitations and participation restrictions on an individual's functioning. My ongoing review of cases within the *DSM-IV-TR* and *ICF* framework encourages me regarding prospects for the *ICF* to inform our understanding of mental disorders and related functioning.

Since working with the *ICIDH-2* and now the *ICF*, I have had the opportunity to work with very talented scholars in counseling, rehabilitation, occupational therapy, physical therapy, speech language pathology, and psychology education. These collaborations have made a great impact on my thinking about the *ICF* and ultimately the content of this text, and so I extend my utmost gratitude to those who worked with me on *ICF*-related projects (in alphabetical order): Susanne M. Bruyère, Lynn F. Bufka, Tim Elliott, Robert Glueckauf, Judy A. Hawley, Debra Homa, John W. Jacobson, John F. Kosciulek, Jayne B. Lux, Kim MacDonald-Wilson, Irmo Marini,

Randolph L. Mowry, Elias Mpofu, Peter Nathan, Patricia B. Nemec, Thomas Oakland, Geoffrey M. Reed, David A. Rosenthal, Caren L. Sax, Marcia J. Scherer, Julie Smart, Donna Fisher Smiley, Susan Stark, Mark Stebnicki, Travis T. Threats, Christine Trask, and Sara A. Van Looy. Finally, a special expression of appreciation and thanks is due to Sheri W. Sussman, Senior Vice President, Editorial, for Springer Publishing, for her remarkable assistance with the conceptualization of this text and tremendous support along the way to its completion.

Foreword

This is an important book, and it conveys a timely message. Written by David Peterson, trained both in rehabilitation psychology and clinical psychology, the book describes and evaluates two influential taxonomies, the *International Classification of Functioning, Disability and Health (ICF:* WHO, 2001) and the *Diagnostic and Statistical Manual of Mental Disorders, 4th Edition, Text Revision (DSM-IV-TR:* APA, 2000). Peterson's book provides compelling support for his conviction that the *ICF*, heretofore of greatest interest to rehabilitation psychologists and their colleagues, and the *DSM*, of primary appeal to clinical psychologists, psychiatrists, and other mental health professionals, work best when used together rather than separately.

As it happens, I was involved very early in an American Psychological Association committee chaired by Stanley Berent of the University of Michigan to help develop the *International Classification of Impairments, Disabilities, and Handicaps: ICIDH* (WHO, 1980), *ICF*'s forebear, as a possible alternative to the *DSM*, then and now owned and largely operated by psychiatrists. Although the committee consisted almost entirely of clinical psychologists, its members saw the *ICIDH*'s potential as a means to capture the psychological, physical, and behavioral disabilities associated with mental disorder in a manner that would avoid many of the psychiatric influences and assumptions implicit in the *DSM*. For several reasons, unfortunately, that effort came to naught. Happily, David Peterson and a diverse group of psychologists became involved later in a more successful effort substantially to convert the *ICIDH* into the *ICF* and to develop a user's guide to the *ICF*.

DSM-I was published in 1952 by the American Psychiatric Association as the first truly national nomenclature of mental disorders. The instrument was designed to be a nomenclature for mental disorders on which psychiatrists could agree, thereby facilitating communication within psychiatry and among mental health professionals. Successive editions and versions of the *DSM*, published in 1968, 1980, 1987, 1994, and the current *DSM-IV-TR* (2000), have included substantially more diagnostic syndromes, greater detail in diagnostic criteria, and substantially greater empirical data supporting syndromes and criteria. Amply praised and criticized, the *DSM* has succeeded in creating a common language used by psychiatrists, clinical psychologists, and other mental health professionals called upon to describe patients' psychopathology, plan treatment, and undertake research on etiology, prognosis, and course.

What *DSM-IV-TR* was not designed to do, and cannot in fact do, is to describe the functional impairments, abilities, and activities associated with psychopathology. As a consequence, for most of the history of the *DSM*, clinicians were left to determine how best to characterize profound differences in functionality among patients with the same or similar *DSM* diagnoses. Some patients who suffer from a major depressive disorder, for example, might have little or no problem continuing to work, attend to their families, and make appropriate decisions in their lives. Other patients with the same diagnosis, however, might be so disabled by this serious mental disorder that institutionalization of some kind may be necessary because they cannot manage on their own. These sorts of real differences in function have real consequences for prognosis and treatment planning. In the absence of a reliable means of characterizing them, clinicians have not been able to undertake research on their role and influence and could not depend upon them for predictive purposes.

ICF was developed by WHO to accompany the WHO's *International Statistical Classification of Diseases and Related Health Problems* (*ICD-10*: WHO, 1992). It is designed to provide information on the broad array of disease and health conditions categorized in *ICD-10*. Emphasizing the importance of functional health as well as disability, the *ICF* describes health and health-related states from the perspective of the body (by classifying body functions and body structures associated with health and disease states as specified in *ICD-10*) as well as from the perspective of the individual and society (by classifying activities and participation associated with health and disease states as specified in *ICD-10*). To this time, the *ICF* has been valued largely by rehabilitation psychologists, nursing personnel, occupational therapists, and physical therapists and their colleagues. All of these professions have historically taken a biopsychosocial view of health and disability.

What the *ICF* is not designed to do is to categorize and classify the mental disorders. That is the role of those chapters of the *ICD-10* that detail mental disorders, as it is of the *DSM-IV-TR* (2000), the taxonomy of mental disorders currently used most widely in the United States.

As complementary instruments, the *ICF* and the *DSM* used together-permit a level of diagnostic detail and functional description of patients previously unavailable. The use of the two instruments in tandem is an exciting prospect. Not only will using these instruments in this way help in treatment planning for individual patients, it will open up the prospect of research that will for the first time reflect differences among diagnostic syndromes in the diversity and nature of their potential to impair and, thereby, to affect prognosis and course.

Human nature being what it is, and as promising as this product of complementary use of these instruments sounds, is it reasonable to hope that busy professionals will take the time and make the effort to come up to speed on a taxonomy with which they are largely unfamiliar? Will rehabilitation psychologists and others involved in the rehabilitation domain take the time and expend the effort to learn the complexities of *DSM* so they can more fully describe patients with functional impairments and disabilities who also suffer from mental disorder? Will clinical psychologists and psychiatrists, busy with their practices or their teaching and research, be willing to learn how to use the *ICF* so they will be able to add dimension, context, and specificity to their *DSM* diagnoses? The chances of this expenditure of effort will be enhanced if the drafters of *DSM-5* dispense with the multiaxial system, a decision rumored to be under consideration. The multiaxial system, introduced in 1980 in *DSM-III*, has proven disappointing because it is difficult to use, hasn't been much used as a result and, hence, hasn't been terribly helpful. That being so, diagnosticians may see in the *ICF* a more reliable and comprehensive alternative for describing the infinite variations in functionality of patients with mood disorder, personality disorder, or anxiety disorder, conditions that manifest themselves in countless and various forms. If the *ICF* enables differentiation among those forms, it would represent an advance for research as well as treatment.

But perhaps I have put the cart before the horse. David Peterson has given us a template for learning the *ICF* and the *DSM* and then using them together to create substantially fuller, more useful descriptions of our patients. I can only hope that rehabilitation psychology, psychiatry, and clinical psychology, as well as the other disciplines for which *ICF* and *DSM* are relevant, will take advantage of Peterson's prescience and hard work. Then we'll be best able to determine what comes next.

Peter E. Nathan, PhD
Distinguished Professor of Psychology and
Public Health Emeritus
University of Iowa Foundation
Iowa City, IA

REFERENCES

American Psychological Association (APA). (1952). *Diagnostic and statistical manual of mental disorders (DSM-I)*. Washington, DC: Author.
American Psychological Association (APA). (1980). *Diagnostic and statistical manual of mental disorders (DSM-III)* (3rd ed.). Washington, DC: Author.

American Psychological Association (APA). (2000). *Diagnostic and statistical manual of mental disorders (DSM-IV-TR)* (4th ed., text revision). Washington, DC: Author.

World Health Organization (WHO). (1980). *International classification of impairments, disabilities and handicaps (ICIDH)*. Geneva: Author.

World Health Organization (WHO). (2001). *International classification of functioning, disability and health (ICF)*. Geneva: Author.

World Health Organization (WHO). (1992). *International statistical classification of disease and related health problems (ICD-10)* (10th revision). Geneva: Author.

Preface

This text explores the psychological aspects of functioning, disability, and health as conceptualized by the World Health Organization's *International Classification of Functioning, Disability and Health* (*ICF*; WHO, 2001) and disorders as diagnosed using the *Diagnostic and Statistical Manual of Mental Disorders, Fourth Edition, Text Revision* (*DSM-IV-TR*; APA, 2000). Diagnostic information complementary to the medical model of mental health care is reviewed within the context of a functioning and health framework as conceptualized in the *ICF*, which is more consistent with contemporary biopsychosocial approaches to mental health service provision (Peterson & Elliott, 2008; Peterson, 2009). The text highlights the importance of the *ICF*'s publication in 2001 as the latest addition to the WHO Family of Health Classifications and the utility of using a biopsychosocial, functional approach to integrate information on mental health, diagnoses, intervention targeting, treatment, and treatment outcomes. In addition to reviewing the *ICF* as an important development in health care, the text will also be a useful survey of psychopathology as classified in the *DSM-IV-TR*.

Readers will learn the utility of the *ICF*'s biopsychosocial approach for conceptualizing and classifying mental health functioning (body functions and structures), disability (activity limitations and participation restrictions), environmental barriers, and facilitators; collaborating with the person being assessed in determining these factors (personal factors), targeting interventions, and evaluating treatment efficacy. The text will offer an initial cross-walking effort between the *ICF* and the *DSM-IV-TR*, exploring the nexus between the conceptual frameworks of the two classification systems.

This text will be useful to any helping professional learning about mental health and illness (rehabilitation counselors, psychologists, psychiatrists, social workers, mental health counselors, marriage and family therapists, nurses, occupational therapists, physical therapists, speech language pathologists, and other rehabilitation health professionals). The text will primarily serve master's and doctoral-level courses addressing the diagnosis and treatment of mental disorders, psychiatric rehabilitation, or the medical and psychosocial aspects of disability. It may also be appropriate for upper-division and advanced undergraduate courses in abnormal or clinical psychology.

In Part I of the text, the focus is on the *ICF* and its predecessors. Preview questions will help prepare the reader for each chapter's content. Clear descriptions of key terms will be provided as concepts are developed within the text. Content of chapters will be illustrated with engaging clinical examples, as well as references for further reading, including journals, textbooks, and Web-based resources. The *ICF* will be frequently referenced and is strongly recommended as a companion resource to Part I of the text.

In Part II of the text, the *DSM-IV-TR* is presented, with some discussion of its relation to the *ICF*. Features similar to Part I will be employed, and within each diagnostic group reviewed the text will directly reference the relevant sections of the *DSM-IV-TR*. Heuristics of the diagnostic groups will be presented without replicating the detail of the *DSM* itself. Part II is designed to be read in tandem with the *DSM* itself.

In Part III of the text, the nexus of the *ICF* and *DSM-IV-TR* are explored. The conceptual frameworks of each system will be compared and contrasted, diagnostic heuristics will be associated with first and second levels of the *ICF* coding system, including relevant body structures (locales in the brain, related endocrine functioning and their *ICF* correlates) and body functions, activity limitations and participation restrictions, and contextual factors (environmental and personal factors).

GOALS OF THE TEXT

1. Develop knowledge and understanding of mental health functioning and impairment based on the emerging international model of health and functioning, the *ICF*, and the diagnostic classification, the *DSM-IV-TR*.
2. Apply the *ICF* conceptual framework to planning mental health assessment and related interventions.
3. Analyze the effect of mental illness and related interventions on activity limitations and participation restrictions and the role of environmental and personal factors in this complex interaction.
4. Review an initial cross-walking effort linking diagnostic information from the *DSM-IV-TR* with the *ICF*'s classification of functioning, disability, and health, with the goal of linking diagnostic information with relevant functional classifications within the *ICF*.

In a text that introduces the *ICF*, it is difficult to avoid being redundant with other similar publications. A variety of reviews have discussed and critiqued the *ICF* (see volume 50 of *Rehabilitation Psychology*, 2005; volume 19 of *Rehabilitation Education*, 2005; and volume 25 of *Disability & Rehabilitation*, 2003). Several book chapters have been written for seminal handbooks in the counseling and psychology professions (Peterson, Mpofu, & Oakland, 2010; Peterson, 2009; Peterson & Elliott, 2008). These publications notwithstanding, any explanation of the *ICF* can and should be referenced back to the *ICF* itself (WHO, 2001).

In order to avoid awkward, frequent, and redundant references, and to improve clarity and style of this text, the descriptions of the *ICF* are presented in a narrative format, within this referenced context and without endless repetitive citations. It is also important to note that the brief overview presented here does not substitute for studying the *ICF* in its entirety, including related literature, and attending training provided by those who are expert in its use (Reed et al., 2005, 2008).

In a text that provides an overview of a system as large and complex as the *DSM-IV-TR* (nearly 1,000 pages in length), opportunity for error is ample; responsibility for error is mine, and corrections or feedback are enthusiastically welcomed. As with the approach to writing about the *ICF*, the same holds true for the overview of the *DSM-IV-TR* presented here. Endless quotes and citations are avoided for the sake of clarity and style, and all mention of the *DSM-IV-TR* is referenced directly to the text itself (APA, 2000). Page number intervals are indicated for each section of the *DSM-IV-TR* reviewed. It is important to note that the overview presented here is no substitute for thorough training and review of the *DSM-IV-TR* under the supervision of a qualified professional.

PART I

The *International Classification of Functioning, Disability, and Health (ICF)*

CHAPTER 1

Importance of the *ICF*

PREVIEW QUESTIONS

1. How prevalent is disability?
2. Who developed the *ICF*, and what is its purpose?
3. What is the relevance of the *ICF*?

A SIGNIFICANT DEVELOPMENT

The *International Classification of Functioning, Disability, and Health* (*ICF*, World Health Organization, 2001a) was published in 2001 as the latest addition to the World Health Organization (WHO) Family of Classifications, as a new taxonomy of health and functioning that promotes the use of universal classifications of function that are complementary to the use of diagnostic information in health care service provision. The *ICF* was developed as a complement to its companion classification, the *International Statistical Classification of Diseases and Related Health Problems, Tenth Revision* (*ICD-10*; World Health Organization, 1992). The *ICD* provides an etiological classification of health conditions (e.g., diseases, disorders, and injuries), whereas the *ICF* provides information on functioning associated with a broad array of health conditions.

The *ICF* was created through an international effort as a means to document the importance of functional health as well as disability. The *ICF* "provides a framework and standard language for the description of health and health related states from different perspectives: The perspective of the body (classification of body functions and of body structures) and the perspective of the individual and the society (classification of activities and participation)" (De Kleijn-De Vrankrijker, 2003, p. 561).

Planning treatments and documenting outcomes of interventions from the body, individual, and societal perspectives can improve the quality of

3

health care service provision and consequently the quality of life of people with disabilities as well as increase the participation of individuals with disabilities in society (Peterson & Threats, 2005). The *ICF* has the potential to improve health care in the broadest sense, while providing specific benefit to people with disabilities, including mental disorders, by using a universal, culturally sensitive, integrative, and interactive model of health and disability that is sensitive to social and environmental aspects of functioning.

The *ICF* is a significant development in health care, as it can be used as a standard for defining concepts, building constructs, hypothesizing relationships, and proposing new theories that will further research and practice in psychology (Bruyère & Peterson, 2005; Bruyère, Van Looy, & Peterson, 2005; Peterson, 2005; Peterson & Paul, 2009; WHO, 2001a). Since the trial version was published in 1980, the *ICF* (at that time called the *International Classification of Impairments, Disabilities, and Handicaps*, or *ICIDH*) has been used as a statistical tool for population studies and in systems of information management; a research tool to measure outcomes, environmental factors, and quality of life; a clinical tool in treatment planning, vocational assessment, and rehabilitation outcome evaluation; a social policy tool for social security planning, compensation systems development, and policy design and implementation; and, lastly, as an educational tool in curriculum design and to raise awareness and take social action (WHO, 2001a, p. 5). As we begin our review of the *ICF* and its importance in health care, we first consider the prevalence of disability and the associated purpose and relevance of the *ICF*.

DISABILITY PREVALENCE

People with disabilities comprise one of the largest collective minority groups in the United States. The U.S. Census Bureau's American Community Survey (ACS) of 2008 suggested that the prevalence of disability, for people age 5 and older in the United States, was over 36.1 million people, roughly 12.1% of the then estimated civilian, noninstitutionalized population (or CNIP; Brault, 2009). Of this number, 13.4 million (37% of those surveyed indicating disability) lived with some cognitive difficulty (associated with a mental or emotional condition), 19.2 million (53.5% of those surveyed) lived with ambulatory difficulty, and 7.2 million (20% of those surveyed) lived with self-care difficulty.

Further, 10.4 million individuals participating in the ACS or 3.5% of the CNIP experienced difficulty hearing, whereas 6.8 million people or

2.3% of the CNIP experienced difficulty seeing; 19.2 million people surveyed or 6.9% of the CNIP reported ambulatory difficulty (i.e., serious difficulty walking or climbing stairs). Participants were also queried regarding difficulty with basic activities around the home associated with caring for oneself, such as difficulty dressing or bathing. An estimated 7.2 million or 2.6% of the CNIP endorsed such self-care difficulty.

More specific to the content of this text, the ACS surveyed for cognitive difficulty because of a physical, mental, or emotional condition (implying psychological or neurological bases) that resulted in serious difficulty concentrating, remembering, or making decisions. About 13.4 million people or 4.8% of the CNIP reported cognitive difficulty as defined by the ACS. More specifically, participants were asked whether they experienced any difficulty doing errands alone, such as visiting a doctor's office or shopping, due to a physical, mental, or emotional condition. About 13.2 million respondents or 5.5% of the CNIP reported difficulty with independent living for these reasons (Brault, 2009).

A different survey, the Survey for Income and Program Participation (SIPP), an established source for disability data since the 1980s (Brault, 2009), in its 2005 iteration used a much larger number of survey items than the ACS, querying activity limitations as well as level of severity of certain limitations (i.e., some difficulty performing an activity vs. cannot perform the activity at all). This more detailed survey resulted in a prevalence estimate of 54.4 million people with disabilities, which was over 18% of the U.S. census estimates for July 2005 (Brault, 2005). The SIPP estimate was nearly 50% higher than the subsequent and more recent ACS survey estimate. The SIPP definition of disability was fundamentally different from the definition used within the ACS, making meaningful comparison of these two surveys difficult.

The 2007 version of the ACS used a different question set from the 2008 iteration and suggested a U.S. prevalence of 41.2 million people living with disability, about 13.5% of the 2007 U.S. population estimate, and over 14% higher than the 2008 ACS estimate. Looking back to 2003, the U.S. Census Bureau estimated that 49.7 million people in the United States lived with some type of long-term health condition or disability (2003). Given these data, during the past 7 years we have a reported range of 36–54 million people, or 12%–18% of the U.S. population, indicating that they have some type of disability. All of these data are based on reports from only those persons who responded to the particular surveys conducted and, thus, may significantly underrepresent persons living with chronic disabilities in the United States. It is also important to consider that all surveys are vulnerable to both sampling (the degree to which the true population was accurately sampled) and nonsampling (survey design, respondent response styles, accurate coding of survey data) errors (Brault, 2009).

Using the highest estimated number of people with disabilities from recent survey data (the 2005 SIPP), 18% is a significant portion of the U.S. population; it is clear that people with disabilities are an important collective minority in the United States. It stands to reason that within the United States we need to work effectively with health care information dealing with functioning, disability, and health. Beyond the bounds of the United States, it has been projected that within the next 8 years, chronic disabling conditions and mental disorders will account for 78% of the global disease burden in developing countries (World Health Organization, 2002, p. 13).

Our health care system will continue to need to adjust to a population of people who are living longer and manage resources around health care interventions that are increasingly more effective and yet remarkably more expensive (Peterson & Aguiar, 2004; Peterson & Elliott, 2008; Tarvydas, Peterson, & Michaelson, 2005). Health care supporting people with disabilities presents serious economic consequences, and costs associated with disability are expected to escalate with the increasing number of persons who will live with a disability over the next several decades (U.S. Department of Health and Human Services, 2000; WHO, 2002).

Historically, people with disabilities have spent over four times as much on medical care, services, and equipment as their nondisabled counterparts (Max, Rice, & Trupin, 1995). A December 2009 press release of the Research Triangle Institute, in collaboration with the U.S. Centers for Disease Control & Prevention, stated that 27% of the U.S. adult health care spending, or 397.8 billion dollars, was associated with disability during the year 2006. The related study was published in the January–February 2010 Public Health Reports.

There are personal consequences associated with disability and potential loss of function, such as decreased employment productivity, impaired quality of life, and difficulty with psychosocial functioning (Hansen, Fink, Frydenberg, & Oxhoj, 2002; Kessler, Greenberg, Mickelson, Meneades, & Wang, 2001). The related economic impact is felt throughout the fabric of society. The current discourse in the United States on health care attests to the fact that our health care system is overwhelmed by the costs incurred in responding to current health care needs, including the acute and long-term needs of people with chronic health conditions (Peterson & Elliott, 2008).

PREVALENCE OF MENTAL DISORDERS

According to the 2004 World Health Report of the World Health Organization, mental disorders were the leading cause of disability in the United
States and Canada for ages 15–44 during the year 2002 (World Health
Organization, 2004). Historically, the Global Burden of Disease Study
found that neuropsychiatric disorders were collectively the third leading
cause of loss of healthy years of life and the leading cause of disability
(Murray & Lopez, 1996). Four of the ten leading causes of disability worldwide were mental disorders, the foremost of which was major depression
(Üstün et al., 2004).

According to the National Comorbidity Survey Replication (NCS-R)
conducted by Kessler and his associates, which surveyed the prevalence,
severity, and comorbidity of 12-month duration *DSM-IV* disorders, prevalence rates for psychiatric diagnoses alone are much higher than either
the ACS or SIPP estimates for a much broader presentation of types of
disability (Kessler, Chiu, Demler, & Walters, 2005b). According to this
survey, an estimated 26.2% of Americans age 18 and older (not including children from age 5–17 as with the ACS and SIPP) have a diagnosable
mental disorder within a given year. Using 2004 U.S. Census residential
population estimates for this age range, 57.7 million adults had a psychiatric diagnosis.

As mentioned earlier, the degree to which a diagnosis is associated
with serious activity limitations or participation restrictions is impossible
to tell from diagnostic information alone, which may account for the
difference between the NCS-R and the ACS and SIPP estimates. The existence of a diagnosis may not be associated with the report of experiencing
a disabling condition (these phenomena will be explored in greater detail
when describing the conceptual framework of the *ICF*). In fact, the
NCS-R survey data queried for severity of impairment associated with
diagnoses, and these findings suggested that the main burden of psychiatric difficulties, those who suffer from a serious mental illness, is con-
centrated to about 6% of the then estimated population, much closer to
the numbers extracted from the ACS data in 2008 (4.8% of the CNIP
reported cognitive difficulty, 5.5% had difficulty doing errands alone,
such as visiting a doctor's office or shopping due to a physical, mental, or
emotional condition).

It is important to note when considering these numbers that nearly
half (45%) of those with any mental disorder met criteria for two or
more disorders, with severity of mental illness strongly associated with

comorbidity (Kessler et al., 2005b). Next, we explore the specific types of mental disorders identified in recent survey research and their prevalence. Details of specific *DSM-IV-TR* diagnoses will be presented in Part II of this text.

Mood Disorders

According to NCS-R, about 20.9 million American adults or 9.5% of the U.S. population, age 18 and older in a given year have a mood disorder, which may include major depressive disorder (the leading cause of disability in the United States for ages 15–44; WHO, 2004), dysthymic disorder (affecting 1.5% of the U.S. population age 18 and older in a given year; Kessler et al., 2005b), and bipolar disorder (affecting 2.6% or 5.7 million adults age 18 and older; Kessler et al., 2005b). Depressive disorders often occur comorbidly with anxiety and substance-related disorders (Kessler et al., 2005b).

Schizophrenia

A fairly dated estimate suggests that about 1.1% of the population age 18 and older in the United States during a given year have the diagnosis of schizophrenia, which equates to about 2.4 million adults (Regier et al., 1993). The current version of the *DSM* suggests that the prevalence rate is about 1%. However, Bhugra (2005) provides more recent estimates of prevalence and an opportunity to review sources of prevalence data in the psychiatric literature and their impact on prevalence rates (see Saha, Chant, Welham, & McGrath, 2005).

As it turns out, international prevalence rates for schizophrenia are much lower than 1%. However, making the distinction between data collected at a given point in time, or over a specific period of time, versus an estimated lifetime prevalence of schizophrenia, the estimates based on a review of 132 core studies were 4.6, 3.3, and 4.0 per 1,000, respectively. These numbers are significantly lower than 1%. It will be interesting to see how the next edition of the *DSM* responds to these more recent data.

Anxiety Disorders

About 40 million American adults age 18 and older or about 18.1% of people in this age group in a given year, have one of the following anxiety disorders: panic disorder, obsessive-compulsive disorder, posttraumatic stress disorder, generalized anxiety disorder, or a type of phobia (social, specific, or agoraphobia). As with mood disorders, anxiety disorder typically occurs with other disorders, specifically, depressive disorders or substance-related disorders (Kessler et al., 2005b). Further, most people with one anxiety disorder will also have another anxiety disorder (Kessler, Bergland, Demler, Jin, & Walters, 2005a).

About 6 million American adults age 18 and older, about 2.7% in a given year, have a panic disorder (Kessler et al., 2005b). Historically, about one in three people with this disorder develop agoraphobia (Robins & Regier, 1991); about 2.2 million or 1% of the same population, have obsessive-compulsive disorder; nearly 7.7 million American adults age 18 and older, about 3.5% of this age group, in a given year have posttraumatic stress disorder (PTSD). There is likely a precipitous rise in PTSD with the ongoing Iraq and Afghanistan conflicts; historically, 19% of Vietnam veterans experienced this diagnosis at some point after their war experience (Dohrenwend et al., 2006; Kessler et al., 2005b).

About 6.8 million American adults or about 3.1% of the same age group have generalized anxiety disorder in a given year, and approximately 15 million of the same population or 6.8% have social phobia. Finally, about 19.2 million of the same population or 8.7% have some type of specific phobia (Kessler et al., 2005b).

Implications of the Prevalence of Mental Disorders

"Mental disorders contribute more to global disability and disease burden than any other category of noncommunicable disease" said Geoffrey Reed, PhD, a WHO psychologist involved in the update to the *ICD* classification system (Martin, 2009, p. 62). Given the prevalence of psychiatric illness and related disability for severe presentations of these illnesses, it stands to reason that the *ICF*, a classification of functioning, disability, and health that can assist with the identification of disability (activity limitations and participation restrictions), as well as assets in functioning, can inform assessment efforts, intervention targeting, the evaluation of the efficacy of such interventions, and related research. Having established the prevalence of disability, and in particular, those of a psychological nature, as well as the significance of the development of the *ICF*, we turn to a discussion of the purpose and relevance of the *ICF*.

PURPOSE OF THE *ICF*

The purpose of the *ICF* is to "provide a unified and standard language and framework for the description of health and health-related states" (WHO, 2001a, p. 3). The aims of the *ICF* as indicated in the document include to

> (1) provide a scientific basis for understanding and studying health and health-related states, outcomes, and determinants; (2) establish a common language for describing health and health-related states in order to improve communication between different users, such as healthcare workers, researchers, policy makers, and the public, including people with disabilities; (3) permit comparison of data across counties, health care disciplines, services and times; and (4) provide a systematic coding scheme for health information systems. (WHO, 2001a, p. 5)

Using the *ICF* in combination with diagnostic information provided by systems like the *DSM-IV-TR* or the *ICD-10* allows the two together to provide more specific and complete conceptualizations of health and human functioning (Bruyère & Peterson, 2005). The *ICD-10*'s primary purpose is to generate diagnoses of diseases, while the *ICF* provides information on functioning and disability associated with various health conditions. Together, the *ICD* and the *ICF* are intended to provide a complementary and meaningful picture of the health of people or populations. One critical reason that these two perspectives are essential to conceptualizing health care is that disease or impairment may be experienced very differently by two individuals; similar health conditions do not imply similar functioning (the related literature is reviewed below in the discussion of models of disability).

The *ICF* represents a new way for the world to conceptualize health and enhance communications regarding health. Research and clinical implementation efforts suggest that the *ICF* is a useful public health tool for classification of health conditions and functional status, and it can be applied to a number of clinical arenas (WHO, 2001a). For example, the *ICF* provides the basis for a systematic coding scheme for global health information systems. Data from these information systems can be used to identify facilitators and barriers that affect the full participation of people with disabilities in society.

Subsequent research may permit comparison of data across countries, health care disciplines, services, and time, contributing to an international database of scientific knowledge of health and health-related states, and thus stimulate research on the consequences of health conditions. The *ICF* and its conceptual framework may assist in preparing the current and next generation of health care and health-related professionals for our increasingly complex health care systems (Peterson & Elliott, 2008).

The *ICF* has the potential to increase communication efficiency among health care providers, clearly target necessary interventions, provide a conceptual framework to analyze the success of interventions, all of which are critical in maintaining quality health care while controlling costs. The *ICF* is useful for a broad spectrum of applications within sectors of health-related settings including insurance or managed care, social security, labor, economics, population surveys, and social policy, including prevention and health promotion (Howard, Nieuwenhuijsen, & Saleeby, 2008), general legislation development, and sectors associated with environmental modification (WHO, 2001a, p. 5).

RELEVANCE OF THE *ICF*

The *ICF* was first drafted in 1980 as the *International Classification of Impairments, Disabilities, and Handicaps (ICIDH)* by the World Health Organization (WHO). The *ICF* developed through years of international participation and systematic revision, including longitudinal consensus building efforts and extensive field testing, and it is a significant development in psychology and general health care. On May 22, 2001, the *ICF* was endorsed by the 54th World Health Assembly for international use and was subsequently accepted by 191 countries as the international standard for classification of health and health-related states. Member states of WHO are charged with implementing the *ICF* in sectors related to health, education, insurance, labor, and legislation (Stucki, Üstün, & Melvin, 2005). The *ICF* is clearly an important international development in health classification that impacts psychology, psychiatry, and all of health care. The *ICF* has been used in a variety of settings for a wide range of applications (Stone, 2008).

International Use

The *ICF* and its conceptual framework have influenced a variety of health care entities abroad with increasing frequency. It has been employed in varying capacities internationally including the United States, Australia, Canada, Germany (Stucki et al., 2005), Italy (Maini, Nocentini, Prevedini, Giardini, & Muscolo, 2008), The Netherlands (Bickenbach, 2003; Holloway, 2004), and Cambodia (Vanleit, 2008). Work on the World

Health Survey, built on the *ICF* conceptual framework, has been implemented in 74 countries (Üstün, Chatterji, Bickenbach, Kostanjsek, & Schneider, 2003).

Specific examples of the *ICF* in international health care enterprises include Europe, Japan, Canada, and Australia. Canada adopted the *ICF* through the Canadian Institute for Health Information, and the Australian Institute of Health and Welfare has applied the *ICF* to its national data dictionaries (Madden, Choi, & Sykes, 2003). Several European countries and Japan are involved in evaluating health outcomes in health resort programs using the *ICF* (Morita, Weigl, Schuh, & Stucki, 2006).

The *ICF* Core Sets

One major *ICF*-related initiative is the construction of the *ICF* Core Sets or subsets of the *ICF* codes used to describe patient functioning, in particular, clinical, research, and health-related settings. In clinical practice, these code subsets can be used in clinical assessment, intervention targeting, and evaluation of treatment outcomes (Grill, Ewert, Chatterji, Kostanjsek, & Stucki, 2005; Stucki et al., 2005).

Core Sets in Germany

Launched in 2001, during the *ICF*'s inaugural year, the *ICF* Core Sets is a joint project of the *ICF* Research Branch of the WHO Collaboration Center of the Family of International Classifications at the Ludwig-Maximilians-University in Munich, Germany, and the Classification, Assessment, and Surveys Team at WHO. Their work began with 12 core sets selected as "most burdensome chronic conditions" in acute hospital and post-acute rehabilitation facilities (Stucki et al., 2005, p. 350). These conditions included neurological conditions (Ewert et al., 2005), cardiopulmonary conditions (Boldt et al., 2005), musculoskeletal conditions (Stoll et al., 2005; Weigl et al., 2006), conditions generally associated with advanced age (Grill et al., 2005b), and relevant to this text, the second largest of the *ICF* Core Sets developed was for that of depression (see Cieza et al., 2004). This core set will be reviewed in some detail in Part III of this text.

Rehabilitation Core Sets in Italy

Researchers in Italy recently evaluated the use of *ICF* Core Sets for implementation in rehabilitation settings. Like the work begun in Germany,

Italian researchers surmised that the complexity and size of the *ICF* are difficult to implement in its entirety within a clinical rehabilitation setting. *ICF* Core Sets or simplified instruments derived from the *ICF* show promise for more targeted classification efforts. The researchers surveyed health professionals regarding difficulties they encountered in using the *ICF* Core Sets. Feedback suggested the need for greater clarity in defining *ICF* constructs within the code and more guidance in the use of qualifiers that determine levels of functioning for a given code (Maini et al., 2008).

Ongoing Core Set Development for Physical Disabilities

International research in the development of core sets is ongoing, addressng a wide variety of disabling conditions (Maini et al., 2008). Physical disorders that have or will have code sets include amputations (Kohler et al., 2009), ankylosing spondylitis (Boonen et al., 2010), cardiopulmonary conditions (Wildner et al., 2005), musculoskeletal conditions in general (Scheuringer et al., 2005), and neurological conditions in general (Stier-Jarmer et al., 2005). The WHO Web site for *ICF*-related research projects indicates ongoing work to generate core sets for other physical disorders including breast cancer, cerebral palsy, dementia, diabetes mellitus, heart disease, multiple sclerosis, obesity, obstructive pulmonary disease, osteoarthritis, osteoporosis, pain management, psoriasis, rheumatoid arthritis, spinal cord injury, traumatic brain injury, and stroke (http://www.icf-research-branch.org).

ICF *Core Sets for Depression*

Disability and *ICF* Core Sets are also underway for mental disorders. Given that mood disorders can be associated with significant loss of functioning and associated quality of life, using *ICF* Core Sets to assist with assessment, intervention targeting, and evaluation of treatment outcomes is desirable.

ICF Core Sets have been constructed for depression (Cieza et al., 2004), both a comprehensive version and a brief version. The depression core set is the second largest code set of the original 12 comprehensive *ICF* Core Sets for chronic disorders (Ayuso-Mateos, 2009; Stucki et al., 2005). A code set is being developed at the Universidad Autónoma de Madrid, Spain, for bipolar disorder (Ayuso-Mateos, 2009). Data available from the depression code set will be considered in Part III of this text.

Cross Walking to Existing Assessment Tools

Shortly after its publication, Cieza et al. (2002), in order to provide some structure for future cross-walking efforts of existing health status measures to the *ICF*, created a set of 10 rules to inform the linking of items from health status measures to the *ICF*. The 10 linking rules proved useful and were associated with a high degree of agreement between health professionals using the rules. Although the *ICF* itself does not dictate what aspects of functioning are classified nor what assessment tools are most relevant for a given situation, a variety of assessment methods are compatible with the *ICF* conceptual framework (Reed et al., 2008).

Within the area of mental health, the *DSM-IV-TR* is currently linked with the *ICD-9* and *-10* codes. As the *DSM-5* is linked to the *ICD-10* and *-11* system updates, linking the *ICF* to the *DSM-5* would provide classification of functioning within a mental health context that moves beyond multiaxial diagnoses alone to descriptions of health and health-related states. These prospects will be explored in greater depth in Part II of this text.

Developing New Assessment Tools

In addition to cross-walking efforts to link existing measures with the *ICF*, new instruments are being developed based on the *ICF* itself (e.g., Jones & Sinclair, 2008; Seekins, Ipsen, & Arnold, 2007). Velozo (2005), who was awarded a NIDRR field-initiated grant to develop a computerized adaptive measurement system for the Activity Dimension of the *ICF*, suggested that Item Response Theory can be used to convert the *ICF* into measurement systems that individualize the assessment process, reduce respondent burden, and increase measurement precision.

Professionals from the disciplines of rehabilitation psychology (DiCowden, 2005), nursing (Coenen, 2005; Harris, 2005), occupational therapy (Velozo, 2005), and physical therapy (Brandt, 2005; Mayo & McGill, 2005) have developed instruments and protocols based on the *ICF* model. Such efforts are essential for the ongoing development of the *ICF*, so that it can reliably be applied in clinical settings. The related literature is expansive and emerging and impossible to review comprehensively in this text.

Informing Scope of Practice

In the United States, the *ICF* framework had a direct impact on the scope of practice statement for the speech language pathology profession (American Speech-Language-Hearing Association [ASHA], 2004;

Threats, 2003) and has influenced activities related to data collection, framing assessment interventions, measuring clinical research outcomes (Threats, 2002), and investigating the role of communication in the quality of life (Threats & Worrall, 2004). The *ICF* has attracted support from other U.S. professional associations as well, including occupational therapy, physical therapy, psychology, recreational therapy, and social work (Reed et al., 2005, 2008).

SUMMARY

Our text began with a prologue and preface that provided a clear context for the author's perspective in writing about the *ICF* and the *DSM-IV-TR*. Our first chapter established the *ICF* as a significant development in health care, within the context of the prevalence of disability in our society. The purpose and relevance of the *ICF* are highlighted, including efforts to date in wide and varied implementation activities on an international scale.

The *ICF* is a relevant development in health care because of its potential to provide health care systems with a common language to enhance diagnostic information with standard descriptions of health and health-related states. Proper implementation of the *ICF* promises to (1) revolutionize the way stakeholders in health care delivery systems think about and classify health, (2) improve the quality of health care for individuals across the world, (3) generate innovative outcome-based research, and (4) influence culturally sensitive global health policy (Stucki, Ewert, & Cieza, 2003).

CHAPTER 2

Historical Context of the *ICF*

PREVIEW QUESTIONS

1. Given the *ICF*'s historical context, what models of disability influenced its development?
2. How did disability policy development in the United States impact the development of the *ICF*?
3. What is the *ICF-CY*?

Having established the importance of the development of the *ICF* in the classification of functioning, disability, and health, we now turn to the *ICF*'s historical development and associated philosophical underpinnings. Over the last 40 years, rehabilitation-related professions have become synonymous with studies of disability (Peterson & Elliott, 2008). As a multidisciplinary field, rehabilitation professionals embrace an activist philosophy that advocates for the improvement of life conditions for persons with disabilities (Frank & Elliott, 2000; Frank, Rosenthal, & Caplan, 2009; Riggar & Maki, 2004; Scherer et al., 2004). The *ICF* and its predecessors, the *International Classification of Impairments, Disabilities and Handicaps* (*ICIDH* and *ICIDH-2*; World Health Organization [WHO], 1980, 1999) reflect important historical developments in disability conceptualization and related policy development and the values espoused in the rehabilitation-related professions.

MODELS OF DISABILITY

Several recent publications have compared and contrasted various models of disability. The *Handbook of Counseling Psychology* (Brown & Lent, 2008) includes a chapter discussing advancements in conceptualizing disability (Peterson & Elliott, 2008) and informs the following brief review. The text *Psychological and Social Impact of Illness and Disability* (Dell Orto &

Power, 2007) provides a detailed review of how disability is defined and conceptualized in the literature (Lutz & Bowers, 2007). An interesting two-part series was published on the evolution of disability models as they applied to psychological injury and law (Schultz, 2008; Schultz & Stewart, 2008). Here, we turn to a discussion of how the dominant models of disability influenced thinking in recent times and how the medical, social, and biopsychosocial models of disability relate to the development of the *ICF*.

ICD-10 and -11

International classification of population health began with a focus on the prevalence of medical diagnoses and causes of death with the *International Statistical Classification of Diseases and Related Health Problems* (*ICD*, now in its 10th revision, WHO, 1992). The *ICD* was first formalized in 1893 as the Bertillon Classification or the International List of Causes of Death (the *ICD* acronym persists to this day). The *ICD* provides an etiological classification of health conditions (e.g., diseases, disorders, and injuries) related to mortality (death) and morbidity (illness). The *ICD* is a good example of the medical model's influence on the diagnostic classification of illness or injury.

Currently, the United States is using the clinical modification of the *ICD-9*, even though the *ICD-10* was approved by the World Health Assembly in 1992, and neighboring Canada has been using the *ICD-10* for some time now. The United States is scheduled to begin using the *ICD-10* in 2013 (Martin, 2009). Meanwhile, the World Health Organization is in the process of updating the *ICD-10* in order to make it a better tool to diagnose and treat disease.

The *ICD-11* is due for publication in 2015. It promises to be a global, multilingual, multidisciplinary system of classification, and its development transparent and free from commercial input. The system's context will allow for interactive information sharing using modern technology and integrated into health informatics systems worldwide. The new system is intended for daily clinical use with simpler diagnostic criteria (Martin, 2009).

Although it continues to be influential, limitations of the medical model and the focus on the civil rights-related and disability activism helped to develop the opposing social model of disability. Although consensus has not been easy to achieve, it is important to define disability so that those who are disadvantaged by their experience of disability can be identified, their life experiences compared with those who are not disabled, and disparities in life experiences can be noted so that inequalities can be observed, measured, and ultimately remedied (Leonardi, Bickenbach, Üstün, Kostanjsek, & Chatterji, 2006).

Although the *ICF* is a useful tool for describing functioning associated with a broad range of disabilities, it was not designed to classify disability exclusively; it also classifies health and health-related states (Bickenbach, Chatterji, Badley, & Üstün, 1999). This represents a fundamental shift away from disease-focused, medical models of health care toward the biopsychosocial model of disability. As the sister classification to the *ICD* and throughout its development, the *ICF* was greatly influenced by the paradigm shift away from medically focused models to consider the influence of psychosocial and environmental factors on disability.

Medical Model of Disability

For many years, the medical model drove assessment practices in health care service provision, focusing on the diagnosis of a disease, disorder, or injury (Wright, 1980). The medical model most commonly relates to an acute treatment process that first identifies a pathogen or cause of injury or other disease process (often classified by the *ICD-10*) and then selects an appropriate treatment protocol for the condition identified (Reed et al., 2008). Within the United States, a classification of procedures associated with treatment of illness or injury employed in this treatment process is the Current Procedural Terminology or CPT codes (American Medical Association, 2010).

Within the medical model, less attention was given to contextual factors (e.g., social and environmental factors) and to the subjective experiences of individuals with disabilities. Disability tended to be conceptualized as a personal problem that required treatment by medical professionals (WHO, 2001a). Contemporary scholarship suggests that behavioral and social factors affect the course of chronic disease and disability over the life span; the medical model and related diagnostic information have been shown to have a limited capacity for assessing and making changes in these areas (Peterson & Elliott, 2008).

It is important to note that the medical model is not without utility. It contributed to advances in science that helped researchers to better describe disease processes and related etiology, allowing more rapid and effective response to the acute needs of persons with physical disabilities and other chronic health conditions. The medical model also informed early initiatives to address issues of improved care, survival, and quality of life (Peterson & Elliott, 2008). In the United States, medical definitions of disability provide the cornerstone for determining disability for legal and occupational purposes and for determining eligibility for financial assistance (Chan & Leahy, 1999, 2005; Tarvydas et al., 2005).

However, the medical model was challenged by the civil rights era and related disability advocacy efforts, encouraging a movement away from the medical model of disability and functioning toward a social model that considered the role of environmental barriers in health and functioning (Peterson & Elliott, 2008; Rusk, 1977; Smart, 2005; Wright, 1980; Wright, 1983). The medical model relies heavily on measures and tests of the disease process; the model places a limited value on subjective reports of quality of life and well-being. More recent assessment paradigms focused less on temporary states measured under these circumstances and more on enduring characteristics of people, such as personal traits, habits, and enduring personality characteristics (e.g., Ong, Peterson, Chronister, Chui, & Chan, 2009; Peterson, 2000; Wiggins, 1996).

Historical evidence suggests that diagnostic information alone, without functional data, may not adequately reflect an individual's health condition (see Peterson, 2005; Reed et al., 2005). Disease or impairment may manifest differently across individuals; similar functioning does not imply similar health conditions. Diagnoses alone have not sufficiently predicted length (McCrone & Phelan, 1994) or outcome of hospitalization (Rabinowitz, Modai, & Inbar-Saban, 1994), level of necessary care (Burns, 1991), service needs (National Advisory Mental Health Council, 1993), work performance (Gatchel, Polatin, Mayer, & Garcy, 1994), receipt of disability benefits (Bassett, Chase, Folstein, & Regier, 1998; Massel, Liberman, Mintz, & Jacobs, 1990; Segal & Choi, 1991), or social integration (Ormel, Oldehinkel, Brilman, & vanden Brink, 1993).

For example, consider someone with a disabling condition secondary to a traumatic accident, one of the results of which is a co-occurring diagnosis of Major Depressive Disorder. According to the *DSM-IV-TR*, the person who is experiencing a major depressive episode must experience at least five of nine possible characteristic symptoms. These symptoms can range from an inability to concentrate to weight gain or loss. The functional implications of any of the nine symptoms may be quite disparate, and the possible combinations of five symptoms required for the diagnosis will have varying clinical presentations. The combinations and presentations possible highlight the fact that diagnostic information alone is limited without clear descriptions of function that informed the diagnosis.

Beyond the variety of presentations of diagnoses and potential functional limitations that may or may not present in an individual, Leonardi et al. (2006, p. 1220) highlight the importance of considering the quality of life experience of a person dealing with health issues. They noted that it is important to distinguish between objective descriptions of the "disability experience" and an individual's satisfaction with that experience: ". . . data about quality of life, well-being, and personal satisfaction with life are useful for health and policy planning; but these data are not necessarily predicted by the presence or extent of disability." In contrast with the medical model, the social model of disability highlights the importance of a person's subjective experience as it relates to facilitators and barriers that the environment may present, their impact on health and functioning, and ultimately an individual's quality of life (Elliott, Kurylo, & Rivera, 2002; Hurst, 2003; Smart, 2005; Ueda & Okawa, 2003).

Social Model of Disability

In the Social model of disability, disability is no longer a simple personal attribute but a complex social construct reflecting the interaction between the individual and his or her environment (WHO, 2001a, p. 20). The social paradigm focuses on the barriers and facilitators to functioning, such as daily activities, life skills, social relations, life satisfaction, and participation in society. This model suggests that any problem related to disability is influenced by, if not due in large part to, societal attitudes and barriers in the environment.

Variations of the social model have appeared within the disability studies literature (Olkin, 1999; Olkin & Pledger, 2003). Within this paradigm, the individual is seen as the organizing core, but impairments are defined by the environment. The environment is typically construed as the ". . . major determinant of individual functioning" (Pledger, 2003; p. 281). The social model highlights the need for increased access and opportunities for people with disabilities and has historically been favored by advocates for the civil rights of persons with disability, who historically have disapproved of the medical model in general.

Hurst (2003) challenged the *ICIDH* development efforts by saying that it perpetuated the medical model, countered the social model of disability, and presented barriers to the understanding of issues related to social justice and disability among health care providers. In response to this criticism, WHO made a concerted effort to involve people with disabilities and disability rights advocates in the *ICIDH* revision process that produced the *ICF*.

Problems associated with exploring the value of the social model of disability include that historically it has neither clearly distinguished who qualifies as a person with a disability nor how disability is measured or determined. Further, researchers in this area have not established a distinct body of scholarship that systematically posits empirically testable and potentially falsifiable hypotheses (Peterson & Elliott, 2008). This may be due in part to the reality that some supporters of the social model of disability regard psychological theory and scholarship as a continuation of the medical model where disability is equated with person-based pathology, largely independent of environmental and social factors (see Olkin & Pledger, 2003).

Biopsychosocial Model of Disability

The *ICF* integrates the medical and social models of disability, addressing biological, individual, and societal perspectives on health in a biopsychosocial approach (Peterson, 2005). The origins of the biopsychosocial framework can be traced back to an article from the 70s arguing for a new medical model for biomedicine (see Engel, 1977). Ultimately, the biopsychosocial model integrates all that is useful in both the medical and social models of disability.

From a disability-rights activist perspective, the interactive model informing the *ICF*'s conceptual framework is complementary to the social model of disability (disability being an interaction between impairment, functioning, and environment). The social model of disability is very helpful in describing how environmental factors are key to understanding disability and how advocacy occurs through social change (Hurst, 2003).

The name of WHO's latest classification system was changed from the *ICIDH* to the *ICF* to reflect the paradigm shift away from a focus on consequences of disease as found in the 1980 version toward a focus on the components of health found in the current version (WHO, 2001a). Rather than an emphasis on "impairment, disability, and handicap" exclusively, the revised classification incorporated the terms *activity* and *participation* to denote positive experiences related to function and health. In the current version of the classification, the term *impairment* is defined as a problem with a body function or structure and the term *handicap* has been replaced with the term *participation restriction*, meaning a problem an individual may experience in life situations.

The evolution of the *ICIDH* to the current iteration of the *ICF* reflects the international zeitgeist to embrace a biopsychosocial model of disability rather than a medical or social model exclusively. We now have at our disposal an etiologically neutral framework and classification that was created through global consensus building, to identify all aspects of a person's health experience at the individual and contextual levels (Stucki et al., 2005). It may be useful to explore the shift from the medical model to the biopsychosocial model of health care as it occurred in the United States through the lens of disability policy development during the 20th century. Reviewed next are disability policy developments leading up to the creation of the *ICIDH*.

DISABILITY POLICY AND THE *ICIDH* AND *ICF*

Disability policy developments in the United States reflect the efforts of people with disabilities and their advocates, who saw the utility of using government structures to address inequities for individuals who have fewer resources (Peterson & Aguiar, 2004). Federal and state funding agencies assumed leadership to resolve the health, vocational, and social inequities faced by persons with disabilities (Peterson & Elliott, 2008). First reviewed are developments in disability policy during the period prior to the creation of the *ICIDH*, largely influenced by world wars, followed by advances in medicine and social awareness that drove more sophisticated policy development throughout the remaining century and into the 21st century. The following review is informed by previously published reviews by Peterson and Aguiar (2004) and Peterson and Rosenthal (2005a).

Policy Developments Prior to the *ICIDH*

Within the United States, there has long existed an historical disparity between resources provided for physical versus mental health services. For example, early rehabilitation services were limited to provision to individuals with physical disabilities (Rubin & Roessler, 2008). Current social discourse identifies this issue as the need for mental health parity. It was not until the Vocational Rehabilitation Act Amendments of 1943 (Barden-Lafollette Act) that rehabilitation services were extended to people with mental health diagnoses (mental retardation and mental illness), as well as people who were blind (Peterson & Aguiar, 2004).

Although recent legislation has begun to address this disparity, there remains a lack of parity between the two health care domains. One of the great values of the *ICIDH* and now the *ICF* is that it was developed to be etiologically neutral; it does not matter whether functional limitations are a result of physical or psychological reasons, as the focus is on functioning, activity limitations, participation restrictions, and contextual factors.

One of the three task forces associated with the *ICIDH* revision process was the International Mental Health Task Force, which from the outset clarified "the distinctions between mental disorders and the disability associated with them while simultaneously aligning these domains of functioning and disability with those associated with physical disorders. The resulting *ICF* is now poised for utilization that will continue this dual trajectory" (Kennedy, 2003, p. 611). Hopefully, an etiologically neutral focus in health care classification can help remedy the disparities that have historically existed between mental and physical health care.

The 1950s ushered in what has been called the *Golden Era of Rehabilitation* (Rusalem, 1976), when federal legislation mandated funds to expand health, vocational, and educational services to persons with disabilities; train professionals to provide these services; and increase architectural accessibility (see Elliott & Leung, 2005). For example, the Vocational Rehabilitation Act (VR Act) Amendments of 1954 (Public Law 565) provided individuals who were blind, poor, aged, or otherwise disabled an income allowance (Supplemental Security Income, [SSI]) as well as major funding for research and demonstration grants. The increase in resources for disability-related research, no doubt, had an impact on scholars' ability to invest time, think creatively, and consider the benefits of movement away from the medical model toward the social model and ultimately the biopsychosocial model of disability conceptualization that currently informs the *ICF*.

The *ICIDH* grew out of the Civil Rights Movement, during which the VR Act Amendments of 1965 expanded funding for services to people with behavior disorders, substance use problems, public offense records, and people from socially disadvantaged backgrounds. The momentum of the 1960s brought the Social Security Act Amendments, establishing Social Security Disability Insurance (SSDI) to pay benefits to people with disabilities who have paid into the federal insurance program. The Vocational Rehabilitation Amendments of 1967 established the National Center for Deaf-Blind Youths and Adults as well as federal funding for pilot projects to serve migrant workers and their families.

The National Commission on Architectural Barriers was authorized by the 1965 Amendments, when the Commission began the process of reviewing the accessibility of public places for individuals with disabilities, leading to the formation of the Architectural Barriers Act (ABA) in 1968. The ABA required accessibility to buildings that were built, leased, or altered with federal funding. The most recent development within the *ICF*'s conceptual framework is its contextual part, including the component of environment. Careful attention to the role of environment in health and functioning is a beneficial manifestation of these civil rights-based initiatives and subsequent government policies.

A review of disability policy from the 1940s through the 1960s demonstrates a shift away from the traditional medical model and the disparity between physical and mental health, toward a more inclusive approach to resourcing both physical and mental health initiatives, and addressing the contextual issues in our environment that present barriers to full participation in society for people with physical disabilities. Although the first iteration of the *ICIDH* did not fully address the role of the environment in human functioning, these policy developments influenced subsequent developments in addressing context within the *ICF*.

During the decade preceding the publication of the *ICIDH* in 1980, the 1970s were characterized as dark times for disability-related policy and services (Rubin & Roessler, 2008). Despite the challenging times, disability policy momentum continued into the early 1970s with the establishment of the Architectural and Transportation Barriers Compliance Board (later renamed the Access Board) in 1973 to ensure that federal agencies complied with the ABA (later considerably expanded in Titles II and III of the Americans with Disabilities Act). The Urban Mass Transit Act began the plan and design of transportation for people with mobility impairments.

Most notable in 1973 was the passing of the policy associated with what came to be known as *the billion dollar program*, the Rehabilitation Act of 1973, which emphasized increased services to persons with the most severe disabilities and greater consumer involvement in the rehabilitation planning process (Rubin & Roessler, 2008). The mid-70s brought policies that mandated free, appropriate, public education to children with disabilities and emphasized education in the most fully integrated and barrier-free environment possible. The Education for All Handicapped Children's Act, which was retitled the Individuals with Disabilities Education Act (IDEA) in its 1990 iteration, sought to influence the achievement of better educational outcomes for children with disabilities. The movement toward considering the role of context or environment continued to manifest in these policy developments.

In 1978, a disability policy was enacted to support independent living services or those services for people with disabilities that were not necessarily tied to a vocational outcome. Centers for independent living partnered with the state-federal vocational rehabilitation system in providing comprehensive support services to people with disabilities. The social perspective on disability was having an impact on U.S. disability policy.

The 1970s disability policy developments reflected emphases on consumerism, informed choice, and full participation of consumers and patients in rehabilitation, vocational rehabilitation, and health-related services. There was also a greater recognition of detrimental effects of societal and individual discrimination against persons with disabilities. It was during the early 70s when work began on the *ICIDH*. Although the construction of the *ICIDH* was an international effort, our review of disability policy development in the United States suggests that these policies had an influence on U.S. participants' contributions to the *ICIDH*, *ICIDH-2*, and ultimately the *ICF*.

Work Begins on the *ICIDH*

Work leading to the development of the *ICIDH* began in 1972, when the WHO laid the groundwork for a classification scheme that addressed the consequences of disease (De Kleijn-De Vrankrijker, 2003). The *ICIDH* was intended to provide a classification of function that complemented the diagnostic and mortality information historically classified by the *ICD*. As the community of rehabilitation practitioners and disability advocates became aware of the *ICIDH* endeavor, in the spirit of the era, great interest developed around the development of a classification system that would take into account the functional impact of impairment and related social consequences.

In 1974, two separate classifications were developed, the first addressing impairments related to changes in health and the second handicaps that considered the role of the environment in disability and functioning. Discussions generated from work since 1972 were formally submitted for consideration at the October 1975 International Conference for the Ninth Revision of the International Classification of Diseases. In May 1976, the 29th World Health Assembly adopted a resolution that approved the trial publication of the supplementary classification of impairments and handicaps as a complement to the *ICD*. The first edition of the *ICIDH* was published in 1980 for trial purposes. This trial edition of the *ICIDH* presented the origins of a more holistic model of disability, stressing the role of environmental determinants in the performance of day-to-day activities and fulfillment of social roles by persons with disabilities (Brandsma, Lakerveld-Heyl, & Van Ravensberg, 1995; De Kleijn-De Vrankrijker, 2003).

Post-*ICIDH* Policy Developments

There was little progress on the *ICIDH* in the decade following its publication for trial purposes in 1980. In the United States, the 1980s was a decade marked by decreased government involvement in education, health, vocational rehabilitation, and disabilities (Peterson & Aguiar, 2004). Notwithstanding this arguably dubious shift in policy, President Bush Sr. brought renewed focus on the status and needs of people with disabilities through his support of the Americans with Disabilities Act (ADA) of 1990. The ADA was established to bring people with disabilities into the economic and social mainstream of American life and to provide enforceable policy that discouraged discrimination against individuals with disabilities.

In the spirit of the *ICIDH*, the ADA established terms that were very functional in nature and addressed environmental contexts in a meaningful way. More specifically, the ADA was developed using two •

critical terms, *impairments* and *disability*, with definitions parallel to those employed in the *ICIDH*. Brown (1993) argued for advantages of linking the *ICIDH* with the ADA such as the creation of a uniform framework for discussion and a standardized measurement tool for data collection. He also provided examples of how ADA goals can be linked directly to *ICIDH* language. For example, *independent living* can be linked with three *ICIDH* handicap domains: *orientation, physical independence*, and *mobility*; the *ICIDH* goals relating to *occupation* could be linked to equal *opportunity* under the ADA, while the goal of *social integration* (*ICIDH* terminology) could be linked to *full participation* (ADA terminology). Last, the term *economic self-sufficiency* as used in the ADA was taken directly from the *ICIDH*. For a succinct overview of contributions of the *ICIDH* in the development of the ADA definitions and implementation, see Nieuwen-huijsen (1995).

The 1992 amendments to the Rehabilitation Act assured increased emphasis on independent living services and highlighted the importance of employment outcomes for persons with disabilities. Specific to the *ICIDH* development efforts, the 1992 amendments empowered people with disabilities by requiring increased participation in the planning and implementation of rehabilitation services. In this same spirit, disability advocates reviewing the *ICIDH* in its 1980 iteration emphasized the need for people with disabilities to be part of the actual classification process not just the health care provider alone. Also, they encouraged ongoing involvement of people with disabilities in the *ICIDH* development efforts. Coordinators of the WHO revision efforts for the *ICIDH* (1980) included people with disabilities and disability advocates in the revision process, which led to important changes in the content and structure of the *ICF* (WHO, 2001a).

Developing the *ICIDH-2*

The revision of the *ICIDH* began with its reprinting in 1993, which ultimately led to the provisionally titled *ICIDH-2*. It was referred to in and incorporated the *Standard Rules on the Equalization of Opportunities for Persons with Disabilities* (United Nations Department of Public Information [UNDPI], 1993), which was adopted by the United Nations General Assembly at its 48th session in December 1993. The *ICIDH-2* was accepted as one of the United Nations' social classifications, subsequently affecting international human rights mandates as well as national legislation. The *ICIDH-2* arguably affected health-related policy development on an international scale.

WHO and its French, Dutch, and North American collaborating centers in 1993 generated the desiderata for continued revision of the *ICIDH* or the *ICIDH-2*. The desiderata suggested that the *ICIDH-2* should:

- Serve the multiple purposes required by different countries, sectors, and health care disciplines
- Be simple enough to be seen by practitioners as a meaningful description of the consequences of health conditions
- Be useful for practice, identifying health care needs and tailoring intervention programs (e.g., prevention, rehabilitation, and social actions)
- Give a coherent view of the consequences of health conditions such that the disablement process, and not just the dimensions of diseases or disorders, can be objectively assessed, recorded, and responded to
- Be sensitive to cultural variations, that is, be translatable and applicable in different cultures and health care systems
- Be usable in a complementary way with the WHO family of classifications (WHO, 2001a, pp. 246–247)

As a member of the WHO's Mental Health Task Force, previously mentioned in the discussion of disability policy and mental health parity, the American Psychological Association (APA) became involved in the revision of the *ICIDH-2* in 1995. The APA's Practice Directorate has worked closely with the WHO since that time. At a 1996 meeting in Geneva, work from various collaborating centers was collated and an alpha draft produced, which was pilot tested from May 1996 through February 1997. Comments and suggestions were compiled at WHO headquarters, and primary issues were identified and circulated to contribute to the ongoing revision process.

In summary, in order to enhance the universal appeal of the *ICIDH-2*, the WHO continued to follow guiding principles in the spirit of the desiderata generated in 1993 during the final revisions. The primary principle held that the classification should contain a culturally meaningful order of categories relying on consensus from potential stakeholders, including professionals in health care service provision, insurance, social security, and other entitlement programs; labor; education; economics; social policy development; and allied corporate entities. Another guiding principle for the *ICIDH-2* revisions was respect for the different languages represented in the international community. They maintained that the *ICF* should be attractive to its users and should appeal to managers and policy makers who would support its use and that it needed to have continuity with previous classification systems in order to complement systems already in place (WHO, 2001a).

Establishing Evidence for Validity and Reliability

Feedback obtained during testing of the Alpha draft of the *ICIDH-2* was used to develop a Beta-1 draft that was tested from June 1997 through December 1998. These results were used to inform development of a Beta-2 draft, which underwent testing from July 1999 through September 2000, which is when the writer became involved with the *ICIDH-2* development efforts.

Feasibility and reliability studies of case evaluations were conducted during the Beta-2 field trials that involved 24 countries, 1,884 case evaluations, and 3,216 evaluations of case summaries. Focus groups and various other studies contributed to the Beta-1 and -2 revision processes. The revisions formulated for the Beta-2 draft of the *ICIDH-2* signified the shift from a focus on impairment and disorder to a focus on health. These revisions were designed to reflect changes in disability policy development and reforms of health care systems internationally and certainly echo our previous discussions regarding models of disability and the evolution of disability policy development in the United States.

International field testing occurred in over 50 countries (WHO, 2001a) at various centers and nongovernmental and intergovernmental organizations affiliated with the United Nations through the efforts of more than 1,800 scientists, clinicians, persons with disabilities, and other experts. Results of the studies led to several conclusions including that the *ICIDH-2* was a useful and meaningful public health tool. It was agreed that training was needed in the implementation of the system, particularly in the application of its conceptual framework.

After preliminary review of the systematic Beta-2 field trial data, the prefinal draft was completed in October 2000 and presented at a revision meeting the following month. Suggestions from the meeting were incorporated into the version submitted to the WHO Executive Board in January 2001. The final draft was presented at the 54th World Health Assembly in May 2001. The Assembly voted for the adoption of the *ICIDH-2* and elected to rename the system from the second edition of the *International Classification of Impairments, Disabilities and Handicaps* (ICIDH-2) to the *International Classification of Functioning, Disability and Health*, or the *ICF* (WHO, 2001a). A summary of the *ICIDH/ICF* revision process can be found in the seventh Annex of the *ICF* (WHO, 2001a).

A Major Concession

The final stages of the *ICF*'s development were marked by a coordinated international effort to build consensus, based on field trial data and expert opinion, as to how the *ICF* would be presented for final approval to the World Health Assembly in 2001 (De Kleijn-De Vrankrijker, 2003). One major concession was negotiated regarding the *Activities* and *Participation* constructs.

Originally, the *Activities* and *Participation* component of the *ICIDH-2* was conceptualized as separate components, *Activities* was separate from *Participation* in separate chapters (as they are still depicted in Figure 3.1). Disability advocates within the United States were particularly invested in keeping these constructs separate and parallel, as it necessitated not only the classification of whether someone could do something (*Activity*) but also whether societal barriers precluded actual *Participation* in his or her context despite ability. Ideally, separate classifications for these two constructs would have allowed the international tracking of data related to what people *can* do (*Capacity*) versus what the environment allows them *to* do (*Performance*).

However, in order for this distinction to be made, international consensus was required as to which items represented *Activities* and which reflected the construct of *Participation*. After years of debate, this consensus could not be adequately achieved, resulting in the collapse of the two chapters into a combined chapter (known as the *d* codes, elaborated on shortly). The *ICF* suggests several different approaches using qualifiers that help to capture what the parallel constructs once captured; in the case of a totally overlapping list of *d* codes, the only way to address the concept of *Participation* as once defined is to use the *d* code *Performance* qualifier (also defined below; Reed et al., 2005; Threats & Worrall, 2004).

Unfortunately, in normative data collection efforts, the data available using separate, nonoverlapping constructs will be lost, particularly for data collection efforts employing the short version of the *ICF* (see Peterson, 2005). This disappointment is qualified, however, because with the use of the *Capacity* and *Performance qualifiers* (defined in the next section), it is possible to capture the essence of participation restrictions as they were formerly classified. Therefore, although an international database capturing these data may be lost, application of the *Capacity* and *Performance* qualifiers allows clinicians to use the *ICF* to emphasize what a person *can* do versus what they actually *do* in their environment. All of these concepts are more thoroughly described in the *ICF* overview that follows.

ICF-CHILDREN/YOUTH (ICF-CY), CHILDHOOD DISABILITY

During the *ICIDH* revision processes of the 90s, a task force was created to specifically address using the *ICIDH* with children. Simeonsson et al. (2003) attempted to incorporate the sensibilities needed when classifying youth who are in constant developmental transition, resulting in the *ICF-Children/Youth (ICF-CY)*. This text does not focus on the *ICF-CY*, but it is clear that a text that focuses on the *ICF-CY* and psychiatric diagnoses of childhood would be a useful reference resource.

The *ICF* has proven useful in working with children. Recent research suggests that the *ICF* itself and the *ICD* can be used together as a common language to document disability characteristics of children in early interventions and in child service systems (Simeonsson, Scarborough, & Hebbeler, 2006).

SUMMARY

We have explored the evolution of the *ICF* within the context of disability policy developments in the United States and the prevailing models of disability to date. It should be clear that the *ICF* is the product of considerable international consensus building efforts and that evidence for validity and reliability have been and will continue to be established by its stakeholders.

We ended this historical discussion with a reference to the children's version of the *ICF*, the *ICF-Children/Youth (ICF-CY)*, which is not a focus for this volume. We continue our focus on the *ICF* with a review of its conceptual framework, defining its parts and components, its coding system, and future efforts for research and clinical implementation.

CHAPTER 3

Overview of the *ICF*

PREVIEW QUESTIONS

1. Describe the *ICF* conceptual framework. What are *Body Functions, Body Structures, Activities, Participation, Activity Limitations, Participation Restrictions, Environmental Factors, and Personal Factors*?
2. How does the *ICF* define *health, functioning, impairment, and disability*?
3. Describe the nature of levels of classification and coding within the *ICF*.
4. How are qualifiers used with Body Functions and Body Structures?
5. How are the *Capacity* and *Performance* qualifiers used with *Activities and Participation*?
6. Describe the *Contextual Factors* and how they are qualified?
7. Describe the Ethical Tenets of the *ICF*, and how do they influence its use?

ENCOURAGEMENT

The size and scope of the *ICF*, with just under 1,500 categories of classification, may make it appear difficult to use at first. However, one could compare its use to that of any comprehensive reference; it is not necessary or practical to read most reference material cover to cover, rather, one searches for specific information according to a specific need. The reader can take comfort in knowing that once familiar with the basic structure of the *ICF*, the user can search purposefully for information related to health and functioning with some facility. To allow quick and easy classification, the WHO has created an electronic version of the *ICF* that is searchable through the *ICF* Browser or CD-ROM (WHO, 2001a). An alphabetical index is also available in the hardcopy version of the *ICF*.

MODEL OF FUNCTIONING AND DISABILITY

The *ICF* is a classification system that uses a universal, culturally sensitive, integrative, and interactive model of health and functioning that provides sensitivity to psychosocial and environmental aspects of health and disability (Simeonsson et al., 2003; Üstün et al., 2003). The model proposed to describe the process of functioning and disability in the *ICF* suggests dynamic and reciprocal relationships between the various health-related conditions within the context of environmental and personal factors.

The *ICF* does not classify people; it describes the situation of the person being evaluated within an array of health or health-related *domains*, which are practical and meaningful sets of related physiological functions, anatomical structures, actions, tasks, or areas of life, within a given context. The *ICF* was designed to classify not only limitations in functioning but also positive experiences with respect to bodily functions, activities, and participation in the environment. Examples of positive experiences include communicating, tending to personal hygiene, working, and studying.

Due to the complexity of interactions in a multidimensional model such as the *ICF*'s model of functioning and disability, the *ICF* text notes that the proposed model is likely incomplete and prone to misrepresentation. This warning notwithstanding, Figure 3.1 provides an illustration of the components and interactions that can be used to describe the relationship between disability and functioning (WHO, 2001a, p. 18). As noted earlier, the *Activities* and *Participation* components are now joined as one *Activities and Participation* component, not separate as Figure 3.1 suggests. WHO created the model to describe the process as an example of the building blocks for users to create their own models and study different aspects of the process of functioning and disability. Figure 3.1 provides a representation of processes associated with disability and function in context.

Universe of Well-Being

The *ICF* conceptual framework portrays health as a dynamic interaction between a person's functioning and disability within a given context. The *ICF* classifies all aspects of human health and some health-related components of well-being. It does not classify circumstances brought about by socioeconomic factors such as race, gender, religion, or culture that may restrict full participation in society for reasons not related to health. However, the *Personal Factors* component within the conceptual framework highlights the need to consider complex social circumstances that

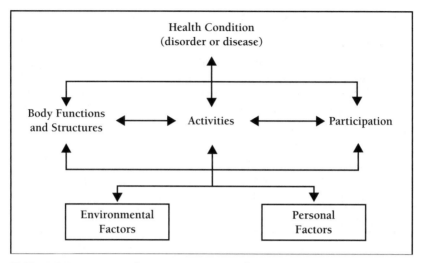

FIGURE 3.1   Interaction between components of *ICF*

Source: *International Classification of Functioning, Disability and Health* (ICF) by the World Health Organization, 2001, Geneva, Author. (Reprinted with permission.)

may influence the information that is currently classified. Note that the terms used in the *ICF* are capitalized to distinguish them from their lay uses (Threats & Worrall, 2004).

The *ICF* defines *well-being* as "encompassing the total universe of human life domains, including physical, mental, and social aspects, that make up what can be called a 'good life'" (WHO, 2001a, p. 211). The *ICF* defines health in terms of the *Universe of well-being* comprised both of *Health domains of well-being*—or those areas of functioning that are a focus of health care professionals—and *Other domains of well-being* that are not typically a focus of health care systems but have a strong relationship to health conditions.

Health

Health refers to components of health, such as seeing, hearing, speaking, remembering, and walking. Health-related components of well-being include employment, education, environment, and transportation. *Health condition* is an umbrella term for an acute or chronic disease, disorder, injury, or trauma (coded using the *ICD-10*). The *ICF* does not draw a rigid line between *Health* and *Health-related domains*; rather, it encourages flexibility to accommodate different conceptualizations of health and health-related states.

Functioning, Impairment, and Disability

Functioning within the *ICF* includes all body functions, structures, activities, and participation in society. It denotes the positive aspects of health and functioning.

Impairments are defined as the manifestations of dysfunction in the body structures or functions rather than as the underlying pathology itself. Etiology of dysfunction is not the focus of the *ICF* but rather is the focus of its sister classification, the *ICD-10*. *Impairments* do not necessarily imply the presence of a disorder or disease but "represent a deviation from certain generally accepted population standards" of functioning (WHO, 2001a, p. 12). Determination of impairment is made by "those qualified to judge physical and mental functioning according to these standards" (p. 12).

Disability refers to any impairments, activity limitations, or participation restrictions, or "the outcome or result of a complex relationship between an individual's health condition and personal factors, and of the external factors that represent the circumstances in which the individual lives" (WHO, 2001a, p. 17). In contrast with *Functioning*, it relates the negative aspects of the interaction between the individual with a health condition and his or her context (Environment and Personal Factors).

Dynamic Interaction and Intervention Targeting

Both functioning and disability are conceptualized within the dynamic interaction between health conditions and contextual factors. The proposed model helps us to understand that difficulty in one aspect of the process does not necessarily imply difficulty in other areas. For example, one may have an impairment such as anxiety but no associated capacity limitation (the person copes well with the anxiety or is treated effectively with medication). On the other hand, one may experience performance problems and capacity limitations without evident impairment (memory difficulties associated with an unidentified case of early onset of Alzheimer's disease). Finally, performance problems may exist without impairments or capacity limitations (a person with Bipolar Disorder is not hired for a job because of stigma associated with the disease, even though the person is compliant with medications, has a stable mood, and can perform the essential functions of the job).

Intervention at any point in the model has the potential to modify one or more entities portrayed in the model. For example, in the second example above, psychological testing may reveal the early dementing process associated with memory loss, identifying the impairment and helping an individual and his or her family cope with and prepare for the disease progression (e.g., requesting pharmacological treatment that has been shown to slow the dementing process). In the last example, disability awareness training or advocacy efforts with the employer may eliminate the prejudice that causes performance difficulty in obtaining gainful employment.

ICF CORE STRUCTURE

The structure of the *ICF* consists of two parts, each with two components. Within the first part, *Functioning and Disability*, the *Body* component consists of two parallel classifications, *Body Functions* and *Body Structures*. Chapters within these classifications are parallel and organized according to body systems. The second component, *Activities and Participation*, covers domains of functioning from both an individual and societal perspective. Components of functioning can be expressed either as nonproblematic functioning or as disabilities (i.e., impairment, activity limitation, or participation restriction). The first part of the *ICF* is interpreted through four separate but related constructs. *Body Functions and Structures* are interpreted through changes in physiological systems or anatomical structures, and *Activities and Participation* are interpreted though *Capacity* and *Performance*. These constructs are defined through the use of qualifiers that are described later.

The second part of the *ICF* classification addresses *Contextual Factors* through two components. The first is *Environmental Factors* or factors in the physical, social, or attitudinal world ranging from the immediate to more general environment. Environmental factors are qualified as either facilitating or hindering functioning. The second component of *Contextual Factors* is *Personal Factors*, which are not currently classified in the *ICF* due to the complex nature of social and cultural variation across the world, but this factor exists in the conceptual framework to call attention to the need to consider unique factors like gender, race, age, fitness, religion, lifestyle, habits, upbringing, coping styles, social background, education, profession, past and current experience, overall behavior pattern and character, individual psychological assets, and other health conditions. A summary of the *ICF* core structure is illustrated in Figure 3.2.

Part 1: Function and Disability		Part 2: Contextual Factors	
Body Functions and Structures	Activities and Participation	Environmental Factors	Personal Factors

FIGURE 3.2   *ICF* core structure

Source: *International Classification of Functioning, Disability and Health* (ICF) by the World Health Organization, 2001, Geneva, Author. (Adapted with permission.)

BODY FUNCTIONS AND BODY STRUCTURES

The *Body Functions and Structures* component of the *ICF* comprises two classifications: physiological functions of body systems or *Body Functions* (including psychological functions) and anatomical parts of the body or *Body Structures* (e.g., organs, limbs, and their components, including the brain and nervous system). *Body Functions* and *Body Structures* are classified in separate but parallel chapters (see Figure 3.3).

Components:	Body Functions	Body Structures	Activities and Participation	Environmental Factors
Code Letter:	*b*	*s*	*d*	*e*
	8 Parallel Chapters		*9 Chapters*	*5 Chapters*
Chapter 1	Mental functions	Structures of the nervous system	Learning and applying knowledge	Products and technology
Chapter 2	Sensory functions and pain	The eye, ear and related structures	General tasks and demands	Natural environment and human-made changes to environment
Chapter 3	Voice and speech functions	Structures involved in voice and speech	Com-munication	Support and relationships
Chapter 4	Functions of the cardiovascular, haematological, immunological and respiratory systems	Structures of the cardiovascular, immunological and respiratory systems	Mobility	Attitudes
Chapter 5	Functions of the digestive, metabolic and endocrine systems	Structures related to the digestive, metabolic and endocrine systems	Self-care	Services, systems, and policies

Continued

Chapter 6	Genitourinary and reproductive functions	Structures related to the genitourinary and reproductive systems	Domestic life	
Chapter 7	Neuromusculoskeletal and movement-related functions	Structures related to movement	Interpersonal interactions and relationships	
Chapter 8	Functions of the skin and related structures	Skin and related structures	Major life areas	
Chapter 9			Community, social, and civic life	

FIGURE 3.3   *ICF*: One-level classification

Source: *International Classification of Functioning, Disability and Health* (ICF) by the World Health Organization, 2001, Geneva, Author. (Adapted with permission.)

For example, within *Body Functions*, "hearing functions" has a corollary within *Body Structures* of "ear and related structures." Both classifications are arranged according to the same body system taxonomy and can be interpreted in terms of changes in physiological systems or in anatomical structures. The criteria for *impairment* are the same for body functions and structures and are classified according to (a) loss or lack, (b) reduction, (c) addition or excess, and (d) deviation. Once present, an impairment is further qualified in terms of severity, which is described next.

Now that we have defined *Body Functions and Structures* within the context of the *ICF*, it may be useful to discuss how the *ICF* overlaps with the *ICD-10* system in this regard. Both classifications address impairments to body structures and related functions but for two different reasons. The *ICF* addresses them to identify problems in related functioning for a given health condition, which may then inform treatment needs, intervention targeting, or even prevention efforts. The *ICD* does so to identify signs and symptoms associated with a disease process or diagnosis and perhaps as a reason for contact with health services (WHO, 2001a, p. 4).

QUALIFIERS

The classification codes are given meaning through the use of various qualifiers, depending upon the component. Codes have no meaning without them. Qualifiers are one or more numbers indicated after a decimal point (or separator) that follows a multilevel code, denoting a magnitude or level of health for that code.

The generic qualifiers noted in Figure 3.4 apply in some fashion across all of the codes. The generic qualifiers describe the extent of problems for a given *ICF* code using the generic scale with some slight modification depending upon the component being qualified. For example, for all instances the scores range from 0 through 4 indicating, respectively, "No," "Mild," "Moderate," "Severe," and "Complete" levels of difficulty, which can be described as impairment, limitation, barrier, facilitator, or difficulty depending upon with which *ICF* construct it is used.

For example, the *Body Function* and *Body Structure* components use a qualifier that addresses severity through values ranging from 0 through 4 indicating, respectively, "No," "Mild," "Moderate," "Severe," and "Complete *impairment*" (WHO, 2001a, p. 47). In contrast, qualifiers for Activities and Participation use the same numbers and severity levels but exchange "impairment" for "difficulty." Qualifiers for Environmental Factors also use the same number and related severity

Code	Level of Problem, Impairment, Difficulty, or Barrier	Qualitative Descriptors for Problem, Impairment, Difficulty, or Barrier	Percentages*
xxxx.0	No	none, absent, negligible . . .	0%–4%
xxxx.1	Mild	slight, low . . .	5%–24%
xxxx.2	Moderate	medium, fair . . .	25%–49%
xxxx.3	Severe	high, extreme . . .	50%–95%
xxxx.4	Complete	total . . .	96%–100%
xxxx.8	not specified		
xxxx.9	not applicable		

FIGURE 3.4   Generic qualifiers

* Percentages are to be calibrated in different domains with reference to relevant population standards as percentiles. "xxxx" stands for a given *ICF* classification code that precedes the qualifier.

Source: *International Classification of Functioning, Disability and Health* (ICF) by the World Health Organization, 2001, Geneva, Author. (Reprinted with permission.)

system but exchange the term *impairment* for *barrier* or *facilitator* as appropriate.

The *Body Structure* component uses the generic qualifier as the first qualifier as well as two additional qualifiers. The second qualifier indicates the nature of the change in a body structure as follows: 0 = no change in structure; 1 = total absence; 2 = partial absence; 3 = additional part; 4 = aberrant dimensions; 5 = discontinuity; 6 = deviating position; 7 = qualitative changes in structure, including accumulation of fluid (p. 105). The third qualifier indicates the location of impairment as follows: 0 = more than one region; 1 = right; 2 = left; 3 = both sides; 4 = front; 5 = back; 6 = proximal; 7 = distal. All three qualifiers have a "not specified" (8) and a "not applicable" (9) qualifier as appropriate.

ACTIVITIES AND PARTICIPATION

The second component under *Functioning and Disability*, *Activities and Participation*, presents a single list of domains that covers a wide range of different aspects of functioning from both individual and societal perspectives. Figure 3.3 lists the nine domains within this component of the *ICF*. The *Body Functions and Structures* component is intended to be complemented by the *Activities and Participation* component. We briefly discussed this component within our historical overview of the *ICF's* development, but the discussion will be more detailed and complete here.

Activity and Participation

An *Activity* is defined as the execution of a task or action by an individual, such as sitting, copying, calculating, or driving. It represents the individual perspective of functioning. *Participation* is involvement in a life situation or the societal perspective of functioning. The domains in this component can be used to describe either or both concepts.

Activity Limitation and Participation Restriction

Activity Limitations are difficulties an individual may have in executing activities, from slight to severe deviation in comparison with someone without a given health condition. *Participation Restrictions* are problems an individual may experience in involvement in life situations, determined by comparing an individual's participation to an individual without disability in that culture or society. Both constructs "are assessed against a generally accepted population standard" (WHO, 2001a, p. 15) for someone without a similar health condition.

The *ICF* proposes four possible conceptualizations of the relationship between *Activities* and *Participation*. The user can code each category as either an activity or participation issue, resulting in two mutually exclusive lists. Australia has adopted this method in their clinical implementation manual. Alternatively, one can use the domains for both activity and participation simultaneously or as an overlapping list, which is how the U.S. version of a clinical implementation manual in progress is proceeding (Reed et al., 2005, 2008; Threats & Worrall, 2004). Two other variations between separate and overlapping lists are referred to in Annex 3 of the *ICF*. Domains within this component are qualified through the constructs of *Capacity* and *Performance*.

CAPACITY AND PERFORMANCE QUALIFIERS

The domains of the *Activities and Participation* component are operationalized through the use of the qualifiers *Capacity* and *Performance*. The *Capacity* qualifier "describes an individual's ability to execute a task or an action," or more specifically, "the highest probable level of functioning that a person may reach in a given domain at a given moment" (WHO, 2001a, p. 15). One must apply the *Capacity* qualifier in the context of a "'uniform' or 'standard' environment, [that thus] reflects the environmentally adjusted ability of the individual" (p. 15). In order to make international comparisons, such environments have to be defined similarly across countries. This situation presents unique standardization challenges that are being addressed in the development of the clinical implementation manual (Reed et al., 2005, 2008; Threats & Worrall, 2004).

The *Performance* qualifier describes "what a person does in his or her current environment" (p. 15). Another way to describe this qualifier is as "involvement in a life situation" or "the lived experience" of a person in the environment (p. 15). Current environment is important to note using the *Environmental Factors* component for this qualifier. One can consider the difference between *Capacity* and *Performance* functioning in order to suggest what could be done to an individual's environment in order to maximize his or her ability and function and to increase opportunity for full participation in society. An example of this may be applications of assistive technologies for persons with disabilities that enable individuals to access vocational, recreational, and community domains, previously unavailable to certain individuals (or groups of individuals) without such support.

Consider another example, a person dealing with schizophrenia as a diagnosis. With proper treatment, a person with schizophrenia may be quite capable of a wide range of activities. However, if due to the stigma associated with mental illness a potential employer is not willing to hire a person so diagnosed, society becomes the barrier to participation in society.

In summary then, *Capacity* relates most closely with what a person can optimally do given his or her *Body Function and Structure*, whereas *Performance* is what a person actually does given his or her context. This presents a "can-do" (*Capacity*) versus "does-do" (*Performance*) paradigm that informs intervention targeting to ameliorate barriers and maximize facilitators within a person's context; more on this in the Contextual Factors section.

The *Performance* and *Capacity* qualifiers are rated on the same 0–4 scale as the first qualifier of *Body Functions and Structures*, substituting the term *difficulty* for *impairment*. *Performance* and *Capacity* can be considered both with and without assistive devices or personal assistance, forming four possible qualifiers (*Performance* with and without assistance and *Capacity* with and without assistance).

CONTEXTUAL FACTORS

Contextual Factors "represent the complete background of an individual's life and living" (WHO, 2001a, p. 16). They include two components, *Environmental* and *Personal Factors*. Disability is defined as "the outcome or result of a complex relationship between an individual's health condition and personal factors, and of the external factors that represent the circumstances in which the individual lives" (WHO, 2001a, p. 17). These contextual factors can present as either barriers to or facilitators of health and functioning in society.

Environmental Factors

Environmental Factors (the physical, social, and attitudinal worlds) are considered as they facilitate or hinder all components of functioning and disability at the *Body Functions and Structures* levels as well as the *Activities and Participation* levels. *Environmental Factors* are organized to focus on two different levels, the individual and societal levels.

The individual level has the most immediate environmental influence, for example, one's home, workplace, or school. Within these contexts, one is influenced by family, peers, acquaintances, and strangers. The physical and material features of the immediate environment are also considered here.

The societal level addresses both formal and informal social structures, services, and overarching approaches or systems in the community or society. Related organization services may include work environment, community activities, government agencies, communication and transportation services, informal social networks, laws, regulations, formal and informal rules, attitudes, and ideologies (WHO, 2001a, p. 17). Figure 3.3 lists the five chapters that comprise *Environmental Factors*. Evaluation of these factors provides opportunity for exploration into determinants and risk factors of health conditions as they exist in the environment.

Qualifiers for Environmental Factors

The *Environmental Factors* are qualified on a scale similar to the generic scale used for *Body Functions*, ranging from 0 to 4—No to Complete— substituting *Barrier* or *Facilitator* for *Impairment*. *Facilitators* according to the *ICF* are factors in a person's environment that, through their absence or presence, improve functioning and reduce disability. *Barriers* are factors that through their absence or presence limit functioning and create disability. *Facilitators*, indicating positive environmental support, are noted with a plus sign; *Barriers* simply follow the decimal point.

There are three suggested coding conventions within the *ICF* for the *Environmental Factors*. They can be coded independently of other components in the *ICF*, coded for every component, or coded for each of the *Performance* and *Capacity* qualifiers under *Activities and Participation*. An example of *Environmental Factors* coding may be the evaluation of an individual's mobility within the community and whether they are able to use public transit effectively to access desired domains (facilitator) or are reliant on others for transportation (barrier). Another example could be the assessment of prevailing attitudes toward disability that create barriers or facilitate inclusion for persons with disabilities.

Personal Factors

Personal Factors may include gender, race, age, fitness, religion, lifestyle, habits, upbringing, coping styles, social background, education, profession, past and current experience, overall behavior pattern and character, individual psychological assets, and other health conditions, all of which can affect health and functioning. As noted earlier, although *Personal Factors* are a consideration within the *Contextual Factors*, they are not described or coded specifically in the *ICF* because they are not considered part of a health condition or health state.

However, *Personal Factors* are considered within the overall model because they may play a role in the manifestation of functioning, disability, or health at any level and also affect the outcome of a given intervention. It is important to note here that disability advocates are encouraging classificatory precision in this important domain, or that code sets are developed to capture this important area (Duggan, Albright, & LeQuerica, 2008; Hurst, 2003) so the *Personal Factors* will likely be a focus of future development within the *ICF* (Duggan et al., 2008).

Having reviewed the major components of the *ICF* and their definitions, Figure 3.5 provides a useful summary table of these terms in their contexts.

LEVELS OF CLASSIFICATION AND CODING

As mentioned previously, *domains* within the *ICF* are practical and meaningful sets of related physiological functions (including psychological functions) and anatomical structures, as well as actions, tasks, and areas of life described from bodily, individual, and societal perspectives that make up the different chapters within each component of the *ICF*. Essential attributes of the domains (e.g., qualities, properties, and relationships) are defined by both inclusions and exclusions; each *ICF* code is designed to be mutually exclusive. The classes and subclasses reflect the various levels that make up the hierarchical order of the *ICF*, with more basic levels comprising all aspects of more detailed levels.

One-Level Classification

The categories of function for a given domain begin at a general level of detail and expand to levels of greater detail. The *One-Level Classification* of the *ICF* expands on the core structure: (1) the *Body Functions* component contains eight chapters that address "physiological functions of body systems (including psychological functions)" (WHO, 2001a, p. 12); (2) the *Body Structures* component contains eight chapters that parallel the *Body Functions* component and deal with "anatomical parts of the body such as organs, limbs, and their components" (p. 12); (3) the *Activities and Participation* component contains nine chapters, with *Activities* addressing "the execution of a task or action by an individual"

Two Parts: (A dynamic interaction)	Part 1: Functioning and Disability		Part 2: Contextual Factors	
Each Part Has Two Components:	Body Functions and Structures	Activities and Participation	Environmental Factors	Personal Factors
Domains (Contain the categories or units of classification of the *ICF*)	1. Body Functions (including Psychological Functioning) 2. Body Structures	Life areas (tasks, actions)	External influences on functioning and disability	Internal influences on function-ing and disability
Constructs (Defined through use of qualifiers that modify the extent or magnitude of function or disability)	Change in body function (physiological) Change in body structure (anatomical)	Capacity: Executing tasks in a standard environment ("can do") Performance: Executing tasks in the current environment ("does do")	Facilitating or hinder-ing impact of features of the physical, social, and attitudinal world	Impact of attributes of the person
Positive Aspect	**Functioning** Functional and structural integrity	Activities Participation	Facilitators	*Not classified in the* ICF
Negative Aspect	**Disability** Impairment	Activity limitation Participation restriction	Barriers/ hindrances	

FIGURE 3.5   Overview of the *ICF*

Note: Units of classification are situations, not people

Source: *International Classification of Functioning, Disability and Health* (ICF) by the World Health Organization, 2001, Geneva, Author. (Adapted with permission.)

and *Participation* addressing "involvement in a life situation" (p. 14); and (4) the *Environmental Factors* component contains five chapters focusing on "the physical, social, and attitudinal environment in which people live and conduct their lives" (p. 171), organized from the immediate to more general environment. The maximum number of codes available at the one-digit level of classification is 34. The one-level classification is illustrated in Figure 3.3.

Two-Level Classification

The *Two-Level Classification* is the first branching level of the *ICF*, comprising specific chapter headings. Alphanumeric codes begin with a letter (*b* for Body Functions, *s* for Body Structures, *d* for Activities and Participation, and *e* for Environmental Factors) and a three-digit numeric classification indicating chapter and specific categories within each chapter. For example, the classification associated with the psychological function of emotion is found in the first chapter of *Body Functions* (its code begins with "b") under the *Specific Mental Function* section, called *Emotional Functions*, or alphanumeric code b152. The two-level items total 362 distinct, three-digit codes.

Detailed Classification

The *Detailed Classification With Definitions* lists all categories within the *ICF* along with their definitions, inclusions, and exclusions, providing greater levels of detail using four- and five-digit numeric codes. The level of classification used depends upon the clinical context. Examining emotional functions once again, examples of level of detail include *Appropriateness of Emotion* (b1520), *Regulation of Emotion* (b1521), and *Range of emotion* (b1522). Code groups also offer an *Other Specified (e.g., b1528)* and *Unspecified (e.g., b1529)* codes for functions not detailed in the current classification.

Codes at the detailed level of classification number up to 1,424 items. However, the *ICF* suggests that typical use of the system in a health or health-related setting for surveys and clinical outcome evaluation will generate a set of 3–18 codes to describe a case with two-level (three-digit) precision. The more precise four-level codes would be used for more specialized services (rehabilitation outcomes, geriatrics, and mental health) and research.

There are two versions of the *ICF*: the full version that provides all four levels of classification detail and the short version that provides two levels of classification. In either case, units of classification are qualified with numeric codes that specify the magnitude or extent of disability or function in a given category as well as the extent to which an environmental factor is a facilitator or a barrier.

Hierarchical and Mutually Exclusive Codes

Within components, as units of classification become more detailed, there is the assumption that more detailed units share the attributes of the broader units in the hierarchy order in which they fall. For example, *Range of Emotion* b1522 shares the attributes of the higher level of classification *Emotional Functions* b152. It is worth mentioning again that categories within the same level are designed to be mutually exclusive. More than one category may be used to accurately classify specific functioning as warranted.

ICF Coding Example

By way of review, the *ICF* has two parts, each with two components. Part 1 of the *ICF* comprises Body Functions and Structures and Activities and Participation. Body Functions have codes beginning with the letter "b," and Body Structures codes begin with the letter "s." Activities and Participation codes begin with the letter "d." The *ICF* also allows for the use of "a" or "p" replacements for "d" if attempting to code Activity or Participation separately. Part 2 of the *ICF* is composed of Environmental and Personal Factors, but Personal Factors are not yet classified in the *ICF*. Environmental Factors codes begin with the letter "e."

The codes themselves begin with the associated chapter number. Looking ahead to our discussion of Figure 3.6, the codes included in the figure all begin with the number 1, because they belong to Chapter 1, Mental Functions. For an example of codes that expand to the fourth level of detail (five digits), the reader is referred to the *ICF*, p. 49, the Orientation Functions (b114) section of Global Mental Functions (b110–b139), which are second-level codes. Orientation functions can be classified more precisely to address Orientation to person (b1142, a third-level code) and even more precisely as Orientation to others (b11421), a fourth-level or five-digit code. This represents the pathway from a two-level code in Mental Functions to a detailed classification as a fourth-level code.

Qualifiers provide inherent meaning to the *ICF* codes, reflect the magnitude of the issue classified, and appear as one, two, or three digits after the decimal point that follows the *ICF* code. Students of the *ICF* will benefit from a review of the second Annex of the *ICF* (pp. 219–233) that provides coding guidelines, including an overview of the *ICF* organization and structure and general and specific coding rules. Annex 4 of the *ICF* (pp. 238–241) provides specific case examples for applying the *ICF*. However, there is work to be done with respect to the consistent clinical implementation of the *ICF*, which we turn to next.

Branch	ICF Code	Two-Level Descriptor
Global Mental Functions (b110–b139)	b110	Consciousness functions
	b114	Orientation functions
	b117	Intellectual functions
	b122	Global psychosocial functions
	b126	Temperament and personality functions
	b130	Energy and drive functions
	b134	Sleep functions
	b139	Global mental functions, other specified and unspecified
Specific mental functions (b140–b189)	b140	Attention functions
	b144	Memory functions
	b147	Psychomotor functions
	b152	Emotional functions
	b156	Perceptual functions
	b160	Thoughts functions
	b164	Higher-level cognitive functions
	b167	Mental functions of language
	b172	Calculation functions
	b176	Mental functions of sequencing and complex movements
	b180	Experience of self and time functions
	b189	Specific mental functions, other specified and unspecified
	b198	Mental functions, other specified
	b199	Mental functions, unspecified

FIGURE 3.6   Body Functions, Chapter 1, Mental Functions, Two-Level Classification of the *ICF*

Source: *International Classification of Functioning, Disability and Health* (ICF) by the World Health Organization, 2001, Geneva, Author. (Reprinted with permission.)

CLINICAL IMPLEMENTATION OF THE *ICF*

Although the *ICF* was adopted as the complement to the *ICD-10*, the 191 member states that are encouraged to use it must generate their own resources necessary to guide its clinical implementation; these efforts have not been consistent or well coordinated across the member states. In order to facilitate implementation of the *ICF* in clinical settings in the United States, the APA and WHO formed a series of interdisciplinary teams of experts to develop *The Procedural Manual and Guide for the Standardized Application of the ICF: A Manual for Health Professionals* (Reed et al., 2005).

Early Stages of the Manual's Development

Reed and associates (2005), some of whom were members of the alpha drafting team for the joint-manual effort, including this author, detailed the initial template development that led to work completed thus far on the implementation manual. Eventually, clinicians provided with a clinical applications manual that associates the *ICF* with contemporary assessment practices will assist novice classification users to orient to the *ICF* effectively and to apply the *ICF* consistently to research and practice.

Current Challenges in Clinical Implementation

The manual development effort proved challenging and is still ongoing. The projected publication date of the manual has been delayed as various complicated issues arise along the way, such as questions regarding interpretation of the codes themselves and the implementation of the *Capacity* and *Performance* qualifiers (Reed et al., 2005, 2008; Threats & Worrall, 2004). The size of the manual has grown over time and generated discussion regarding the utility of a paper manual versus an electronic computerized matching system approach to implementing the *ICF*. The manual is currently undergoing a multidisciplinary, final editing process, so it may be published by the time this text is published.

All of the research on the development of the *ICIDH* will not necessarily generalize to the *ICF* as it is currently constructed, given the significant changes to the classification system (see Peterson & Rosenthal, 2005a,b). The creation of *The Manual* adds another layer of complexity to *ICF* implementation. Once the manual is published, studies will need to be conducted that evaluate the clarity of the manual, the utility of the manual in clinical practice, and ultimately the application of the *ICF* given the new implementation guidelines. Complementary training will be developed to promote consistent coding of guidelines from the WHO and its collaborating centers (Reed et al., 2008).

Clinical judgment, assessment biases, and interactional dynamics between rater and participants are further areas of complexity to address in standard use of the *ICF*, so much work lies ahead. A thorough review of the American Psychological Association's (APA) collaboration with the World Health Organization (WHO) in the development of a clinical implementation manual can be found in Reed and associates (2005, 2008).

ASPECTS OF THE *ICF* APPLICABLE TO MENTAL DISORDERS

Since the focus of this text is the nexus between the *ICF* and the *DSM-IV-TR*, we conclude this overview of the *ICF* by highlighting aspects of the *ICF* most relevant to mental health functioning and mental disorders. Research and practice inform us that the relationship between psychological health and physical health is complex, reciprocal in some instances, and almost always mutually influential (APA, 2000). It is artificial in most instances to try to separate psychological factors from physical impairment. As we describe aspects of the *ICF* that would most typically be associated with mental disorders, it is important to acknowledge that nearly every aspect of the *ICF* could be impacted by psychological factors.

One-Level Classification

The obvious chapter within the *Body Structures* component of the *ICF* that relates to mental disorders is Structures of the Nervous System, Chapter 1. The functional parallel chapter under *Body Functions* is Mental Functions, Chapter 1. There are other chapters in this component of the *ICF* that relate to very specific aspects of health and functioning in *DSM-IV-TR*-diagnosed mental disorders, which are explored in Part III of this text.

The chapters most relevant to mental disorders in the *Activities and Participation* component of the *ICF* include Chapter 1, Learning and Applying Knowledge; Chapter 2, General Tasks and Demands; and Chapter 3, Communication; Chapter 7, Interpersonal Interactions and Relationships; Chapter 8, Major Life Areas; and Chapter 9, Community, Social, and Civic Life, relate closely to the psychosocial sequelae of mental disorders.

Finally, the chapters most relevant to mental disorders in the Environmental Factors section of the *ICF* include Chapter 3, Support and Relationships; and Chapter 4, Attitudes; Chapter 5, Services, Systems, and Policies, could certainly be a relevant domain to classify when planning mental health service provision.

Two-Level Classification

The Two-Level Classification contains the *ICF* chapters and the first branching level in the classification. The short version of the *ICF* contains only two levels of classification, and it is likely that most international initiatives involving data sharing will occur at this level of detail. The detailed classification may have as many as five levels of classificatory precision and will likely be reserved for special applications in research, assessment, and practice. Here, we discuss one instance of where Two-Level classification codes will relate to mental disorders.

Whether the diagnostic system is the *ICD* or the *DSM-IV-TR*, Chapter 1, Mental Functions, will be one of the most frequently used chapter of codes in the *ICF* for mental disorders. Chapter 1 with its first level of branching is presented in Figure 3.6.

Because the *ICF* is a recommended companion text to Part 1 of this text, including all 1,424 *ICF* codes in this text is not necessary, but Figure 3.6 is included as a point of focus for discussion. It is not difficult to imagine that disturbances in mood, anxiety, and perception (i.e., psychotic symptoms) would impact the detailed global and specific mental functions listed in Figure 3.6. The reader is referred to the *ICF* Detailed Classification with definitions to review the 14 pages that expand these branches to the fourth and fifth level of detail.

The challenge for the manual in development for the *ICF* is to provide guidance on how each of these constructs is operationalized. For example, b144 memory functions; what model of memory is proposed as the standard? What assessment instruments and what metrics will inform its qualification? Similarly, consider code b126, Temperament and personality functions. By what theory and/or factor analysis will temperament and personality be defined? What instruments will best capture these complex constructs?

In Part III of this text, we present results from the study that established two *ICF* Core Sets for depression. The specific Core Sets are presented in their entirety to provide an example of the comprehensive application of the *ICF* in describing the functional aspects of a given mental disorder. The results and discussion portions of the publication are reviewed in light of future Core Set development.

Having provided an overview of the *ICF*, its conceptual framework, and its component parts, we now turn our focus to the ethical clinical implementation of the *ICF* in clinical practice and research.

CHAPTER 4

Collaborative Clinical Practice and Research

PREVIEW QUESTIONS

1. What are the 11 provisions for ethical use of the *ICF*? How do they correspond with Kitchener's (2000) 5 ethical principles?
2. How can the *ICF* be used to encourage contemporary thinking on mental health parity in health care?
3. What improvements need to be made in the *ICF*?
4. What future research efforts lie ahead for the *ICF*?

In this chapter, we focus on the collaborative nature of classifying health and functioning using the *ICF*, the collaboration necessary for ongoing development of the *ICF*, and related ethical issues for research and practice. We complete Part I of the text with a discussion of the future prospects for the *ICF* in this light and with a brief summary of what we have covered so far in the first part of the text.

ETHICAL ISSUES

According to the World Health Organization (World Health Organization [WHO], 2001a), even a well-developed tool can be misused and cause harm. Although WHO suggests that the units of classification within the *ICF* are not people, but situations of functioning (WHO, 2001a), Duchan (2004) posited that the *ICF* is potentially dehumanizing if it is misused to represent individuals by a series of numbers. The developers of the *ICF* appeared to forecast this vulnerability, creating an annex at the end of the document consisting of 11 ethical provisions intended to guide the ethical use of the classification system.

We review the 11 provisions for ethical use of the *ICF* and discuss them in relation to Kitchener's (2000) five principles for thinking well in psychology-related professions. When used in an ethical manner, the *ICF* is a tool that can be used for enhancing psychological treatment outcomes and encouraging mental health parity and related social justice. This section draws from a similar discussion published in a special issue of *Rehabilitation Education* (Peterson & Threats, 2005).

ETHICAL PROVISIONS OF THE *ICF*

The *ICF* incorporates a set of ethical provisions that are complementary to major ethical tenets previously identified in counseling and psychology (Kitchener, 2000). When applied in an ethically responsible manner, the *ICF* is used withconsumer participation in a collaborative and informational process; it is not something that is done to the consumer (Peterson & Threats, 2005; Threats & Worrall, 2004). The *ICF* is unique among classification systems in that the 11 ethical provisions are actually a part of the overall classification system. In order to maintain the spirit of its intended use, it is important for *ICF* users to be informed by the ethical provisions when applying the *ICF* to practice.

The 11 ethical provisions were established in the sixth Annex of the *ICF* to reduce the risk of disrespectful or harmful use of the classification system. The provisions address three general areas: (1) respect and confidentiality, (2) clinical use of the *ICF*, and (3) social use of *ICF* information (WHO, 2001a, pp. 244–245). The sixth Annex of the *ICF* prefaces the *Ethical Guidelines for the Use of ICF* as follows:

> Every scientific tool can be misused and abused. It would be naïve to believe that a classification system such as *ICF* will never be used in ways that are harmful to people. As explained in Appendix 5, the process of the revision of *ICIDH* has included persons with disabilities and their advocacy organizations from the beginning. Their input has lead to substantive changes in the terminology, content and structure of *ICF*. This annex sets out some basic guidelines for the ethical use of *ICF*. It is obvious that no set of guidelines can anticipate all forms of misuse of a classification or other scientific tool, or for that matter, that guidelines alone can prevent misuse. This document is no exception. It is hoped that attention to the provisions that follow will reduce the risk that *ICF* will be used in ways that are disrespectful and harmful to people with disabilities. (WHO, 2001a, p. 244)

The 11 provisions are listed here according to three broad themes.

Respect and Confidentiality

1. *ICF* should always be used so as to respect the inherent value and autonomy of individual persons.
2. *ICF* should never be used to label people or otherwise identify them solely in terms of one or more disability categories.
3. In clinical settings, *ICF* should always be used with the full knowledge, cooperation, and consent of the persons whose levels of functioning are being classified. If limitations of an individual's cognitive capacity preclude this involvement, the individual's advocate should be an active participant.
4. The information coded using *ICF* should be viewed as personal information and subject to recognized rules of confidentiality appropriate for the manner in which the data will be used.

Clinical Use of *ICF*

5. Wherever possible, the clinician should explain to the individual or the individual's advocate the purpose of the use of *ICF* and invite questions about the appropriateness of using it to classify the person's levels of functioning.
6. Wherever possible, the person whose level of functioning is being classified (or the person's advocate) should have the opportunity to participate and in particular to challenge or affirm the appropriateness of the category being used and the assessment assigned.
7. Because the deficit being classified is a result of both a person's health condition and the physical and social context in which the person lives, *ICF* should be used holistically.

Social Use of *ICF* Information

8. *ICF* information should be used, to the greatest extent feasible, with the collaboration of individuals to enhance their choices and their control over their lives.
9. *ICF* information should be used toward the development of social policy and political change that seek to enhance and support the participation of individuals.
10. *ICF*, and all information derived from its use, should not be employed to deny established rights or otherwise restrict legitimate entitlements to benefits for individuals or groups.

11. Individuals classed together under *ICF* may still differ in many ways. Laws and regulations that refer to *ICF* classifications should not assume more homogeneity than intended and should ensure that those whose levels of functioning are being classified are considered as individuals (WHO, 2001a, pp. 244–245).

KITCHENER'S ETHICAL PRINCIPLES

The ethical provisions set forth in the *ICF* complement Kitchener's Foundational Principles for Thinking Well (Kitchener, 2000), which are derived from Beauchamp and Childress "common morality" in biomedical ethics (1994, p. 102). Kitchener's five principles are nonmaleficence, beneficence, autonomy, fidelity, and justice, and they have been used to inform the development of ethical codes in counseling and psychology-related professions (Cottone & Tarvydas, 2007; Peterson & Murray, 2006). The philosophical underpinnings of the Disability Rights Movement are not unlike the values espoused in Kitchener's ethical principles (Riggar & Maki, 2004) and likely influenced the creation of the ethical provisions in the *ICF* given the participation of stakeholders sympathetic to the movement.

According to Kitchener (Kitchener, 2000), *nonmaleficence* means not causing others harm, including avoiding actions that risk harming others. *Beneficence* means doing good or benefiting others, including balancing the potential consequences of an action, both beneficial and harmful. *Autonomy* addresses freedom of action and choice, promoting autonomous action that is reciprocal in nature. *Fidelity* connotes faithful, loyal, honest, and trustworthy behavior. Finally, *justice* deals with issues of fairness, crossing individual, interpersonal, organizational, and societal spheres of existence. Table 4.1 highlights the relationships between the 11 *ICF* ethical provisions and Kitchener's (Kitchener, 2000) ethical principles (Peterson & Threats, 2005). It is arguable that all of the provisions in some way avoid doing harm (nonmaleficence) and attempt to do good (beneficence), thus all 11 provisions could be associated with these two constructs. Table 4.1 illustrates key emphases within a given provision as they relate to Kitchener's Principles.

MENTAL HEALTH PARITY

If health care professionals value the dignity and worth of all people, then all persons with disabilities, regardless of the origin of impairment, should be afforded the same dignity, rights, and opportunities. The ethical tenets

TABLE 4.1 Proposed Correspondence Between Kitchener's Ethical Principles (Kitchener, 2000) and the *ICF* Ethical Provisions

ICF Ethical Provisions	Nonmaleficence	Beneficence	Autonomy	Fidelity	Justice
1	X	X	X		
2	X	X		X	X
3	X		X		
4			X	X	X
5	X		X		
6			X		
7			X		X
8			X		
9					X
10					X
11	X	X			

Source: Peterson and Threats (2005).

of the *ICF* are consistent with this perspective. Such has not been the case in the United States with respect to third-party reimbursement for health care services, where mental health-related services are often relegated to mental health carve out resources that are not as well resourced as services for physical medicine.

Recently in the United States, mental health care parity legislation was passed, which promises to challenge the lack of parity with respect to third-party resources provided for the treatment of physical versus mental disabilities. The *ICF* has brought international attention to this dilemma through the associated Mental Health Task Force (Kennedy, 2003).

The *ICF* is etiologically neutral; for example, difficulties in attention are classified the same regardless of whether they are caused by problems with pain (physical medicine) versus depression (psychiatric medicine). The *ICF* conceptual framework promotes mental health care parity by definition, as no distinction is made as to the cause of difficulty with attention. Etiological factors can be inferred from the body structure codes of the *ICF* and with associated classification by the *ICD-10*. However, when functioning becomes the focus of describing health, the differences between physical and mental impairments diminish, ultimately providing support for the mental health parity movement (Peterson & Threats, 2005).

If health care classification becomes more etiologically neutral and focuses on functioning (what a person does, what he or she can do given the opportunity), the rationale for mental health parity becomes more salient. Hopefully, the *ICF* will continue to play an important role in achieving mental health parity and in treating people with mental disorders comparably to people dealing with physical disorders. For a thorough review of the important work of the Mental Health Task Force described in our historical development discussion of the *ICF*, see Kennedy (2003).

SOCIAL JUSTICE

The United Nations recognized the *ICIDH*'s value and endorsed its use "as a basis for human rights advocacy around the world" (Üstün, Chatterji, Bickenbach, Kostanjsek, & Schneider, 2003, p. 569). However, the original *ICIDH* (WHO, 1980) was developed in close circles of rehabilitation professionals who did not systematically consult with people with disabilities. As efforts began in 1993 to revise the classification system, input was sought from the disability community, including individuals with disabilities and related organizations. Disabled Peoples' International contributed its time and energies to the revision process, and the *ICF* reflects their important input (Duggan, Albright, & LeQuerica, 2008; Hurst, 2003; WHO, 2001a, p. 242).

Advocacy

Advocacy is an ethical responsibility of all health care professionals. The ethical provisions of the *ICF* encourage health care professionals to use the *ICF* to facilitate the empowerment and inclusion of persons with disabilities in society. One way to advocate social justice for those who may be marginalized by society is to include them in the development of practical solutions (Peterson & Threats, 2005). The *ICF* was revised to its current iteration with significant input from all of its stakeholders, an example of social justice in action (WHO, 2001a).

Inclusion in the Classification Process

The *ICIDH*'s revision process included people with disabilities in important decision-making processes, and the ultimate product, the *ICF*, reveals the fruit of their efforts (Simeonsson et al., 2003). Because of consumer involvement with its development, the instructions for use of the *ICF* delineate that the individual whose situation is being classified should participate in classifying and qualifying levels of functioning. Those being evaluated are especially encouraged to take the lead in deciding how the environment is classified as a facilitator or barrier to functioning (Hurst, 2003; WHO, 2001a).

The disability community was also involved in and had an important impact on the identification of key constructs within the classification during latter phases of the development of the *ICF* (see Hurst, 2003; Üstün et al., 2003). For example, the term *handicap* was eliminated from the classification because of its pejorative connotations in English. *Disability* was purposefully avoided as a name of any component of the *ICF* and is used as an umbrella term that is operationalized as *Activity Limitations* or *Participation Restrictions*.

Environmental Task Force

Another important outcome of the disability community's involvement was the establishment of the Environmental Task Force (ETF), one of three task forces created for the recent revision process. ETF was funded by the Centers for Disease Control and chaired by Rachel Hurst, a disability rights activist (Hurst, 2003). People with disabilities were the majority of the members of the ETF, representing WHO-based geographic regions and expertise in environmental factors and disability. The work of the ETF resulted in the development of the *Environmental Factors* component of the *ICF*, which encouraged consideration of the influence of interactions between an individual and his or her environment rather than focusing on the person's impairment exclusively (Schneidert, Hurst, Miller, & Üstün, 2003).

The contextual factors (*Environmental* and *Personal Factors*) developed in collaboration with the disability community provided a more holistic picture of health and functioning. Classifying health and functioning in light of contextual factors will lead to more effective health care service provision for people with disabilities and greater social justice. Social policy developers can consider contextual factors and related databases when establishing legislation, services, and interventions for people with disabilities (Hurst, 2003; Schneidert et al., 2003).

FUTURE DEVELOPMENT EFFORTS

WHO wrote in the eighth Annex of the *ICF* that the *ICF* is owned by all its users. As our literature review suggests in Part I of this text, WHO and its collaborating centers have done considerable work since the *ICF*'s publication in 2001, but there is much left to be done by the international community owners of this important but nascent system. WHO suggested the following foci for future work with the *ICF*:

1. Promote the use of the *ICF* at the country level for development of national databases.
2. Establish an international dataset and the framework to permit international comparisons.
3. Identify algorithms for eligibility for social benefits and pensions.
4. Study disability and functioning of family members (e.g., a study of third-party disability due to the health condition of significant others).
5. Develop the *Personal Factors* component.
6. Develop precise operational definitions of categories for research purposes.
7. Develop assessment instruments for identification and measurement.
8. Provide practical applications by means of computerization and case recording forms.
9. Establish links with quality-of-life concepts and the measurement of subjective well-being.
10. Research into treatment or intervention matching.
11. Promote use in scientific studies for comparison between different health conditions.
12. Develop training materials on the use of *ICF*.
13. Create *ICF* training and reference centers worldwide.
14. Research environmental factors to provide the necessary detail for use in describing both the standardized and current environment. (WHO, 2001a, pp. 251–252)

We can take some comfort as we review the reference section of this text that many initiatives related to these 14 future work goals have resulted in peer-reviewed publications and seminal reference texts. It is an exciting time to be involved with the development of the *ICF* as its owners take responsibility for making the system the best it can be for society.

FUTURE RESEARCH EFFORTS

The following areas of suggested research are not exhaustive and are based on recent reviews of the literature generated by *ICF* stakeholders. Some recommendations for future research are drawn from previous reviews of the *ICF* research landscape (Peterson, 2005; Peterson & Rosenthal, 2005b; Peterson, Mpofu, & Oakland, 2010).

Validity Studies

The model of disability and functioning proposed by WHO requires further study to establish evidence of construct- and criterion-related validity. Further operationalization and quantification of *ICF* codes and qualifiers are necessary. Researchers must collect data on the various constructs presented, explore associations, and hypothesize and confirm causal links. As the *ICF* Core Set research progresses, and researchers focus on more specific applications of the *ICF*, evidences for validity of specific applications will become apparent (Peterson & Paul, 2009).

Medical Informatics

Chute (2005) proposed that the evolving knowledge base of medical information has outgrown our ability to consume it effectively. Systems like the *ICF* and its sister classification the *ICD*, in electronic and searchable formats, can help construct shared semantics, vocabularies, and terminologies that are accessible and clinically useful in a way that helps us to use medical knowledge effectively for treating people in health care settings. Chute argued that although medical informatics is a very complex area of research, measures and classifications of functioning are the overall metric of organic well-being and thus important to include in this evolving research area.

For example, common taxonomies used between psychiatry, neuropsychology, neurology, physiatry, speech language pathology, occupational therapy, and physical therapy may facilitate better coordination of subacute rehabilitation services provided for people with traumatic brain injury. The *ICF* can provide direction, consistency, and assurance to manage the ever-increasing amount of medical information in these areas of rehabilitation health care (Rock, 2005).

Savova, Harris, Pakhomov, & Chute (2005) presented a method of semantic processing of a portion of the *ICF* (*Self-Care*), using Natural Language Processing (NLP) techniques (a subfield of artificial intelligence and linguistics that studies the problems of automated generation and understanding of natural human languages) or computational methods of processing information to autocode text descriptions of health care scenarios. Although their study suggested that some ambiguities existed within the *ICF* itself, overall they were able to provide relevant and complete coverage for the *ICF Self-Care* domain.

Sundar, Daumen, Conley, and Stone (2008) demonstrated that the *ICF* could be used effectively to retrieve information using the subject headings from the bibliographic database of the Center for International Rehabilitation Research and Information Exchange (CIRRIE). Nearly two-thirds of the subject headings were mapped to equivalent *ICF* codes using only the two-level code set (a more detailed level of classification is available and may have resulted in higher matching).

The Lister Hill National Center for Biomedical Communications applied the *ICF* to the United States National Library of Medicine's (NLM) Unified Medical Language System (UMLS) data system (Bodenreider, 2005). The UMLS can be used to develop computer systems that work with the meaning of the language of biomedicine and health. The NLM produces and distributes the UMLS Knowledge Sources (databases) and associated software tools (programs) for use by system developers in building or enhancing electronic information systems that create, process, retrieve, integrate, and/or aggregate biomedical and health data and information, as well as in informatics research. Preliminary efforts have focused on mapping the *ICF* into the UMLS. *ICF* concepts were associated with a related term within the UMLS, so that in the future the *ICF* could be cross-referenced with other information systems that are already mapped to the UMLS. Previous UMLS initiatives were primarily influenced by the medical model. The biopsychosocial approach embraced by the *ICF* has challenged the UMLS to develop new categories to better reflect functional information rather than diagnostic information alone.

The NLM's university-based Biomedical Informatics Research Training Programs are currently located in 18 leading research institutions across the United States, and they are exploring a wide range of related foci including bioinformatics and computational biology, clinical research translational informatics, and public health informatics. As these efforts advance, the *ICF* can advance with them. Contemporary conceptualizations of the biological foundations of impairments that guided the construction of the *ICIDH* and *ICF* will need to be updated to reflect developments in science at the cellular and molecular levels (WHO, 2001a).

Future Cross-Walking Efforts

Efforts to map the *ICF* onto items of contemporary instruments in health care are ongoing and are a critical aspect of future success of the *ICF*. As evidence accumulates, various health care disciplines can create bridging texts and documents to facilitate the *ICF*'s dissemination into their respective classification protocols (Stucki, Ewert, & Cieza, 2003; Stucki, Üstün, & Melvin, 2005). This text is a modest effort at establishing a link between the *ICF* and the *DSM-IV-TR*, and it is hoped that it will be revised to reflect links with the *DSM-5* when it is released in 2013.

Developing International Collaborations

The *ICF* provides a lexicon for an increasingly unified global discourse about the health and well-being of groups including people with disabilities. Researchers involved in clinical practice and in using the *ICF* need to continue developing international and interdisciplinary collaborations to facilitate this discourse (Martin, 2009). Ongoing clinical implementation efforts will help us understand the *ICF*'s utility in conceptualizing functioning, disability, and health within this international and multidisciplinary paradigm.

Refining Contextual and Personal Factors

The *ICF* as it currently exists in its 2001 iteration will benefit from ongoing development efforts (Jones & Sinclair, 2008). Hurst (2003) contends that with the introduction of the constructs of *Environmental Factors* and *Participation*, the *ICF* can go a long way toward enhancing service provision for people with disabilities by making the focus of interventions the environment. The most recent addition to the *ICF*, *Environmental Factors*, will remain an active area of development in future iterations of the *ICF*.

Others believe that the *ICF* is still missing important aspects of life and living currently summarized under the *Personal* component of *Contextual Factors*. Ueda and Okawa (2003) suggest that the entire "subjective dimension" or "experience" is missing from the *ICF* entirely. They define the "Subjective experience of disability" as:

> a set of cognitive, emotional and motivational states of mind of any person, but particularly of a person with health condition and/or disability . . . It is a unique combination of, on one hand, a disability experience, i.e. a reflection (influence) of existing health conditions, impairments, activity limitations, participation restrictions and negative environmental factors (obstacles) into the person's mind (negative subjective experience), and on the other hand an experience of a positive nature, which includes, among other things, the psychological coping skills developed, often unconsciously, in order to overcome these negative influences (positive subjective experience). (p. 599)

It is reasonable to propose that there may be considerable overlap between *subjective experience* and *Personal Factors*, which are currently undefined within the *Contextual* part of the *ICF*. To the *ICF*'s credit, developing this component is prioritized as important future work for the *ICF* (WHO, 2001a, p. 251). Classifying the subjective experience of a person with a disability may present initially as an incomprehensible Rosetta stone, but with careful science and creativity it can become a part of the *ICF* classification system (Peterson & Threats, 2005).

Civil Rights and Social Policy Development

Although the rights of people with disabilities vary considerably from country to country, one way to advance the civil rights of people with disabilities throughout the world is to establish an international dialogue using a common language to describe health and human functioning. An example of such a dialogue is the 2003 special edition of the international journal *Disability and Rehabilitation* (Vol. 25), which featured 16 articles from a group of international scholars focusing on the *ICF*. In the United States, the May 2005 issue of the journal *Rehabilitation Psychology* was published and featured a five-article special section on the *ICF*. The 2005 volume of *Rehabilitation Education* was another example of disseminating information related to the development and future implementation of the *ICF*.

The potential applications of the *ICF* to social policy initiatives are significant. Functional information can be correlated with distributions of wealth to assess economic need. Entitlement programs can use standard functional criteria that are informed by international research to distribute benefits and evaluate the effectiveness of their distribution (Schraner, De Jonge, Layton, Bringolf, & Molenda, 2008). Collecting data with specific and standard benchmarks can inform future development and revision of regulations and guidelines associated with social policy.

When we improve the quality of life and health of persons with disability, in addition to enhancing those people's quality of life, we are also helping their families, social networks, and society as a whole, and at the same time, using the *ICF* as a tool for social justice (Jones & Sinclair, 2008; Peterson & Threats, 2005). Society has everything to gain from improving the health care of people with disabilities, as there are clear direct and indirect financial benefits in improving a person's health and functioning (Üstün et al., 2003; WHO, 2002).

CONCLUSION TO PART I

In Part I of this text, we have reviewed why the *ICF* is an important international development that is now in use in many countries in varying capacities. Disability is ubiquitous in our world, and it is an important consideration in coordinating available health care resources internationally. The *ICF* promises to inform our international health efforts by providing a unified language of health and functioning that will facilitate the exchange of information that is unprecedented in modern times. Future assessment, treatment, and research efforts using the *ICF* can revolutionize the way we think about physical and psychological functioning, disability, and health; improve the quality of care for individuals internationally; generate and disseminate universal research data on disability and functioning; and ultimately influence culturally sensitive global health policy.

We carefully considered the historical context of the *ICF*'s development, particularly with respect to the role that disability policy in the United States played in the *ICIDH* and the *ICF*. The evolution of widely accepted models of disability paralleled the *ICF*'s development into its current form. We completed this historical discussion with seminal events that formalized the published version in 2001.

An overview of the *ICF* was attempted, which in summary comprises two parts, each with two components. Each component within the *ICF* consists of various domains composed of the categories that comprise the actual units of classification, which can be coded and qualified numerically to represent the health and health-related states of an individual. The qualifiers describe the extent of problems for a given code using the same generic scale with slight modifications depending on the component qualified (see Figure 3.4). Figure 3.5 provides a complete overview of the *ICF* concepts presented.

We ended Part I of the text with a discussion of collaborative assessment with the *ICF*, including a presentation of *ICF*'s ethical provisions in light of ethical principles in psychology. These ethical principles will guide future clinical and research efforts of *ICF* stakeholders as the *ICF* evolves to its next iteration.

Those who want to learn more about the *ICF* should consult the *ICF* document (WHO, 2001a) for more precise coding guidelines, paying close attention to annexes at the end of the document, specifically, Annexes 2, 3, and 4, seek training from WHO affiliates knowledgeable in the *ICF*, and anticipate the release of the Manual from the American Psychological Association/World Health Organization (see Reed et al., 2008).

PART II

The *DSM-IV-TR*

We began in Part I with an overview of the *ICF* and its sister classification the *ICD*. We established that the *ICF* is a very significant development in health care on a global scale. We then established the prevalence of mental disorders more specifically and previewed the application of the *ICF* to describing health and health-related states for people with mental disorders.

After a review of the historical conceptions of the disability construct, we provided a comprehensive overview of the *ICF*'s two parts, each with two components, and we defined the key constructs within the *ICF* conceptual framework. We then reviewed the importance of collaborative assessment and research approaches with the *ICF* and discussed future prospects for the *ICF* generally.

In Parts II and III of our text, we bring our focus fully on applying the *ICF* to the *DSM-IV-TR*. It is important for new mental health professionals to be aware of the systems used by common third-party payers. Diagnostic codes from the *ICD-9-CM* and the *DSM-IV-TR* are frequently required in order to be reimbursed for services. Investing time in becoming familiar and the *ICD* with the *DSM* is time well spent for emerging mental health professionals. Associating the diagnostic information of the *DSM* with useful health and functioning data via the *ICF* can inform and improve the assessment, intervention targeting, and evaluation of treatment efforts in mental health services.

When the author was first exposed to the *ICF*, it was over a dozen years after having worked with the *DSM*. It seemed obvious to the author at that time of discovery, that the *ICF* and the *DSM* could be used together much in the way that the *ICF* and *ICD* are companion classification systems. Moreover, the multiaxial approach to differential diagnosis within the *DSM* was quite complementary to the *ICF* conceptual framework (e.g., Axes III, IV, and V). It is with this expectation that we begin our overview of the *DSM-IV-TR*.

DSM-IV-TR as a Companion Text

Just as the *ICF* was recommended as a companion text while reading Part I of this text, Part II provides brief summaries of diagnoses presented in the *DSM-IV-TR* (hereafter the *DSM*), which should be used as an accompanying text for the following review. Relevant page numbers for the *DSM* follow each heuristic presentation of the various diagnostic groups and subgroups.

The explanation of mental disorders from the *DSM* is a basic summary that guides readers through the *DSM* itself. The author attempted to provide a useful, abbreviated review of the *DSM*, without the use of endless quotation marks in order to enhance the readability of complex material. All *DSM*-related material included in this text is and should be considered as cited directly back to the *DSM-IV-TR* (APA, 2000), with page intervals provided at the end of summaries, directing the reader to the actual material for further review.

The conceptualizations of *DSM* mental disorders in Part II of this text are heuristics to facilitate learning of the *DSM* itself. Heuristics are by definition simplifications of complex constructs and are used to help learners discover or learn for themselves. Summarizing nearly 1,000 pages of a complex diagnostic system is no small task; this being the first edition of this text, there will no doubt be recommendations and corrections to embrace for subsequent editions, not to mention updating to the *DSM-5*. The reader is recommended to review Part II of this text systematically with the *DSM* itself. There really is no substitute for reviewing the actual volume of the *DSM*, receiving appropriate and sufficient supervision in its use, and then using the *DSM* directly when engaging in the diagnostic process.

Other Companion Materials to the Text

Extremely useful support materials are available for the *DSM-IV-TR*. First, the *DSM-IV-TR Case* Book (Spitzer et al., 2002) provides clinical examples of the application of the coding system to clinical vignettes. Second, American Psychiatric Publishing, Inc. operates a Web site one can subscribe to, with key resources for mental health professionals and students, centered around the *DSM-IV-TR*. The Web site provides expanded material on diagnostic criteria, differential diagnostic advice, case vignettes, multidisciplinary treatment guidelines, and the latest research (see www.psychiatryonline.com).

DSM-IV Sourcebook

Although the *DSM-IV-TR* itself is quite long, nearly 1,000 pages in length, it is informative for those new to the system that there exists a comprehensive set of four volumes recording the clinical and research support for the *DSM*'s development. The *DSM-IV Sourcebook* contains 150 literature reviews (the first three volumes) and reports related to data reanalyses, clinical field trials, and executive summaries as to how these data were used (the fourth and final volume). This does not include the many papers published in peer-reviewed journals that also record efforts to empirically validate the multi-axial system. That is not to say that all efforts published support the system as constructed, and in fact some are quite critical of it (Martin, 2009). See the critiques of *DSM* section at the end of Chapter 5 for further discussion.

Need for Adequate Training and Supervision

This review is not a substitute for adequate advanced training in psychopathology, the *DSM-IV-TR* itself, and subsequent clinical training and supervision in its application to practice. The actual introduction to the *DSM-IV-TR* recommends that it not be applied mechanically by untrained individuals (p. xxxii). This overview does provide a useful primer to the *DSM-IV-TR* as well as its relationship to the *ICF* as they are currently constructed. It also represents an initial cross-walking effort between the conceptual frameworks of the two classification systems.

To avoid awkward prose, the *DSM-IV-TR* is not precisely referenced at every possible opportunity. As mentioned above, all descriptions of the *DSM* should be and are so referenced to the original document (APA, 2000).

Clarification of Terms Used in Part II

In Part I of this text, we discussed the different conceptions of disability over the last century. The standard of using person-first language when addressing people with disabilities has made its way into contemporary guides of writing and practice. Inflammatory or derogatory terminology regarding people with disabilities is not acceptable in any social discourse.

Mental Disorder. It is acknowledged in the *DSM* that there are problems with the term *mental disorder* but that "the problem raised by the term 'mental' disorders has been much clearer than its solution" (APA, 2000, p. xxx). I acknowledge the sensitivity of the concept of "mental disorder," but in writing about the *DSM*, which systematizes the diagnosis of the same, it would be very awkward if not impossible to avoid the use of the term *mental disorder*.

Historically, mental disorders have also been written about using other terminology. *Psychiatric disabilities* harkens from the specialty discipline of psychiatric rehabilitation (MacDonald-Wilson & Nemec, 2005). The terms *emotional disorder* and *mental illness* also frequently find their way into our social discourse (Hong, 2009).

When writing about the *DSM*, it is not possible to write about its contents directly without using the term *disorder,* which for some disability advocates may reflect insensitivity toward the spirit of disability-sensitive language. Part II of this text will use the term *mental disorder* because of its consistency with the *DSM-IV-TR*.

Psychiatry Versus Psychology. The term *psychiatric* means of or pertaining to psychiatry, which relates to a specific profession in mental health services; medical doctors with special training in brain–behavior relationships and the pharmacological treatment of mental disorders. We do not use the term *psychiatric diagnoses* over mental disorders because of the nomenclature used in the *DSM*, and to be inclusive of the broad range of professionals who frequently use *DSM* diagnoses.

Psychological means of or pertaining to psychology, which is a broader discipline of the study of the mind. Because the term *psychology* is more inclusive and relates to many professions outside of psychiatry, including psychology, social work, marriage and family therapy, mental health counseling, rehabilitation counseling, occupational therapy, physical therapy, physiatry, and speech language pathology, this term is preferred and used in the title and throughout the text as appropriate. Coincidentally, this term and its derivatives are also used throughout the *DSM* itself.

CHAPTER 5

Introduction
to the *DSM-IV-TR*

PREVIEW QUESTIONS

1. How has the *DSM* evolved since its inception?
2. How is the *DSM-IV-TR* organized?
3. How does the *DSM-IV-TR* define mental disorder?
4. Describe the five axes of the *DSM*.
5. How are *DSM* diagnoses qualified (i.e., course, severity)?

Published by the American Psychiatric Association (2000), the *DSM-IV-TR* (hereafter the *DSM*) is based on an extensive empirical foundation and is used for clinical, research, and educational purposes. The *DSM* is used by psychiatrists, other physicians, psychologists, social workers, nurses, occupational and rehabilitation therapists, counselors, and other health and mental health professionals working within inpatient, outpatient, partial hospital, primary care, and other clinical and public health settings (p. xxiii).

THE *DSM* AND THE *ICD-10*

The *ICF* was described in Part I of this text as a sister classification to the *ICD-10*. The *DSM* and the *ICD* systems also share an important history. Those developing the *ICD-10* and *DSM-IV* "worked closely to coordinate their efforts, resulting in much mutual influence" (APA, 2000, p. xxix). The primary function of the *ICD* system has been to delineate categories to facilitate the collection of basic health statistics, and this information can be used to inform efforts to decrease the burden of global health. In contrast, the *DSM* system was constructed with medical nomenclature to more specifically facilitate clinical practice and research.

Because of its importance in the classification of mental disorders internationally, and specifically with third-party payers and government health initiatives in the United States, the Appendix contains an outline of the *ICD-10 Classification of Mental and Behavioral Disorders*, the mental and behavioral disorders portion of the *ICD-10* system. The reader can compare and contrast the code structure of the *ICD-10* with the *DSM-IV-TR* (which currently includes both *ICD-9 CM* and *ICD-10* code sets for mental disorders) and see the results of WHO/APA code revision coordination efforts and the consequent similarities (as well as differences) across major diagnostic groups and specific subgroups (see Appendix; the 2007 version of the *ICD* is available online at http://www.who.int/classifications/apps/ICD/ICD10online/).

HISTORY OF THE *DSM*'S DEVELOPMENT

This historical review is drawn from a more comprehensive one within the *DSM* itself (APA, 2000). Classification of mental disorders in the United States began with the 1840 census, where the frequency of one category, "idiocy/insanity," was surveyed. By 1880, one category grew to seven, of which only a few are current in our contemporary discourse of mental illness, but they include mania, melancholia, monomania, paresis, dementia, dipsomania, and epilepsy. In 1917, collaborating agencies coordinated the first effort to gather uniform statistics regarding mental illness across mental hospitals in the United States.

After World War II, veterans returned to United States to outpatient treatment centers with a wide variety of presentations of psychological difficulties, and subsequently the U.S. Army and Veterans Administration developed a much broader nomenclature to capture the problems presented. At that same time, the *ICD* system created the first section for mental disorders within the sixth version of the *ICD*.

DSM-I

The first edition of the *DSM* was a variant of the *ICD-6*, called the *Diagnostic and Statistical Manual: Mental Disorders* (*DSM-I*; American Psychiatric Association [APA], 1952), published in 1952, the first official manual of mental disorders to focus on clinical utility. Adolf Meyer's psychobiological view on the etiology of mental disorders (see Winters & Bowers, 1957) influenced the first version of the *DSM* through the inclusion of the term *reaction* throughout. His perspective argued that mental disorders represented reactions of one's personality to psychological, social, and biological influences.

DSM-II

There were minimal changes between the *DSM-I* and the first printing of the *DSM-II* (APA, 1968). Although innovations in diagnostic methodologies were available, none were employed in the *DSM-II*, which co-occurred with the *ICD*-8 revision processes. The first version of the *DSM* and its second revision were similar in all but one respect, which was movement away from embracing any particular etiological framework, such as that suggested by Meyer's psychobiological approach, and thus the elimination of the term *reaction* throughout.

There was a very important change in the sixth printing of the second edition of the *DSM* (APA, 1973) that is not mentioned in the *DSM-IV-TR* historical recounting of its development. In 1973, the debate over the inclusion of homosexuality as a mental disorder within the *DSM* was settled by eliminating it as a mental disorder. An apparent compromise diagnosis was substituted by incorporating the new diagnosis, Sexual Orientation Disturbance. As the Civil Rights Movement had an impact on the *ICF* and its conception of disability, so also did the movement have a positive impact on mental health professionals' view on sexual orientation. Different expressions of sexual orientation were no longer systematically pathologized, going a long way toward enhancing the mental health of people who are gay, lesbian, or bisexual. Within the *ICD-10* system, homosexuality is listed along with heterosexuality and bisexuality as qualifiers for the context of psychological and behavioral disorders associated with sexual development and orientation and not disorders in and of themselves.

DSM-III

The World Health Organization (WHO) sponsored a comprehensive review of diagnostic issues associated with mental disorder taxonomies by British psychiatrist Erwin Stengel, whose report was credited with having great influence on future iterations of the *DSM*, given his comprehensive review of diagnostic issues, which resulted in advances in diagnostic methodology (see also Stengel, 1957). His work encouraged the use of explicit definitions to increase the reliability of clinical diagnoses. Although completed before the second revision of the *DSM*, these advances were not employed until the third revision of the *DSM*.

The third revision of the *DSM* (APA, 1980) was coordinated with the ninth revision of the *ICD* system and published in 1980. Stengel's work inspired several innovations for the third revision, including more explicit diagnostic criteria, the introduction of the multiaxial framework, and the use of theoretically neutral (with respect to etiology) presentations of diagnostic criteria. Revisions to improve clarity and consistency of the *DSM-III* resulted in the publication of the *DSM-III-R* in 1987 (APA, 1987).

DSM-IV

Because of the innovations developed for the *DSM-III*-R, the fourth revision of the *DSM* (APA, 1994) was uniquely informed by an empirical literature that grew out of the specificity of the multiaxial system. Most diagnoses in the *DSM* now have specific, associated empirical research bases and available research datasets to inform future revision processes.

The fourth revision of the *DSM* was published in 1994 and was informed by a three-stage empirical process: "(1) comprehensive and systematic reviews of the published literature, (2) reanalyses of already-collected datasets, and (3) extensive issue-focused field trials" (APA, 2000, p. xxvi). Specific procedures employed are described in detail within the *DSM* on pages xxvi–xxvii.

The revision process for the *DSM-IV* involved over 60 professional associations (e.g., American Psychiatric Association, American Health Information Management Association, American Psychological Association, National Center for Health Statistics, and WHO) and over 1,000 people involved with task forces, administrative staff, and other participants. Those with specific expertise were assembled into groups to address the various diagnostic areas within the *DSM*.

Those who were involved in the *DSM* revision process were charged with recognizing the breadth of available evidences and opinions regarding psychiatric conditions, including international perspectives, when formulating suggestions for revisions. Conferences, workshops, and critiques were conducted to provide conceptual and methodological guidance.

Another important influence on the fourth revision effort was the collaboration between the *DSM* work groups and the WHO's efforts on revising the ninth revision of the *ICD*. New developments within the *ICD* informed the selection of some literature review and data reanalysis efforts. Collaborations coordinated between developers of the *DSM* and *ICD* provided greater congruence and reduced "meaningless differences in wording" between them (APA, 2000, p. xxix).

DSM-IV-TR Revision Process

The interval of time between the revision of the *DSM-III* and III-R, as well as to the fourth revision, was 7 years. The revision of the *DSM-IV* to the fifth revision was projected at least 12 years in the future (at that time, this implied 2012, which has since been delayed to 2013). Given developments in research and practice, this time span jeopardized the currency of the empirical basis of the *DSM* for applications to education, research, and practice.

The Text Revision of the fourth edition of the *DSM* (APA, 2000) was begun in 1997, 3 years after the publication of the fourth revision, but a full 5 years since the last literature review update. Work groups were established to correspond with the *DSM-IV* revision process. A major literature review was conducted to ensure that its empirical basis was still up to date. An effort was made to correct any factual errors discovered since its publication in 1994. An effort was also made to enhance the educational value of the *DSM*.

At the time of the Text Revision publication in 2000, the official *ICD* coding system used in the United States was the ninth revision Clinical Modification (*ICD-9-CM*), whereas throughout most of the world they had advanced to the *ICD-10* system. Thus, the *ICD-9-CM* codes for selected general medical conditions and medication-induced disorders were included in Appendix G for referencing Axis III concerns consistent with the United States. In addition, the *ICD-10* codes from Chapter 5, "Mental and Behavioural Disorders," associated with the *DSM* classification system are listed in Appendix H of the *DSM-IV-TR* to remain current with the international adoption of the *ICD-10*. Because of the collaborative effort between the developers of the *ICD* and *DSM*, the *DSM-IV-TR* codes are fully compatible with codes and terms in the *ICD-9-CM* and the tabular index of the *ICD-10* (APA, 2000, p. 883).

Specific to the Text Revision effort, only the text sections were updated (e.g., Associated Features and Disorders, Prevalence). No substantive changes were made to criteria sets, no new disorders were added, no new subtypes inserted into diagnostic categories, and no changes were made to the appendix reviewing proposed diagnostic additions. Changes included in the Text Revision are listed in Appendix D of the *DSM-IV-TR*.

OVERVIEW OF THE *DSM-IV-TR*

Having reviewed the historical development of the *DSM*, next we provide a basic overview of the *DSM-IV-TR* (hereafter the *DSM*). First presented is the organization of the classification system, followed by the *DSM* definition of mental disorder and a presentation of some of the methods used to describe specific diagnoses within the *DSM*.

Organization of the *DSM-IV-TR*

The *DSM* begins with an introduction to its use, followed by the systematic listing of the codes and categories of the *DSM-IV-TR* classification. A description of the multiaxial system is provided, followed by diagnostic criteria and descriptive text for each disorder. The system concludes with 11 appendixes, which are described later.

Descriptive Text

The text of the *DSM* describes each disorder according to several content areas as appropriate. *Diagnostic Features* lists diagnostic criteria with illustrative examples. *Subtypes* (mutually exclusive and exhaustive subgroups within a diagnosis) and/or *Specifiers* (specify a more homogenous subgroup within a disorder who share certain features) provides specific explanations of terminologies, subtypes of certain diagnoses, and their potential courses. Recording procedures are provided for each diagnostic category, including names of diagnoses, the associated *ICD-9-CM* codes, and instructions for applying subtypes and/or course specifiers (described in greater detail below).

Once these key features of a diagnosis are presented, detailed information is presented under other headings that address clinical features associated with a disorder (but not required to assign the diagnosis), other mental disorders often associated with a diagnosis (and whether they precede, co-occur, or result from a given disorder), predisposing factors to a condition, associated laboratory findings (biometrics, psychometrics, and medical lab results), variations and prevalence influenced by demographics, and features of prevalence, course, and familial patterns. All diagnoses contain a section discussing *Differential Diagnosis* or how to differentiate a given disorder from other disorders that share similar characteristics.

Organization of Disorders

There are 16 major diagnostic classes in the *DSM* and additional sections, "Other Conditions That May Be a Focus of Clinical Attention" and "Additional Codes" that are described at the end of Table 5.1. The first section is devoted to disorders typically first diagnosed in childhood or adolescence, but this distinction is not an absolute one, as often these issues do not become a focus of clinical attention until adulthood. On the other hand, the remaining diagnoses in the *DSM* may be relevant to children as well. Their primacy in the organization of the *DSM* relates to the typical order of clinical focus when working with patients; in this instance, any childhood history of mental disorders.

TABLE 5.1 Major Diagnostic Classes of the *DSM-IV-TR*

Major Diagnostic Class (*DSM-IV-TR* page numbers are listed in parentheses)	Specific Disorders
Disorders usually first diagnosed in Infancy, Childhood, or Adolescence (39)	Mental Retardation (coded on Axis II), Learning Disorders, Motor Skills Disorders, Communication Disorders, Pervasive Developmental Disorders, Attention-Deficit and Disruptive Behavior Disorders, Feeding and Eating Disorders of Infancy or Early Childhood, Tic Disorders, Elimination Disorders, Other Disorders of Infancy, Childhood, or Adolescence
Delirium, Dementia, and Amnestic and Other Cognitive Disorders (135)	Delirium, Dementia, Amnestic Disorders, Other Cognitive Disorders
Mental Disorders due to a General Medical Condition not Elsewhere Classified (181)	i.e., Catatonic Disorder Due to . . . Personality Change Due to . . . Mental Disorder NOS Due to . . .
Substance-Related Disorders (191)	Alcohol-Related Disorders, Amphetamine (or Amphetamine-Like)-Related Disorders, Caffeine-Related Disorders, Cannabis-Related Disorders, Cocaine-Related Disorders, Hallucinogen-Related Disorders, Inhalant-Related Disorders, Nicotine-Related Disorders, Opioid-Related Disorders, Phencyclidine (or Phencyclidine-Like)-Related Disorders, Sedative-, Hypnotic-, or Anxiolytic-Related Disorders, Polysubstance-Related Disorders, Other (Unknown) Substance-Related Disorders
Schizophrenia and Other Psychotic Disorders (297)	i.e., Schizophrenia; Schizophreniform, Schizoaffective Disorders; Delusional Disorder; Brief Psychotic Disorder, Shared Psychotic Disorder; Psychotic Order Due to . . .; Substance-Induced Psychotic Disorder; Pyschotic Disorder NOS
Mood Disorders (345)	Depressive Disorders, Bipolar Disorders
Anxiety Disorders (429)	i.e., Panic Disorder, Agoraphobia, Specific Phobia, Social Phobia, Obsessive-Compulsive Disorder, Posttraumatic Stress Disorder, Acute Stress Disorder, General-ized Anxiety Disorder, Anxiety Disorder Due to . . ., Substance-Induced Anxiety Disorder, Anxiety Disorder NOS

(Continued)

TABLE 5.1 (Continued)

Major Diagnostic Class (*DSM-IV-TR* page numbers are listed in parentheses)	Specific Disorders
Somatoform Disorders (485)	i.e., Somatization Disorder, Undifferentiated Somatoform Disorder, Conversion Disorder, Pain Disorder, Hypochondriasis, Body Dysmorphic Disorder, Somatoform Disorder NOS
Factitious Disorders (513)	
Dissociative Disorders (519)	Dissociative Amnesia, Fugue, Identity Disorder, and Disorder NOS; Depersonalization Disorder
Sexual and Gender Identity Disorders (535)	Sexual Dysfunctions, Sexual Desire Disorders, Sexual Arousal Disorders, Orgasmic Disorders, Sexual Pain Disorders, Sexual Dysfunction Due to a General Medical Condition, Paraphilias, Gender Identity Disorders
Eating Disorders (583)	i.e., Anorexia Nervosa, Bulimia Nervosa, Eating Disorder NOS
Sleep Disorders (597)	Primary Sleep Disorders (Dyssomnias, Parasomnias), Sleep Disorders Related to Another Mental Disorder, Other Sleep Disorders
Impulse-Control Disorders Not Elsewhere Classified (663)	i.e., Intermittent Explosive Disorder, Kleptomania, Pyromania, Pathological Gambling, Trichotillomania, Impulse-Control Disorder NOS
Adjustment Disorders (679)	
Personality Disorders (685)	Coded on Axis II, i.e., Paranoid, Schizoid, Schizotypal Antisocial, Borderline, Histrionic, Narcissistic, Avoidant, Dependent, Obsessive-Compulsive Personality Disorders; Personality Disorder NOS
Other Conditions That May Be a Focus of Clinical Attention (731)	Psychological Factors Affecting Medical Condition, Medication-Induced Movement Disorders, Other Medication-Induced Disorder, Relational Problems, Problems Related to Abuse or Neglect, Additional Conditions That May Be a Focus of Clinical Attention
Additional Codes (743)	These codes are used when there are no diagnoses or if the diagnoses are deferred for Axes I or II, or for the Unspecified Mental Disorder (nonpsychotic) diagnosis.

The next three sections were organized in the *DSM-III* under the title "Organic Mental Syndromes," but this heading has since been abandoned due to the growing evidence of the biopsychosocial nature of mental disorders. Nevertheless, their position is appropriate in the *DSM* with respect to the differential diagnostic process. Delirium, Dementia, and Amnestic and Other Cognitive Disorders; Mental Disorders due to a General Medical Condition; and Substance-Related Disorders should be ruled out before proceeding to subsequent diagnostic classes.

To facilitate the differential diagnostic process, complete lists of these conditions are provided near the beginning of the classification to remind us of their importance. The specific text and criteria for these disorders are included in related diagnostic sections further along in the manual. Exclusion criteria, discussed below, provide specific guidance to users of the *DSM* for specific mental disorders. For example, if someone presents with a history of heroin dependence and symptoms of depression, the need to rule out the depressive influence of heroin is required before deciding on the utility of the diagnosis of Major Depressive Disorder.

The remaining sections of the *DSM* are organized according to shared phenomenological features. The one exception is for Adjustment Disorders, which is organized according to dysfunctional reaction to a stressor (e.g., depression, anxiety). The last section of disorders is a collection of "Other Conditions That May Be a Focus of Clinical Attention."

Appendixes

The *DSM* has 11 appendixes. Appendix A provides six decision trees that illustrate the hierarchical structure of the *DSM*. The following diagnoses are used to instruct users of the *DSM* in the differential diagnostic process: Mental Disorders due to General Medical Condition, Substance-Induced Mood Disorders, Psychotic Disorders, Mood Disorders, Anxiety Disorders, and Somatoform Disorders.

Appendix B contains Criteria Sets and Axes Provided for Further Study. Preliminary study information is provided for an extensive list of proposed diagnoses. Also, alternative dimensional descriptors are proposed for Schizophrenia and an alternative criterion B for Dysthymic Disorder. Three new axes are also proposed: Defensive Functioning Scale, Global Assessment of Relational Functioning Scale (GARF), and Social and Occupational Functioning Assessment Scale (SOFAS).

Appendix C provides a list of technical terms used to apply the criteria sets in the *DSM* to clinical practice. Appendix D highlights changes from the *DSM-IV* to the *DSM-IV-TR*. Appendixes E and F provide very useful alphabetical and numerical listings of all *DSM* diagnoses with their *ICD-9-CM* codes. Skipping ahead to Appendix H, the *ICD-10* codes are listed for all *DSM* diagnoses, to facilitate international communication where the *ICD-10* system is already in use.

Appendix G is important with respect to Axis III of the *DSM* (Axes are described below). Axis III considers the role that general medical conditions may play in a given mental health context. *ICD-9-CM* codes are provided here for selected general medical conditions. Also, *ICD-9-E* codes for certain medications that can cause Substance-Induced Disorders are also provided. These E codes can also be placed on Axis I immediately following the related disorder listing.

Appendix I provides two resources to enhance cultural competency in the differential diagnostic process. First, an outline for cultural formulation, which the clinician can use to systematically evaluate and report the impact of a person's cultural context. The second part includes a glossary of culture-bound syndromes found in the literature. The last two Appendixes list *DSM-IV* contributors and Text Revision advisors.

Multiaxial Assessment

The *DSM* employs a multiaxial system to classify mental disorders. Five domains address various mental disorders, general medical conditions, psychosocial and environmental problems, and level of functioning, each with its own contribution to diagnosing, treatment planning, and prediction or evaluation of treatment outcomes. The multiaxial system promotes a biopsychosocial model, consistent with the conceptual framework of the *ICF*. Users of the *DSM* may choose to employ it without the multiaxial framework; those guidelines are on page 37 of the *DSM*.

The five axes of the *DSM* are:

- Axis I   Clinical Disorders
            Other Conditions That May Be a Focus of Clinical
            Attention
- Axis II   Personality Disorders
            Mental Retardation
- Axis III   General Medical Conditions
- Axis IV   Psychosocial and Environmental Problems
- Axis V   Global Assessment of Functioning (p. 27)

Axis I

All disorders are classified on this axis with the exception of Personality Disorders and Mental Retardation, which are reported on Axis II. Typically, the main diagnosis is indicated on Axis I. If more than one diagnosis is indicated on Axis I, the main one is listed first. If it so happens that the main reason for treatment is on Axis II, it is so indicated with the qualifying phrase "Principal Diagnosis" or "Reason for Visit." Axes I and II can be coded to indicate that there is no diagnosis at present (code V71.09) or that diagnosis is deferred in order to gather more information (code 799.9).

Axis II

On Axis II, Mental Retardation and Personality Disorders are listed. In addition, notations of prominent maladaptive personality features and defense mechanisms may also be listed as foci of clinical attention. The premise for separating Axis II from Axis I disorders, historically, was to be sure to draw attention to those diagnoses that may be overshadowed by more dramatic diagnoses; a florid psychosis might draw greater attention than the existence of Borderline Intellectual Functioning. As with Axis I diagnosis, Axis II diagnosis may be deferred, as indicated by the code 799.9, or if no Axis II diagnosis is present, it should be coded as V71.09.

Axis III

Axis III is used to list general medical conditions that are distinct from mental disorders classified in the *DSM*. General medical conditions may be relevant to understanding or treating a mental disorder, and listing them in the multiaxial assessment encourages thoroughness in evaluation and enhances communication among health care providers. Appendix G of the *DSM* lists *ICD-9-CM* codes for selected general medical conditions, including medication-induced disorders, to facilitate coding on Axis III. See Table 5.2 for a listing of medical areas addressed.

There are a number of reasons to consider Axis III in conceptualizing a given case. In some instances, the medical condition may be etiologically related to the mental disorder (e.g., hypothyroidism influencing depressive symptoms). Alternatively, an Axis I disorder may be a psychological reaction to a general medical condition on Axis III (e.g., Adjustment Disorder with Depressed Mood in response to an amputation). In some cases, Axis III conditions may impact the choice of pharmacotherapy for a given Axis I

TABLE 5.2 Axis III: Categories of General Medical Conditions

Disease Types (see pages 867–879 of *DSM-IV-TR*)

Circulatory System

Congenital

Digestive System

Endocrine, Nutritional, and Metabolic

Genitourinary System

Hematological

Infectious

Medication-Induced Disorders (see pages 879–882 of *DSM-IV-TR*)

Musculoskeletal System and Connective Tissue

Neoplasms (abnormal mass of tissue)

Nervous System

Overdose, Poisoning

Pregnancy, Childbirth, and the Puerperium (the time immediately following childbirth)

Respiratory System

Sense Organs: Eye, Ear, Nose, Throat

Skin and Subcutaneous Tissue

condition (e.g., the existence of arrhythmias and stimulant treatment for ADHD). If no Axis III issues exist, "None" is indicated; if more information is required, "Deferred" may be appropriate.

Axis IV

Axis IV, Psychosocial and Environmental Problems, is used in the multiaxial system to highlight issues that may affect diagnosis, treatment, and prognosis of Axes I and II disorders. Issues may include a negative life event, problems in the environment, interpersonal difficulties, lack of social support, or other contextual problems. Issues on Axis IV may initiate or exacerbate an Axis I or II disorder or may result from them. These contextual issues may play an important role in intervention targeting, treatment planning, and evaluation of treatment outcomes.

The *DSM* suggests that only those issues that existed within the past year should be included on Axis IV. However, if a significant life event prior to that time period continues to affect current functioning, for example, Posttraumatic Stress Disorder following a distant traumatic event, related psychosocial and environmental problems should be noted.

TABLE 5.3 Axis IV: Psychosocial and Environmental Problems

Problem Types (APA, 2000, p. 32)	Examples (see pp. 31–32 of DSM)
Primary support group	Problems with health, death, separation, abuse, neglect, discord, system changes
Related to the social environment	Problems with death, social support, acculturation, discrimination, life changes
Educational	Problems with literacy, academic performance, discipline, school resources
Occupational	Problems with maintaining employment, work stress, job satisfaction, interpersonal issues
Housing	Homelessness, unsafe or inadequate housing, issues with neighbors or landlord
Economic	Financial distress, inadequate welfare support
Access to health care services	Inadequate access to required services, transportation, and insurance coverage
Interaction with the legal system/ crime	Arrest, incarceration, litigation; victim of a crime
Other psychosocial/environmental	Disasters, war, violence, discord with caregivers; lack of social services

Finally, when a psychosocial or environmental problem is the main reason for clinical contact, it can also be recorded on Axis I with a code derived from "Other Conditions That May Be a Focus of Clinical Attention" (p. 731). See Table 5.3 for a summary of categories and related problems noted on Axis IV. The general categories, related problems, and specific examples may be included under Axis IV.

Axis V

Axis V is used to indicate an individual's overall level of functioning given the data on the first four axes. Functioning is addressed in global terms with a single measure called the Global Assessment of Functioning Scale (GAF). The greatest utility of the GAF is it provides a single measure that can be compared over time to provide some indication of the effects of treatment or the progression of a mental disorder.

Assignment of a GAF score is not supposed to take into account impairment in functioning that is related to physical or environmental limitations. Rather, its focus is on psychological, social, and occupational functioning. The GAF is divided into 10 ranges of functioning, 10 points each ranging from 0 (inadequate information) to 100 (Superior functioning). Each

10-point range is assigned based on either symptom severity or level of functioning. The *DSM* recommends reporting the lowest of the two. GAFs can be assigned for the current period, highest level of functioning within the past year, or as a comparison between admission and discharge in a hospital; these contexts are addressed in parentheses following the GAF score.

Pages 32–34 of the *DSM* provide detailed instructions on how to use the GAF. The details of using the GAF, including the table of 10 categories and four-step process for determining a GAF, will not be replicated here. The reader is referred directly to the *DSM* for a careful review of the use of the GAF.

In Appendix B of the *DSM*, there are proposed axes for further study, in which the clinician is offered several alternatives to the GAF that focus on particular areas of functioning. The Social and Occupational Functioning Assessment Scale (SOFAS) provides an estimate of social and occupational disability independent of the severity of psychological symptoms (see pp. 817–818). A Defensive Functioning Scale allows the clinician to evaluate the concept of defense mechanisms as they impact functioning (see pp. 807–810). Finally, a Global Assessment of Relational Functioning (GARF) is a systems-based corollary to the GAF, providing an overall judgment of the functioning of a family or "ongoing relational unit" (see pp. 814–816).

To the *DSM*'s credit, acknowledging the unique contribution of some measures of functioning is progressive and in keeping with the literature that suggests diagnoses alone do not present the entire health picture. However, the detail available within the *ICF* to assess functioning stands in stark contrast to the GAF, GARF, and the SOFAS, global measures that do not capture differences between, as with the *ICF*, Capacity and Performance. The SOFAS provides some insight into the fact that symptom severity does not necessarily impact social and occupational functioning in kind. Perhaps in the future, Axes IV and V can be informed by the *ICF*, and the Personal Factors component of the *ICF* can be informed by Axis IV criteria.

Mental Disorder in the *DSM*

In its introduction, the *DSM-IV-TR* provides a definition of mental disorder, which stands to reason given that the term is used within its title, and the classification relates to various presentations of mental disorders. According to the most recent iteration of *DSM*, and as it was defined for the *DSM-III* and *DSM-III-R*, a mental disorder is:

> . . . conceptualized as a clinically significant behavioral or psycho-
> logical syndrome or pattern that occurs in an individual and that
> is associated with present distress (e.g., a painful symptom) or

disability (i.e., impairment in one or more important areas of functioning) or with a significantly increased risk of suffering death, pain, disability, or an important loss of freedom. In addition, this syndrome or pattern must not be merely an expectable and culturally sanctioned response to a particular event, for example, the death of a loved one. Whatever its original cause, it must currently be considered a manifestation of a behavioral, psychological, or biological dysfunction in the individual. Neither deviant behavior (e.g. political, religious, or sexual) nor conflicts that are primarily between the individual and society are mental disorders unless the deviance or conflict is a symptom of a dysfunction in the individual, as described above. (APA, 2000, p. xxxi)

Most diagnoses within the *DSM* include a clinical significance criterion, usually worded ". . . causes clinically significant distress or impairment in social, occupational, or other important areas of functioning" (p. 8). If the presenting impairments that are potentially associated with a given mental disorder do not rise to the level of causing significant difficulty, such a diagnosis may be unwarranted. The *DSM* encourages the use of multiple data sources to inform such decisions, including the individual being evaluated, clinical observation, standardized testing, and information from family members and other third parties. The *ICF* encourages the use of similar resources in establishing foci of clinical attention and levels of Activity Limitations and Participation Restrictions associated with a given health condition.

Users of the *DSM* need adequate clinical training and experience in the diagnosis of mental disorders. Further, when establishing the existence of a mental disorder, it is important to realize that the diagnostic criteria in the *DSM* are "meant to serve as guidelines to be informed by clinical judgment and are not meant to be used in a cookbook fashion" (p. xxxii). If the clinical presentation falls short in meeting the minimum criteria of a given diagnosis, but the symptoms that are present are persistent and severe, the diagnosis may still be a proper one. Conversely, considerable departure from the guidelines will ultimately reduce the *DSM's* utility to consistently communicate the presence of mental disorders.

Exclusion Criteria

Because the diagnoses provided in the *DSM* are not mutually exclusive, resulting in different types of possible relationships among disorders, the *DSM* provides guidance for selecting the most appropriate diagnosis through the use of exclusion criteria. The differential diagnostic process is informed by these exclusion criteria. Pages 5–7 of the *DSM* spell out in detail the different wordings of exclusion criteria that are used throughout the *DSM*. An important exclusion criterion relates to determining the role of substance abuse or dependence in psychological difficulty. All substance-induced disorders carry two specific criteria to help determine whether symptoms are the direct physiological effect of a substance (see p. 7).

Generally speaking, the *DSM* exclusion criteria help with avoiding the use of unnecessary multiple diagnoses. However, there may be cases where two diagnoses are appropriate, despite exclusion criteria provided. For example, the boundary between Panic Disorder with Agoraphobia and Social Phobia is not easy to ascertain. Although the "not better accounted for . . ." exclusion criterion refers each of these diagnoses to the other in this fashion, in some cases both diagnoses might be appropriate. The "not better accounted for . . ." exclusion criterion is an excellent example of the role of clinical judgment in the use of the *DSM* in assigning diagnoses.

"Criteria have never been met for . . ." exclusion creates a lifetime hierarchy between different diagnoses. For example, Major Depressive Disorder is not an appropriate diagnosis once a Manic Episode has occurred, after which one is instructed to use Bipolar I Disorder as the appropriate diagnosis. "Criteria are not met for . . ." helps distinguish between disorders or subtypes of disorders. "Does not occur exclusively during the course of . . ." is used in situations in which symptoms of one disorder are associated features or a subset of the symptoms of a given proper diagnosis.

Severity and Course Specifiers

Specifiers are used to reflect severity (Mild, Moderate, and Severe) and course (Remission or Prior History) of a diagnosis. In most cases, diagnoses are used to reflect current status; however in the case, for example, of a diagnosis with a high incidence of relapse, like alcohol abuse or dependence, indicating the remission status is clinically useful.

Severity

Severity specifiers are used only when the full criteria for a disorder are met, and they are based on the number and intensity of the signs and symptoms of the mental disorder and resulting impairment in occupational or social functioning. Severity specifiers are defined as follows:

> **Mild:** Few, if any, symptoms in excess of those required to make the diagnosis are present, and symptoms result in no more than minor impairment in social or occupational functioning.

Moderate: Symptoms or functional impairment between "mild" and "severe" is present.

Severe: Many symptoms in excess of those required to make the diagnosis, or several symptoms that are particularly severe, are present, or the symptoms result in marked impairment in social or occupational functioning (p. 2).

Course

Course specifiers include:

In Partial Remission: The full criteria for the disorder were previously met, but currently only some of the symptoms or signs of the disorder remain.

In Full Remission: There are no longer any symptoms or signs of the disorder, but it is still clinically relevant to note the disorder—for example, in an individual with previous episodes of Bipolar Disorder who has been symptom free on lithium for the past 3 years. After a period in full remission, the clinician may judge the individual to be recovered and, therefore, would no longer code the disorder as a current diagnosis. The differentiation of the "In Full Remission" from recovered requires consideration of many factors, including the characteristic course of the disorder, the length of time since the last period of disturbance, the total duration of the disturbance, and the need for continued evaluation or prophylactic treatment.

Prior History: For some purposes, it may be useful to note a history of the criteria having been met for a disorder even when the individual is considered to be recovered from it. Such past diagnoses of mental disorder would be indicated by using the specifier Prior History (e.g., Separation Anxiety Disorder, Prior History, for an individual with a history of Separation Anxiety Disorder who has no current disorder or who currently meets criteria for Panic Disorder) (p. 2).

Some diagnoses in the *DSM* are provided with more specific definitions of these severity and course specifiers, which are discussed under those specific diagnoses.

Recurrence

Related to severity and course in the *DSM* is the concept of Recurrence. It allows the clinician to note whether symptoms of a previously resolved diagnosis have returned (*current*) or some but not all have returned (*provisional*);

the clinician can decide that it is a recurrence of a condition even before all criteria are formally met (e.g., having met the criteria for a Major Depressive Episode for only 10 rather than 14 days).

If recurrence is suspected but the clinician is unsure, the Not Otherwise Specified (NOS) qualifier is appropriate. Further, if symptoms are present but not clinically significant, current or provisional may not be appropriate, but "Prior History" course specifier may be a clinically useful qualifier to the diagnosis. The NOS and Provisional specifiers are defined next.

Diagnostic Uncertainty

Not Otherwise Specified

Not Otherwise Specified (NOS) is used to indicate that symptoms of a disorder are present but their number and severity are not clear at present. A complete description for the use of NOS can be found on page 4 of the *DSM*, but in summary, it is used when general guidelines for a disorder are appropriate, but symptoms may be below diagnostic thresholds or are atypical or mixed in presentation; symptoms are not yet classified as a diagnosis in the *DSM* but cause clinically significant distress or impairment; the cause (etiology) is unclear, such as in cases involving substance-induced disorders, or; there is incomplete or contradictory information (see page 4).

Provisional

The specifier *provisional* is appropriate when there is a strong presumption that the full criteria will be met for a mental disorder diagnosis, but sufficient information is not yet available. *Provisional* also has an important use in addressing *recurrence*.

CRITIQUES OF THE *DSM-IV-TR*

Dimensional Versus Categorical Systems

Dimensional models of classification classify clinical presentations based on quantification of attributes rather than the assignment to categories. Dimensional systems work well with phenomena that are distributed continuously and that do not have clear boundaries.

The *DSM* stakeholders in the revision process were hesitant to adopt a dimensional system approach, arguing that numerical systems are much less familiar and vivid than categorical names for mental disorders and that dimensional systems have yet to be proven more effective or useful. They admitted that more research and increased familiarity with dimensional approaches would prove useful in research and clinical practice. Their assessment was prophetic in that one of the most important proposed changes in the *DSM-5* is the use of dimensional scales (see discussion of the *DSM-5* revision process at the end of Part II of this text).

Difficult to Use?

Some have argued that both the *ICD* and *DSM* systems are difficult to use. According to Reed, the *DSM-IV-TR* requires one to recall 20–35 pieces of information to make one or more of over 400 diagnoses. Others suggest that both the *DSM* and *ICD* are limited in their ability to describe patient problems in a meaningful, clinically accurate manner, which does not lend itself to the efficient use of very limited treatment resources (as cited in Martin, 2009).

This writer's opinion about the *DSM* specifically is not that it is difficult to use in and of itself but it does require a significant, detailed knowledge base in psychopathology and patience with the systematic differential diagnostic process. Mental disorders are complex in their presentations, so it is not surprising that a related diagnostic classification is equally complicated.

The use of the *DSM* also requires considerable experience in clinical decision making and confidence in using sound clinical judgment to make distinctions among diagnoses that at times lack clearly demarcated boundaries. That is not to deny, of course, that the *DSM* will continue to benefit from ongoing revisions that are informed by research and contemporary clinical practice.

Generally speaking, society has become increasingly fast paced and impatient with anything less than drive-through or microwave speed. Systems that require careful clinical deliberation and the application of sophisticated diagnostic criteria may try the patience of much of the public. Our managed care environment has also placed great strain on time and resources used for any particular clinical context (Tarvydas, Peterson, & Michaelson, 2005). I believe that the depth and breadth that the *DSM* offers to clinicians in diagnosing mental disorders, while detailed and complex, are clinically useful and ultimately to the benefit of the consumer of mental health services; it informs the judgment of clinical professionals using the *DSM*; and it guides researchers who are informed by its content.

Martin's (2009) opinion regarding the incomplete picture painted by diagnoses alone, particularly with the pressures of managed care, is consistent with our review of the limitations of diagnostic information in Part I of this text. Herein lies the benefit of incorporating the *ICF* into the assessment, treatment, and research of people with mental disorders. The *ICF* provides the functional complement to diagnostic systems in mental health.

ICD-11 and the *DSM*

According to Geoffrey Reed, WHO psychologist involved in the eleventh revision of the *ICD* system, there is widespread sentiment that having two classification systems for mental disorders is not helpful to the related professions. He noted important distinctions between the two systems.

SUMMARY

First, the *ICD* system is created by a large multidisciplinary global health agency with a constitutional public mission to help reduce the disease burden of mental disorders without respect for profit. In contrast, the *DSM* is produced by a single national professional association for psychiatrists in the United States, which generates considerable revenue for the organization.

Reed predicted that the *ICD* will eventually supersede the *DSM* for international mental health efforts. The *ICD-11* will be published in 2015, and promises to be a clinically useful tool that captures patient conditions, and will embrace electronic technology to allow interactive information sharing. The *ICD-11* will be global, multilingual, multidisciplinary, transparent, and free from commercial input. Reed opined that while the *ICD-11* may gain dominance in the classification of mental disorders, the *DSM* will continue to serve as an important reference text of psychiatric diagnoses in the United States (Martin, 2009).

CHAPTER 6

DSM-IV-TR: First Priority of Differential Diagnoses

PREVIEW QUESTIONS

1. Describe several information resources that can be used with *DSM-IV-TR*.
2. How are levels of severity established in mental retardation?
3. Carefully review each diagnosis summary and the associated page numbers for the complete description within the *DSM-IV-TR*.
4. Lookup case vignettes in the *DSM-IV-TR Case Book* for each disorder presented.

USE OF THE *DSM-IV-TR* WITH THIS SECTION OF THE TEXT

This review of the spectrum of diagnoses in the *DSM* provides a useful overview for those learning about the *DSM* and the differential diagnostic process. This text is intended to be used along with the *DSM* itself; the author recommends that the reader review the associated sections of the *DSM* indicated by page number while reading the heuristics presented here. A discussion of the *DSM* in the context of the *ICF* will be the focus of Part III of this text.

DSM-IV-TR Case Book

A learning companion to the *DSM*, the *DSM-IV-TR Case Book* (Spitzer, Gibbon, Skodol, Williams, & First, 2002) provides case examples and the opportunity to apply the concepts and terminology of the *DSM-IV-TR* to clinical vignettes. Vignettes are concise but rich in content and are

followed by an explanation of the differential diagnostic process employed. A handy index allows one to seek out vignettes portraying specific
diagnoses.

A Guide to Treatments That Work

Editors Nathan and Gorman have updated the third edition of *Treatments That Work* (2007), a detailed evaluative review of current research
on empirically supported treatments, with chapters written by clinical psychologists and psychiatrists who are major contributors to their
literature. This is an excellent resource for treatment planning based
on information from the *DSM*. Intervention targeting and evaluation
of *Treatments That Work* outcomes can be informed and facilitated by
application of the *ICF*'s conceptual framework and code sets (Peterson,
Mpofu, & Oakland, 2010).

Online Resource for Psychotropic Treatments

A very useful resource for remaining current on pharmacological treatments,
including recent "black box" updates, changes in dosing strategies, and
approval of new uses of psychotropic drugs, can be found on MedlinePlus,
at http://medlineplus.gov/ under the "Drugs and Supplements" tab. The
Web site also provides many useful features, like health topics on disease
and wellness, a medical encyclopedia with pictures and diagrams, a medical dictionary, directories of health care professionals including local
resources, and current health news.

What Makes a Diagnosis?

There are many details for each diagnosis reviewed here that are elaborated
upon in the nearly 1,000 page *DSM*, and for practical purposes many of
them will not be repeated here. The reader is encouraged to review the
page numbers from the *DSM* indicated in each relevant section of this text
in order to review each diagnosis in all of its detail.

   One criterion that exists for nearly every diagnosis in the *DSM* is that
the constellation of symptoms for a given disorder and the associated deficits cause significant distress or impairment in social, occupational, or other
important areas of functioning. The significance threshold is determined
using symptoms reported, objective testing and other medical evidences
when available, and sound clinical judgment.

DISORDERS USUALLY FIRST DIAGNOSED IN INFANCY, CHILDHOOD, OR ADOLESCENCE

This grouping within the *DSM* identifies diagnoses typically encountered during infancy, childhood, or adolescence. In reality, these diagnoses may not be detected until adulthood. Further, diagnoses from the rest of the *DSM* may occur in childhood, and adults may be diagnosed with mental disorders from the grouping when appropriate, so professionals specializing in any specific developmental range need to be familiar with the entire diagnostic system. Relevant diagnoses contain information that informs the use of *DSM* with infants, children, and adolescents.

The *ICF-CY*

It is appropriate within this diagnostic category to revisit a point made earlier in Part I of this text, which is the existence of a Children and Youth version of the *ICF* (*ICF-CY*; Simeonsson et al., 2006). Simeonsson and colleagues (2003) revised the *ICIDH/ICF* to include aspects that address the sensibilities needed when classifying youth. Although this text does not focus on the *ICF-Y*, a future version of a similar text focusing on mental disorders found with infants, children, and adolescents, and the role of how the *ICF-Y* may inform working well with these mental disorders, may result in a very useful resource (see also Simeonsson et al., 2006).

Next, we turn to brief descriptions of diagnoses found in this grouping of mental disorders. The reader should also review the relevant sections within the *DSM-IV-TR* itself, to understand more completely how the *DSM* defines a given condition.

Mental Retardation

The diagnosis of mental retardation is appropriate when subaverage intellectual functioning and co-occurring impairments in adaptive functioning are detected before age 18. Mental health professionals will find it useful to understand the degrees of severity used to qualify the level of impairment associated with the diagnosis. Along with the impaired adaptive functioning, IQ ranges are used to establish levels of mental retardation. See Table 6.1 for a listing of degrees of severity of mental retardation according to IQ levels.

TABLE 6.1 Degrees of Severity of Mental Retardation (APA, 2000, p. 42)

ICD-9-CM Codes	Severity	IQ Level
317	Mild	50–55 to about 70
318.0	Moderate	35–40 to 50–55
318.1	Severe	20–25 to 35–40
318.2	Profound	Below 20 or 25

Pages 41–49 of the *DSM* provide detailed criteria for the diagnosis of mental retardation. As with most diagnoses in the *DSM*, the section begins with an overview of diagnostic features, which provides clarification of concepts involved with the disorder. Next, the specific subcategories of Mental Retardation, Mild, Moderate, Severe, Profound, and Severity Unspecified are clarified for enhanced diagnostic precision, and recording procedures are clarified. The "Associated Features and Disorders" section provides an overview of prevalence and comorbidity data, predisposing factors to mental retardation, and associated examination and laboratory findings. Next, specific culture, age, and gender features are noted, as are prevalence, course, and familial patterns of the diagnosis. The section concludes with instructions on differential diagnosis, relationship to other classifications of Mental Retardation, and a summary table of the diagnostic criteria.

Learning Disorders

If academic functioning is substantially below one's expected performance given the context (age, intelligence, and education), a Learning Disorder may be appropriate to diagnose. There are several subtypes in this grouping, including Reading Disorder, Mathematics Disorder, Disorder of Written Expression, and the expected Learning Disorder NOS. Pages 49–56 provide detailed information as outlined for Mental Retardation.

Motor Skills Disorder

The Motor Skills diagnostic category contains no unique subtypes. The single diagnosis in the category, Developmental Coordination Disorder, is appropriate when motor coordination is substantially below that expected for a given age and intelligence level. See pp. 56–58 of the *DSM* for diagnostic details.

Communication Disorders

The Communication Disorders group has five subtypes. Expressive Language Disorder is an impairment in expressive language development. Pages 58–61 detail diagnostic features. Mixed Receptive-Expressive Language Disorder involves, as the name suggests, difficulty in not only expressive but also receptive language development (pp. 62–64). There is no diagnosis for Receptive Language Disorder alone.

Three more subgroups remain in the Communication Disorders category. Phonological Disorder is the failure to use developmentally expected speech sounds at an appropriate age and is detailed on pp. 65–66. Stuttering is a disturbance in the normal fluency and time patterning of speech, as described on pp. 67–69. Finally, Communication Disorder NOS may address an anomaly not covered in the five subgroups, such as peculiarities in vocal tone and volume.

Pervasive Developmental Disorders

This particular diagnostic group has received a lot of attention recently from the popular press, due to the apparently high prevalence of Autism. Pervasive Developmental Disorders (PDDs) are characterized by severe deficits and pervasive impairments in multiple areas of development, which may include impairments in reciprocal social interaction, communication, typical interests, behaviors, and activities. There are five subgroups in this diagnostic group.

Autistic Disorder

Autistic Disorder is a PDD where there is markedly impaired development in social interaction and communication, along with very restricted interests and activities. Pages 70–75 provide considerable detail about this disorder.

Rett's Disorder

Rett's Disorder is a PDD characterized by several specific deficits that develop after a normal period of functioning after birth (i.e., 5 months of normal motor development). Between ages 5 and 48 months head growth decelerates, and between 5 and 30 months there is a loss of previously acquired purposeful hand skills and subsequent development of characteristic stereotyped hand movements that appear like hand washing. In the first few years after development of the disorder, there is a loss of social interest, which may reemerge later in development to some degree.

The disorder is also associated with problems in the coordination of gait or trunk movements and severe psychomotor retardation. There is also severely impaired expressive and receptive language development. This diagnosis has appeared only in females to date; more details can be found on pp. 76–77 in the *DSM*.

Childhood Disintegrative Disorder

Childhood Disintegrative Disorder is characterized by a marked regression in several areas of functioning following a period of at least 2 years of apparent normal development. Between ages 2 and 10 years, there is a clinically significant loss of previously acquired skills in language, social skills, adaptive behaviors, bowel and bladder control, play, or motor skills (see pp. 77–79 in the *DSM*).

Asperger's Disorder

Asperger's Disorder, or Asperger's Syndrome as it is known, shares many of the features of Autistic Disorder, except there are no significant delays or deviance in language acquisition. Further, with Asperger's Disorder, there are no noticeable cognitive delays during the first 3 years of development, although in retrospect to many parents or caregivers, while cognitive difficulties were not noticed, unusual behaviors typically appeared during this time period (see pp. 80–84 in the *DSM*).

The last of the five subgroups for this diagnostic category is PDD NOS, including Atypical Autism. All of the symptoms reviewed earlier may be present at subthreshold level, or develop at an atypical time. In such cases, PDD NOS is an appropriate diagnosis.

Attention-Deficit and Disruptive Behavior Disorders

This diagnostic group contains four subgroups, largely related by some difficulty regulating behavior in a socially appropriate manner.

Attention-Deficit/Hyperactivity Disorder

In Attention-Deficit/Hyperactivity Disorder (ADHD), there exists an inordinate, persistent pattern of inattention and/or hyperactivity-impulsivity, present prior to age 7, and these symptoms must interfere with social, academic, or occupational functioning. Subtypes of this diagnosis include three variants: predominately inattentive, hyperactive-impulsive, or combined type. There is, of course, ADHD NOS, with two particular instances not covered in the ADHD diagnostic criteria. First, for those whose onset is after age 7 and second, for those demonstrating inattention, but rather than hyperactivity they struggle with sluggishness, daydreaming, and hypoactivity (see pp. 85–93 in the *DSM*).

Conduct Disorder

Conduct Disorder manifests as a repetitive and persistent pattern of violating either the basic rights of others or major age-appropriate societal norms or rules. The diagnosis indicates whether the problem behaviors manifested during childhood versus adolescence; adults may also receive this diagnosis as long as they do not meet the criteria for Antisocial Personality Disorder. There are four groupings of problem behaviors: aggressive behavior, nonaggressive behavior, deceitfulness or theft, or serious violations of rules (see pp. 93–99 in the *DSM*).

Oppositional Defiant Disorder

Behaviors associated with Oppositional Defiant Disorder (ODD) are of a less severe nature than those for Conduct Disorder. ODD relates to a pattern of negativistic, hostile, and defiant behaviors (e.g., losing temper, defying rules, deliberately annoying people, being spiteful or vindictive). Although all of the features of ODD are present in Conduct Disorder, behaviors associated with ODD typically do not rise to the level of aggressive and destructive activities nor patterns of theft or deceit. There is, of course, the NOS diagnosis for Disruptive Behavior Disorder (see pp. 100–102 in the *DSM*).

Feeding and Eating Disorders of Infancy or Childhood

All disorders in this group are characterized by persistent disturbances in feeding and eating. There are three subtypes of diagnoses in this diagnostic group, Pica, Rumination Disorder, and Feeding Disorder of Infancy or Early Childhood. The reader will note that Anorexia Nervosa and Bulimia Nervosa are in a different category of Eating Disorders further on in the *DSM*.

Pica

If an infant or child eats one or more nonnutritive substances on a persistent basis for at least 1 month, to the point of requiring clinical attention and not as a less salient feature of Mental Retardation or another PDD, the diagnosis of Pica is appropriate. Infants and younger children with this disorder tend to eat things like paint, plaster, string, hair, or cloth. Older children may consume animal droppings, sand, insects, leaves, or pebbles. Adolescents and adults may consume clay or soil (see pp. 103–105 in the *DSM*).

Rumination Disorder

If after a normal period of functioning, an infant or child repeatedly regurgitates and re-chews food, and this lasts at least 1 month, Rumination Disorder is an appropriate diagnosis. As with Pica, this disorder may not be appropriate if such behaviors co-occur with Mental Retardation or PDD and if the symptoms do not require specific clinical attention (see pp. 105–106 in the *DSM*).

Feeding Disorder of Infancy or Early Childhood

This diagnosis features persistent failure to eat adequately. It may manifest as failure to gain weight or significant weight loss over 1 month. Onset must be before the age of 6 years (see pp. 107–108 in the *DSM*).

Tic Disorders

Four disorders exist in this section of the *DSM*: Tourette's Disorder, Chronic Motor or Vocal Tic Disorder, Transient Tic Disorder, and Tic Disorder NOS. Generally speaking, a tic is a sudden, rapid, recurrent, nonrhythmic, stereotyped motor movement, or vocalization. Tics may be simple (involving only a few muscles or sounds, like eye blinking, nose wrinkling, neck jerking, shoulder shrugging, facial grimacing, and abdominal tensing) or complex (hand gestures, jumping, touching, pressing, stomping, facial contortions, repeatedly smelling an object, squatting, deep knee bends, retracing steps, twirling when walking, and assuming and holding unusual postures; see pp. 108–111 in the *DSM*).

Tourette's Disorder

Tourette's Disorder is characterized by multiple motor tics and one or more vocal tics, occurring many times each day for more than a year. There may be periods of less than 3 months without such tics, and the diagnosis remains appropriate. The tics must occur before 18 years of age and not be the direct physiological effect of a substance or medical condition (see pp. 111–114 in the *DSM*).

Chronic or Transient Tic Disorders

Chronic Motor or Vocal Tic Disorder is associated with the presence of either a vocal or motor tic, but not both. Transient Tic Disorder can be both, lasts for at least 4 weeks, but no longer than 12 months (otherwise

Tourette's Disorder would be more appropriate). Tic Disorder NOS is characterized by tics that do not meet other criteria for more specific tic disorder (see pp. 114–116 in the *DSM*).

Elimination Disorders

Encopresis

Encopresis relates to children who are 4 years or older (or have the mental age of 4 if developmentally delayed), who have repeated passage of feces into inappropriate places, like clothing or the floor. It most often is involuntary, but it may be intentional, and occur at least once a month for at least 3 months. There are subtype qualifications involving constipation; see pages 116–118 in the *DSM* for greater detail.

Enuresis (Not Due to a General Medical Condition)

Enuresis involves repeated voiding of urine during the day or at night into bed or clothes, after the age when continence is expected (chronological or mental age of 5 years old). Enuresis must occur at least twice weekly for at least 3 months or cause significant distress or impairment. Subtypes indicate whether enuresis occurs during the waking hours (Diurnal Only), during nighttime sleep (Nocturnal Only), or both (see pp. 118–121 in the *DSM*).

Other Disorders of Infancy, Childhood, or Adolescence

Disorders that do not fit into the subgroups above are included here, including Separation Anxiety Disorder, Selective Mutism, Reactive Attachment Disorder of Infancy or Early Childhood, Stereotypic Movement Disorder, and a NOS category, reviewed from pages 121–134 in the *DSM*. It is also noted within this diagnostic area that children or adolescence may be experiencing difficulties requiring clinical attention that are not defined as mental disorders specifically, and these are listed on p. 731 of the *DSM* under Other Conditions That May Be A Focus of Clinical Attention.

DELIRIUM, DEMENTIA, AND AMNESTIC AND OTHER COGNITIVE DISORDERS

This section of the *DSM* contains disorders associated with a significant change in cognition relative to previous functioning. For each disorder, the cause is either a general medical condition (not always identifiable) and/or a substance (illicit, prescribed, or a toxin).

Delirium

Delirium is characterized by a disturbance of consciousness and change in cognition that develop over a short period of time. The presentation can be dramatic and quite debilitating, and it is attributed to either a general medical condition, substance-induced, or multiple etiologies (see pp. 136–147 in the *DSM*).

Dementia

Dementia, in contrast with Delirium, can be more insidious and its course more gradual, causing multiple cognitive deficits including impairment in memory. A variety of presumed etiologies may be indicated, including Dementias of the following types: Alzheimer's, Vascular, Other General Medical Condition (i.e., HIV; head trauma; Parkinson's, Huntington's, Pick's, or Creutzfeldt-Jakob disease; Other General Medical Conditions), Substance-induced Persisting, Due to Multiple Etiologies, or NOS. See pp. 147–171 of the *DSM* for detailed descriptions of the various types of Dementias.

Amnestic Disorder

An amnestic disorder is specific to memory impairment in the absence of other cognitive deficits. Amnestic disorders are listed according to presumed etiology, the same as Delirium disorders are listed (see pp. 172–179 in the *DSM*).

Cognitive Disorder NOS

Cognitive Disorder NOS is used when none of the following delirium, dementia, or amnestic disorders applies, and it is not better accounted for Delirium, Dementia, or Amnestic Disorder NOS (see pp. 179–180 in the *DSM*). Typical presentations of Cognitive Disorder NOS are comparatively mild, evidenced by standardized testing in the context of a coexisting, systemic, general medical condition or central nervous system dysfunction. Postconcussional disorder following head trauma may be associated with impairment in memory or attention and a diagnosis of Cognitive Disorder NOS.

MENTAL DISORDERS DUE TO A GENERAL MEDICAL CONDITION

As mentioned previously in the discussion addressing the organization of the *DSM*, disorders related to general medical conditions are more proximal in the order of presentation to draw clinician's attention to the influence of such conditions on mental disorders. This is not unlike how the *ICF* conceptual framework highlights Body Functions and Structures first and that associated impairments are interpreted within the subsequent context of Activities and Participation.

Within the section Mental Disorders Due to a General Medical Condition, diagnoses are listed to draw attention to their relative order in the differential diagnostic process. Three of these diagnoses are listed in this section of the *DSM* with their full criteria. Seven of those listed are detailed within other relevant sections of the *DSM*.

Related Conditions Placed in Other Sections of the *DSM*

The seven conditions included in Mental Disorders Due to a General Medical Condition, but have criteria listed in other sections of the *DSM*, include Delirium, Dementia, Amnestic Disorder, Psychotic Disorder, Mood Disorder, Anxiety Disorder, Sexual Dysfunction, and Sleep Disorder Due to a General Medical Condition.

Catatonic Disorder Due to a General Medical Condition

Catatonic Disorder Due to a General Medical Condition is appropriate in the presence of catatonia presumably due to the direct physiological effects of the same. Catatonia may manifest as motoric immobility, excessive motor activity, extreme negativism or mutism, peculiarities of voluntary movement, echolalia (involuntary or voluntary repeating what is heard), or echopraxia (mimicking movements that are seen). See pp. 185–187 in the *DSM* for detailed criteria.

Personality Change Due to a General Medical Condition

Personality Change Due to a General Medical Condition is different from enduring personality traits addressed on Axis II of the *DSM*; the changes that are brought about by a medical condition are more variable in their onset and course. In all cases of this diagnosis, the change represents a change from premorbid personality traits and/or behaviors.

Children with this disorder may manifest a marked deviation from normal development as opposed to personality per se. Adults with this disorder may manifest personality changes that include affective instability, poor impulse control, outbursts of aggression or rage notably out of proportion for a given stressor, marked apathy, suspiciousness, or paranoid ideation.

There are eight subtypes of this diagnosis, including Labile Type, Disinhibited Type, Aggressive Type, Apathetic Type, Paranoid Type, Other Type, Combined Type, and Unspecified Type (see pp. 187–190 in the *DSM* for more details).

SUBSTANCE-RELATED DISORDERS

There are over 100 pages in the *DSM* dedicated to Substance-Related Disorders. This section of the *DSM* is a rich resource for understanding the complexities of substance abuse and addiction, including specific aspects of substance intoxication, abuse, dependence, and withdrawal.

Types of Substances

Substances may include any drug of abuse (including alcohol, caffeine, and nicotine), a prescribed medication, or a toxin. These substances are divided into 11 classes: Alcohol; Amphetamines; Caffeine; Cannabis; Cocaine; Hallucinogens; Inhalants; Nicotine; Opioids; Phencyclidine; and Sedatives, Hypnotics, or Anxiolytics. Of course, a Polysubstance category exists. There are a number of other substances, such as over-the-counter medications and prescribed drugs that may be a factor in substance abuse or dependence (examples are listed on p. 191 in the *DSM*).

Substance Use Disorders

Substance-Related Disorders are divided into two different groups. First, Substance Use Disorders involve substance abuse or dependence.

Substance Dependence

Substance dependence involves a cluster of cognitive, behavioral, and physiological symptoms that indicate continued use of a given substance despite significant related problems. Repeated substance use leads to tolerance, withdrawal, and compulsive drug-taking behavior. Two specifiers within this diagnostic category indicate With Physiological Dependence (when evidence of tolerance or withdrawal exist) and Without Physiological Dependence.

All substance categories except Caffeine can manifest symptoms of Dependence, which is defined as a cluster of three or more of possible symptoms occurring at any time in a 12-month period: (1) tolerance;

(2) withdrawal; (3) taking a substance in larger amounts or over a longer period than was originally intended; (4) unsuccessful efforts to discontinue use; (5) spending a great deal of time acquiring, using, or recovering from the substance; (6) giving up or reducing important social, occupational, or recreational activities; and (7) continued use despite recognizing the contributing role of the substance to a psychological or physical problem (see pages 192–198 of *DSM*).

Course Specifiers in Substance Dependence

Six course specifiers are available for this diagnosis. Four of the Remission specifiers require that none of the criteria for Dependence or Abuse is present for at least 1 month (abstinence for at least 1 month). The interval of time that has passed since cessation of substance use determines whether they are in Early versus Sustained Remission. Because the first 12 months following dependence have a high potential for relapse, this period is designated Early Remission. After 12 months of Early Remission have passed with no abuse or dependence, Sustained Remission is achieved.

The continued presence of one or more of the criteria for Abuse or Dependence determines whether they are in Partial versus Full remission. In Partial Remission, at least one of the criteria for Dependence or Abuse has been met, intermittently or continuously, during the period of remission. For Full Remission, no criteria for Abuse or Dependence have been met during the period of remission.

These specifiers do not apply if someone is On Agonist Therapy (like the opioid agonist therapy methadone) or In a Controlled Environment (sober living home or locked hospital unit), which are the remaining two specifiers. Keeping the first four remission specifiers straight can be a challenge for newcomers to the *DSM*, so Table 6.2 is included here to provide a visual summary of criteria for remission (see pp. 192–198 in the *DSM* for the complete review of Substance Dependence).

Substance Abuse

The diagnosis of Substance Abuse is not used if Substance Dependence is more appropriate. It does not involve caffeine or nicotine. Substance use, misuse, or hazardous use is not the same as meeting the criteria for Substance Abuse as a diagnosis. Substance Abuse is a maladaptive behavior pattern of substance use manifested by recurrent and significant adverse consequences related to the repeated use of substances. The durational

TABLE 6.2 Course Specifiers for Substance Dependence

Remission Specifier	Duration Criteria
Early Partial Remission	For 1 month, but less than 12 months, one or more criteria for Dependence or Abuse have been met, but full criteria for Dependence have not been met.
Early Full Remission	For 1 month, but less than 12 months, no criteria for Dependence or Abuse have been met.
Sustained Partial Remission	For 12 months or longer, full criteria for Dependence have not been met; however, one or more criteria for Dependence or Abuse have been met.
Sustained Full Remission	For 12 months or longer, none of the criteria for Dependence or Abuse has been met at any time.

Note: These remission specifiers can be applied only after no criteria for Dependence or Abuse have been met for at least 1 month. These specifiers do not apply if the individual is on agonist therapy or in a controlled environment. (See pages 195–197 of *DSM* for details and a graphic representation of course specifiers).

requirement is a 12-month period of behavior "or been persistent" (p. 198). See pp. 198–199 in the *DSM* for detailed criteria for defining maladaptive behavior associated with Substance Abuse.

Substance-Induced Disorders

The second group within Substance-Related Disorders involves Substance-Induced Disorders, which address the effects of substance intoxication, withdrawal, and a variety of substance-induced dysfunction (e.g., psychosis, amnesia, etc.). Pages 199–296 of the *DSM* outlines in great detail the manifestation of these effects across the 11 classes of substances. It is important to note that substance use disorders of abuse, intoxication, or withdrawal do not use the course specifiers employed in substance dependence. There is no diagnosis in the *DSM* "substance abuse in sustained remission," although the author frequently sees such use in reviewing many mental health-related reports.

We have just reviewed the diagnoses that the *DSM* presents as the first priority of the differential diagnostic process. Ruling out the existence of these disorders allows careful consideration of other disorders that share phenomenological features, to which we turn in our next chapter.

CHAPTER 7

Disorders With Shared Phenomenological Features: Part I

PREVIEW QUESTIONS

1. What are the essential features of Schizophrenia?
2. What is a Major Depressive Episode?
3. What is a Manic or Mixed Episode?
4. What are the differences between Bipolar I and Bipolar II disorders?
5. After carefully reviewing diagnostic summaries provided in this chapter, go directly to the *DSM* page intervals indicated and carefully review the diagnoses in their entirety.

The remaining diagnoses in the *DSM*, apart from the Adjustment Disorders and Other Disorders section, are organized according to shared phenomenological features (e.g., bizarre behavior, disturbances in mood, and anxiety). As with the prior sections, the brief reviews serve to orient the reader to these mental disorders, and the reader is encouraged to review each diagnostic section of the *DSM* in its entirety.

SCHIZOPHRENIA AND OTHER PSYCHOTIC DISORDERS

The mental disorders in this section of the *DSM* include psychotic symptoms as a prominent aspect of their presentation. That is not to say that psychosis is the most important aspect of the disorders, nor do they share a common etiology. Further, diagnoses found in other sections of the *DSM* may present psychotic features. Historically, the term *psychotic* has had a wide range of interpretations (see p. 297 in the *DSM*). The contemporary use of the term psychotic in the *DSM* refers to the presence of certain symptoms that vary somewhat depending upon the diagnosis. In addition to the following diagnostic groups, there is, of course, Psychotic Disorder NOS for psychotic presentations that do not meet the criteria for these specific disorders (see pp. 298–343 in the *DSM* for details).

Schizophrenia

Schizophrenia is diagnosed after 6 months of a presenting constellation of symptoms associated with impaired occupational or social functioning. These symptoms present for more than 1 month and include delusions, hallucinations, disorganized speech (frequent derailment and incoherence), grossly disorganized or catatonic behavior, and negative symptoms (affective flattening, alogia, or avolition). The progression of Schizophrenia has been conceptualized as prodromal, active, and residual phases; the aforementioned symptoms are part of the active phase of the disorder.

Two main types of symptoms surface in Schizophrenia. Positive symptoms are characterized by an excess or distortion of normal functions, whereas negative symptoms reflect a diminution or loss of normal functioning. Subtypes of Schizophrenia include Paranoid, Disorganized, Catatonic, Undifferentiated, and Residual Type. A variety of course specifiers are provided for use after the disorder has existed for more than 12 months. Some have opined that these subtypes are of limited utility in clinical and research settings.

Other subtyping schemes for Schizophrenia are possible and are being explored, including a dimensional alternative noted in Appendix B of the *DSM*, consisting of three dimensions of interest: psychotic, disorganized, and negative dimensions (see pp. 297–303 for very detailed explanation of diagnostic criteria and course specifiers for the current conceptualization of Schizophrenia).

Schizophreniform Disorder

Schizophreniform Disorder shares the same diagnostic features as Schizophrenia, except the symptoms have lasted only 1–6 months, and there is not necessarily a decline in functioning (see pp. 317–319 in the *DSM* for associated features and disorders).

Schizoaffective Disorder

In Schizoaffective Disorder, a mood episode (Major Depressive, Manic, or Mixed Episode) and active-phase symptoms of schizophrenia occur together. The co-occurrence of these symptoms is preceded or followed by at least 2 weeks of delusions or hallucinations without prominent mood symptoms. For some individuals with Schizoaffective disorder, symptoms can last for years or even decades. There are two subtypes of this disorder, Bipolar Type and Depressive Type, depending on the manifestation of mood disturbance (see pp. 319–323 in the *DSM*).

Delusional Disorder

In delusional disorder, at least 1 month of nonbizarre delusions (situations that occur in real life) have occurred without other active-phase symptoms of Schizophrenia. There are five subtypes of this disorder: Erotomanic, Grandiose, Jealous, Persecutory, Somatic, Mixed, and Unspecified Types (see pp. 323–329 in the *DSM* for details).

Brief Psychotic Disorder

Brief Psychotic Disorder lasts more than 1 day and remits by 1 month's time. This disorder is specified as With Marked Stressors, Without, or With Postpartum Onset (see pp. 329–332 in the *DSM*).

Shared Psychotic Disorder

Shared Psychotic Disorder presents as a delusion in an individual who is influenced by someone, typically an individual who is closely involved, who has a longer-standing delusion with similar content. The alternative French label "Folie a Deux" implies the fruitless shared delusion of two people. This diagnosis presents an example where the definition of psychotic is actually that of a delusion (see pp. 332–334 in the *DSM*).

Psychotic Disorder Due to a General Medical Condition and Substance-Induced Psychotic Disorder

For both of these subgroups, psychotic symptoms are judged to be a direct physiological consequence of either a general medical condition for the former or a drug of abuse, a medication, or toxin exposure for the latter (see pp. 334–343 in the *DSM* for specific criteria with specifiers).

MOOD DISORDERS

The Mood Disorder section of the *DSM* is organized first with an explanation of what are mood episodes (Major Depressive, Manic, Mixed, and Hypomanic episodes), followed by the criteria for the diagnoses that incorporate these definitions. The disorders are divided into Depressive Disorders, Bipolar Disorders, and two disorders based on etiology of mood difficulty (General Medical Condition and Substance Induced). Most Mood Disorders can be specified as to With/Without Interepisode Recovery (see pp. 424–425 in the *DSM*), Seasonal Pattern (pp. 425–426), and in the case of the Bipolar Disorders, Rapid Cycling (pp. 427–428). See pp. 410–428 in the *DSM* for the entire presentation of Specifiers Describing Current or Most Recent Episode.

Mood Episodes

Major Depressive Episode

A Major Depressive Episode is at least 2 weeks of depressed mood or loss of interest or pleasure in nearly all activities. Children may appear irritable rather than sad. This must also be accompanied by at least four additional symptoms of depression that persist for most of the day, almost every day, for at least 2 consecutive weeks. The list of additional symptoms includes changes in appetite or weight, sleep, or psychomotor activity; decreased energy; feelings of worthlessness or guilt; difficulty thinking, concentrating, or making decisions; or recurrent thoughts of death or suicidal ideation, plans, or attempts.

Some people may emphasize somatic complaints (aches and pains) rather than reporting feelings of sadness. During an episode, many people experience irritability. Page 356 of the *DSM* provides a detailed listing of the criteria for a Major Depressive Episode, including the nine symptoms of which five must be present to meet the criteria for the diagnosis (see the entire section, pp. 349–356 in the *DSM*). Severity/Psychotic/Remission specifiers are reviewed on pp. 411–413 in the *DSM*.

Manic Episode

A Manic Episode is a distinct period during which there is an abnormally and persistently elevated, expansive, or irritable mood that lasts at least 1 week (less if hospitalization is required). The mood disturbance must be accompanied by at least three of seven additional symptoms including inflated self-esteem, grandiosity, decreased need for sleep, pressure of speech, flight of ideas, distractibility, increased involvement in goal-directed activities or psychomotor agitation, and excessive involvement in pleasurable activities with a high potential for painful consequences.

Elevated mood in a Manic Episode is euphoric, unusually good, cheerful, or high, relatively excessive from a person's baseline approach to life.

Accompanying expansive mood includes unceasing and indiscriminate enthusiasm for interpersonal, sexual, or occupational interactions. The person's mood may change toward irritability when wishes are not granted. Lability of mood is also a hallmark of a Manic Episode (see pp. 357–362 of the *DSM* for greater detail. Severity/Psychotic/Remission Specifiers are outlined and described on pp. 413–415 in the *DSM*).

Mixed Episode

A Mixed Episode is a period of at least 1 week where the criteria for both a Manic Episode and a Major Depressive Episode are met nearly every day. Rapidly alternating moods are accompanied by symptoms of a Manic Episode. Symptoms typically include agitation, insomnia, appetite dysregulation, psychotic features, and suicidal thinking (see pp. 362–365 of the *DSM*. Severity/Psychotic/Remission Specifiers for Mixed Episode are described on pp. 415–417 of the *DSM*).

Hypomanic Episode

A Hypomanic Episode is not severe enough to cause marked impairment in functioning or to require hospitalization. It is defined similarly to a Manic Episode, but the durational criterion is only 4 days in length, rather than a week or more, and only three or more symptoms from a list of seven must be present. Elevated mood in a Hypomanic Episode is described as euphoric, unusually good, cheerful, high, just as a Manic Episode is manifested. Uncritical self-confidence may exist as opposed to grandiosity, and impulsive activity also occurs but without the level of impairment characteristic of a Manic Episode (see pp. 365–368 in the *DSM*).

Major Depressive Disorder

Major Depressive Disorder is diagnosed when there is one or more Major Depressive Episodes, without a history of Manic, Hypomanic, or Mixed Episodes. It cannot also be better accounted for by Schizoaffective Disorder and cannot be superimposed on Schizophrenia, Schizophreniform, Delusional, or Psychotic Disorders. There must never have been a Manic or Mixed Episode, else Bipolar I Disorder is more appropriate. The same holds for Hypomanic Episode and Bipolar II Disorder.

Major Depressive Disorder is qualified as either a Single Episode or Recurrent. An episode is considered ended when the full criteria for the disorder is not met for at least 2 consecutive months. The following specifiers can be employed: Severity (Mild, Moderate, or Severe); With or Without Psychotic Features; In Partial or Full Remission; Chronic (see page 417 of *DSM*); and With Catatonic Features, With Melancholic Features, With Atypical Features, or With Postpartum Onset (see pp. 417–423 in the *DSM*; see pp. 369–376 in the *DSM* for details on specifiers and associated features and disorders).

Dysthymic Disorder

Dysthymic disorder is appropriate when there has been at least 2 years of depressed mood for more days than not, accompanied by other depressive symptoms that do not meet the criteria for a Major Depressive Episode. For children, the mood presentation may be that of irritable, and required duration is only 1 year. Specifiers for the disorder include Early Onset (before 21 years old), Late Onset (at age 21 or older), and with Atypical Features (mood reactivity, increased appetite and weight gain, hypersomnia, leaden paralysis, and a long-standing pattern of extreme sensitivity to perceived interpersonal rejection; see pp. 420–421 in the *DSM*; see pp. 376–381 in the *DSM*).

Depressive Disorder NOS

The NOS category is used to diagnose problematic depression that does not meet the criteria for Major Depressive Disorder, Dysthymic Disorder, Adjustment Disorder with Depressed Mood or with Mixed Anxiety, and Depressed Mood. As with other NOS diagnoses, Depressive Disorder NOS can also be used when there are symptoms about which there is inadequate or contradictory information.

Bipolar I Disorder

Bipolar I Disorder is distinct from Bipolar II Disorder, in that there are one or more Manic or Mixed Episodes, for which Bipolar II Disorder there are only Hypomanic Episodes. For Bipolar I Disorder, Manic or Mixed Episodes are usually accompanied by Major Depressive Episodes. Bipolar I Disorder, Single Manic Episode, is used to first diagnose the disorder. Subsequent diagnoses take into account the nature of the most recent mood episode.

For Bipolar I Disorder Most Recent Episode Depressed, the following specifiers can be employed: Severity/Psychotic/Remission status, Chronic, With Catatonic Features, With Melancholic Features, With Atypical Features, and With Postpartum Onset. For Bipolar I Disorder, either Single

Manic Episode, Most Recent Episode Manic, or Most Recent Episode Mixed, the following specifiers can be employed: Severity/Psychotic/Remission status, With Catatonic Features, and With Postpartum Onset (see pp. 383–392 in the *DSM* for more specific guidance on the use of these specifiers).

Bipolar II Disorder

Bipolar II Disorder is characterized by one or more Major Depressive Episodes accompanied by at least one Hypomanic Episode. The presence of a Manic or Mixed Episodes precludes this diagnosis. The current or most recent mood episode is noted by specifying "Hypomanic" or "Depressed."

For Bipolar II Disorder, Depressed, the following specifiers can be employed: Severity (Mild, Moderate, or Severe); Without or With Psychotic features; In Partial or Full Remission; Chronic, and; With Catatonic, Melancholic, or Atypical Features, and; With Postpartum Onset (see pp. 392–397 in the *DSM*).

Cyclothymic Disorder

If for 2 years or more, someone experiences numerous periods of hypomanic symptoms that do not meet the criteria for a Manic Episode and numerous periods of depressive symptoms that do not meet the criteria for a Major Depressive Episode, Cyclothymic Disorder is the appropriate diagnosis. There are no specifiers that apply to this Mood Disorder (see pp. 398–401 of the *DSM* for more specific information).

Bipolar Disorder NOS

As with other NOS diagnoses, Bipolar Disorder NOS is appropriate when there are bipolar features that do not meet the criteria for types I or II or Cyclothymic Disorder or if there are symptoms about which there is inadequate or contradictory information (see pp. 400–401 of the *DSM* for more specific information).

Mood Disorder Due to a General Medical Condition; Substance-Induced Mood Disorder

These diagnoses are appropriate when there is prominent and persistent disturbance of mood that appears to be a direct physiological consequence of either a general medical condition or that is substance induced (see pp. 401–404 of the *DSM* for more specific information).

Substance-Induced Mood Disorder

For this disorder the effects of a substance are judged to be responsible for the disturbance in mood. The full criteria for a Major Depressive, Manic, Mixed, or Hypomanic episode do not need to be met for this diagnosis. See pp. 405 through 409 of the *DSM* for specific details on diagnostic features, subtypes, specifiers, and other diagnostic details.

Mood Disorder NOS

The utility of the NOS diagnosis for Mood Disorder is in covering those cases where the criteria for neither Depressive Disorder NOS nor Bipolar Disorder NOS are met. For example, in the case of acute agitation with no known physiological cause.

ANXIETY DISORDERS

Panic Attacks and Agoraphobia co-occur in several mental disorders in this grouping as well as in other groups (Mood Disorders, Substance-Related Disorders) and some General Medical Conditions (cardiac, respiratory, vestibular, and gastrointestinal). Consequently, criteria sets are offered for Panic Attack and Agoraphobia separately at the beginning of this section of the *DSM*. Anxiety Disorder NOS is available for conditions presenting with anxiety that do not meet the criteria for the following disorders.

Panic Attack

A Panic Attack is experienced as a sudden onset of intense apprehension, fearfulness, or terror, often associated with feelings of impending doom. It causes great discomfort in the absence of any real danger. At least 4 of 13 possible somatic or cognitive symptoms must be present. Symptoms associated with Panic Attack include shortness of breath, palpitations, chest pain or discomfort, choking or smothering sensations, and fear of losing control. Full criteria and subtypes of Panic Attacks are listed on pp. 430–432 in the *DSM*.

Agoraphobia

Agoraphobia is anxiety related to places or situations from which escape might be difficult or embarrassing. One may avoid contexts in which help may not be available in the event of having a Panic Attack or panic-like symptoms (being in public or at home alone, being in a crowd of people, traveling by bus or plane, being on a bridge or an elevator). See pp. 432–433 in the *DSM* for detailed features and criteria for Agoraphobia.

Panic Disorder Without or With Agoraphobia

Panic Disorder Without Agoraphobia presents with recurrent unexpected Panic Attacks, about which there is persistent concern. Panic Disorder With Agoraphobia includes both Panic Attacks and symptoms of Agoraphobia (see pp. 433–441 in the *DSM*).

Agoraphobia Without History of Panic Disorder

Agoraphobia Without History of Panic Disorder presents criteria for Agoraphobia and panic-like symptoms but without a history of unexpected Panic Attacks. To qualify for this diagnosis, the full criteria for Panic Disorder must never have been met. Many people presenting with Agoraphobia do have a history of Panic Disorder, but many more are diagnosed with Agoraphobia alone; the *DSM* suggests that there are difficulties confirming this with clinical data, as some person so diagnosed may actually be dealing with a Specific Phobia (see pp. 441–443 in the *DSM*).

Specific Phobia

Specific Phobias cause clinically significant anxiety provoked by the presence of specific feared objects or situations, often associated with avoidance behavior. Exposure to the stressor almost invariably provokes an immediate anxiety response. Although adults with this disorder may realize that their fears are excessive, children with this disorder may not.

Subtypes of phobias include Animal Type, Natural Environment Type, Blood–Injection–Injury Type, Situational Type, and Other Type. Having one phobia increases the likelihood of having another phobia of the same subtype (e.g., fear of snakes and spiders; see pp. 443–450 in the *DSM*).

Social Phobia (Social Anxiety Disorder)

Significant anxiety that is provoked by certain types of social or performance situations in which embarrassment might occur suggests the diagnosis of Social Phobia. The diagnosis is appropriate only if the anxiety significantly interferes with daily functioning or if the person is remarkably distressed about the phobia. Some people may cope with their anxiety by avoiding anxiety-provoking situations. An individual may be very fearful of doing something, but if it is not a part of the daily routine, or there is no marked distress about the fear, then it is not diagnosable (e.g., fear of mountain climbing; see pp. 450–456 in the *DSM*).

Obsessive-Compulsive Disorder

Obsessive-Compulsive Disorder is identified by two phenomena. Recurrent Obsessions (persistent ideas, thoughts, impulses, or images experienced as intrusive and inappropriate) may cause marked anxiety or distress, and Compulsions (repetitive behaviors like praying, counting, hand washing, checking), may be acted on to neutralize anxiety (not for pleasure or gratification), which may or may not be related to an obsession. Either phenomena can occur apart from and unrelated to the other, or they can occur as a Compulsion in response to an Obsession (see pp. 456–463 in the *DSM* for complete criteria and a detailed discussion of the differential diagnostic process for this disorder).

Posttraumatic Stress Disorder

Posttraumatic Stress Disorder (PTSD) consists of the reexperiencing of an extremely traumatic event (involving actual or threatened death or serious injury, witnessing or learning of the same) accompanied by symptoms of increased arousal and avoidance of stimuli associated with the trauma. Three specifiers indicate whether the duration of symptoms is less than 3 months (Acute), lasts longer than 3 months (Chronic), or whether 6 months had passed between the traumatic event and the onset of symptoms (see pp. 463–468 in the *DSM*).

Acute Stress Disorder

Acute Stress Disorder is similar to that of PTSD. This diagnosis is appropriate if symptoms occur within 1 month after exposure to an extremely traumatic event and last at least 2 days in duration. The same types of potential stressors indicated for PTSD (see p. 463 in the *DSM*) pertain to Acute Stress Disorder (see pp. 469–472).

Generalized Anxiety Disorder

The existence of persistent and excessive anxiety and worry (apprehensive expectation about a number of events or activities), occurring more days than not for a 6-month period, supports the diagnosis of Generalized Anxiety Disorder (GAD). Exclusion criteria for this disorder, in relationship with other anxiety and mood disorders, are complex (the reader is referred to pp. 472–476 in the *DSM*).

Anxiety Disorder Due to General Medical Condition/Substance-Induced Anxiety Disorder

As with other psychological difficulties caused by general medical conditions or induced by substances, this category allows the classification of diagnoses associated with clinically significant anxiety as a result of the same (see pp. 476–484 in the *DSM*). As with other *DSM* diagnoses, a Not Otherwise Specified option is available for Anxiety Disorder when anxiety and phobic avoidance are present but the symptoms do not meet complete criteria for other such diagnoses just reviewed.

SOMATOFORM DISORDERS

Somatoform disorders share the feature of the presence of physical symptoms that suggest a general medical condition that is not fully explained by a general medical condition, by the direct effect of substance, or by another mental disorder (such as Panic Disorder). Although Factitious Disorders and Malingering are intentional, the symptoms in a Somatoform Disorder are not under voluntary control. The NOS version of this disorder allows for coding disorders that do not meet the specific criteria for the following disorders (p. 511 in the *DSM*).

Somatization Disorder

Formerly called hysteria, Somatization Disorder manifests with a pattern of multiple clinically significant somatic symptoms. The symptoms must affect at least four different sites on the body or related functions (see page 486 of the *DSM* for a list in order of frequency of occurrence). Examples of symptoms include some combination of pain, gastrointestinal, sexual, and voluntary motor or sensory ("pseudoneurological") symptoms.

The combination of symptoms must occur before age 30 and last for a period of several years. Symptoms are considered significant if they lead to some type of treatment (e.g., medication) or cause significant impairment in social, occupational, or other important areas of functioning (see pp. 486–490 in the *DSM*).

Undifferentiated Somatoform Disorder

Undifferentiated Somatoform Disorder is similar to but below the threshold for a diagnosis of Somatization Disorder, lasting at least 6 months. Symptoms for this disorder frequently include chronic fatigue, loss of appetite, or gastrointestinal or genitourinary symptoms. There may be a single circumscribed symptom, but more often there are multiple physical symptoms (see pp. 490–492 in the *DSM*).

Conversion Disorder

Conversion Disorder symptoms suggest that some type of neurological or other general medical condition is causing deficits in voluntary motor or sensory function, but their etiology is unexplained. Conversion symptoms do not conform to known anatomical pathways and physiological mechanisms, rather they follow the individual's conceptualization of a condition. For example, a paralysis of sorts may relate to an entire body part, rather than components of it associated with a given neural pathway. Symptoms are often inconsistent; when attention is directed elsewhere, a formerly paralyzed body part may inadvertently move for some purposeful task.

It is important to note that there are a broad range of neurological conditions that may be misdiagnosed as Conversion Disorder (e.g., multiple sclerosis, myasthenia gravis). There are four subtypes for this diagnosis: With Motor Symptom or Deficit, With Sensory Symptom or Deficit, With Seizures or Convulsions, and With Mixed Presentation.

Psychological factors are judged to be associated with the symptoms or deficits, due to the fact that conflicts or stressors precede, and initiate or exacerbate, symptoms or deficits. Symptoms are not feigned as in Factitious Disorder or Malingering, but determining whether this is so can be difficult. This diagnosis is not given if culturally sanctioned behavior or experience account for symptoms nor for symptoms limited to pain or sexual dysfunction exclusively (see pp. 492–498 in the *DSM*).

Pain Disorder

Pain is the main focus of clinical attention with Pain Disorder, and psychological factors are judged to have an important role in its severity and course. This disorder is not diagnosed if better accounted for by Mood, Anxiety, or Psychotic disorders or if it is related to Dyspareunia (under Sexual Pain Disorders). There are three subtypes and two specifiers with this diagnosis. Subtypes include Pain Disorder Associated With: Psychological Factors, Both Psychological Factors and a General Medical Condition, and a General Medical Condition. These can be specified as Acute or Chronic (see pp. 498–503 in the *DSM* for more detail).

Hypochondriasis

Based on misinterpretation of bodily symptoms or bodily functions (although a coexisting general medical condition is possible), Hypochondriasis manifests as a preoccupation with the fear of having or the idea that one has a serious disease. Symptoms of this disorder persist despite assurance from a medical professional and persist for at least 6 months. The person is able to acknowledge that exaggeration of the extent of disease is a possibility, but if there is no insight into concerns being excessive or unreasonable, the specifier With Poor Insight is used (see pp. 504–507 in the *DSM*).

Body Dysmorphic Disorder

A person with Body Dysmorphic Disorder is preoccupied with an imagined or exaggerated defect in physical appearance. Individuals with this disorder may describe their preoccupations as "intensely painful," "tormenting," or "devastating." Self-consciousness about appearance may lead to avoidance behavior (see pp. 507–510 in the *DSM*).

FACTITIOUS DISORDER

Factitious Disorder is a diagnosis alone in its category. Factitious Disorder manifests as physical or psychological symptoms that are intentionally produced or feigned in order to assume the sick role. Judgment that the symptoms are feigned comes from exclusion of possible causes and direct evidence. Individuals with this disorder may present their problems in a vague and inconsistent manner but with a dramatic flair. The presence of factitious symptoms does not mean that true physical or psychological conditions are not also present.

There are three subtypes of this disorder: With Predominantly Psychological Signs and Symptoms, With Predominantly Physical Signs and Symptoms, and With Combined Psychological and Physical Signs and Symptoms.

The difference between Malingering and Factitious Disorder is the motivation for feigning illness. With Malingering, the motivation is obvious and recognizable when environmental circumstances are known (e.g., feigning disability to gain an entitlement). With Factitious Disorder, the motivation is to assume the sick role, in the absence of any other external motivator (see pp. 513–517 in the *DSM*). Under some circumstances, Malingering may be considered adaptive (e.g., feigning heart pain in a hostage situation), but Factitious Disorder always implies psychopathology.

DISSOCIATIVE DISORDERS

Dissociative Disorders involve a disruption in the usually integrated functions of consciousness, memory, identity, or perception, which can occur suddenly or gradually and be either transient or chronic. If dissociative symptoms accompany Acute Stress Disorder, PTSD, or Somatization Disorder, an additional diagnosis of a dissociative type is not appropriate.

Multicultural competency is an asset when addressing Dissociative Disorders, as dissociative states may play an important part in cultural or religious activities in many societies. In most instances where dissociative symptoms are culturally sanctioned, they do not lead to seeking help or cause distress and therefore are not diagnosable.

Dissociative Amnesia

The inability to recall important personal information, usually of a traumatic or stressful nature, is Dissociative Amnesia. The inability to recall is too extensive to be attributed to plain forgetfulness.

There are five subtypes of amnesia noted in the *DSM*. *Localized amnesia* relates to forgetting a circumscribed period of time, usually within a few hours of a very traumatic event. *Selective amnesia* presents as the ability to recall some, but not all, of the events during a circumscribed period of time. Less common are the three remaining subtypes. *Generalized amnesia* involves the failure to recall one's entire life. *Continuous Amnesia* relates to forgetting events subsequent to a specific time, up to and including the present. Finally, Systematized Amnesia is loss of memory for certain categories of information, such as all memories associated with one particular person (see pp. 520–523 in the *DSM*).

Dissociative Fugue

The sudden, unexpected travel away from home or work, accompanied by an inability to recall the past and confusion about personal identity, or the assumption of a new identity, is Dissociative Fugue. Travel may range from short trips to complex wanderings over weeks or months, and the traveler may not demonstrate any overt psychopathology. Once returned to the prefugue state, there may be no memory of travel (see pp. 523–526 in the *DSM*).

Dissociative Identity Disorder

Better known under its former name Multiple Personality Disorder, Dissociative Identity Disorder is associated with the presence of two or more distinct identities or personality states that recurrently take control of a person's behavior, accompanied by an inability to recall important personal information that is too extensive to be explained by ordinary forgetfulness. In children, symptoms cannot be attributed to imaginary playmates or other fantasy play.

The disorder is characterized by a fragmented identity rather than multiple, separate personalities per se. Each personality state may present as a distinct personal history, self-image, and even a separate name, and at least two of the identities recurrently take control of the person's behavior. The disorder reflects a failure to integrate various aspects of identity, memory, and consciousness (see pp. 526–529 in the *DSM* for more details regarding the complex diagnostic and associated features for this disorder).

Depersonalization Disorder

The persistent and recurring sensation of being detached from one's mental processes or body, accompanied by intact reality testing, is associated with Depersonalization Disorder. The individual with this disorder may feel like an automaton (acting in a mechanical or unemotional way) or as if in a dream or movie. In clinical samples, this condition is diagnosed twice as often for women as for men.

There may be the sense of being outside of oneself. Sensory anesthesia, or a sense of lacking control over oneself, may be present. Depersonalization itself is a normal phenomenon, so the diagnosis should only be made if the symptoms are causing significant distress or impairment in functioning (see pp. 530–532 in the *DSM*).

Dissociative Disorder NOS

This category exists for disorders where there are some dissociative symptoms, but the criteria are not met for the other dissociative disorders. The *DSM* lists six instances: presentation of some aspects of Dissociative Identity Disorder, Derealization unaccompanied by depersonalization, brainwashing, dissociative trance disorder, loss of consciousness, and Ganser syndrome (see pp. 532–533 in the *DSM* for more details).

CHAPTER 8

Disorders With Shared Phenomenological Features: Part II

REVIEW QUESTIONS

1. What are the sexual dysfunctions included in the *DSM-IV-TR*?
2. What are paraphilias?
3. Describe several of the Impulse-Control Disorders.
4. Describe the three clusters of Personality Disorder. What are their related diagnoses?
5. After carefully reviewing diagnostic summaries provided in this chapter, go directly to the *DSM* page intervals indicated and carefully review the diagnoses in their entirely.

SEXUAL AND GENDER IDENTITY DISORDERS

This section of the *DSM* addresses Sexual Dysfunctions, Paraphilias, and Gender Identity Disorders.

Sexual Dysfunctions

Characterized by disturbance in sexual desire and the sexual response cycle (defined on pp. 535–536), Sexual Dysfunctions cause marked distress and interpersonal difficulty. Seven categories of Sexual Dysfunction are reviewed briefly below (see pp. 535–558 in the *DSM* for greater detail than presented here).

Sexual Desire Disorders

The two disorders in this group include Hypoactive Sexual Desire Disorder and Sexual Aversion Disorder. The first is a deficiency or absence of sexual fantasies and desire for sexual activity, the second is the aversion to and active avoidance of genital sexual contact with a sexual partner (see pp. 539–542 in the *DSM*).

Sexual Arousal Disorders

The two disorders in this group include Female Sexual Arousal Disorder and Male Erectile Disorder. The first addresses a woman's inability to attain, or to maintain until completion of sexual activity, an adequate lubrication-swelling response of sexual excitement. The second involves a man's inability to attain, or to maintain until completion of the sexual activity, an adequate erection (see pp. 543–547 in the *DSM*).

Orgasmic Disorders

Three diagnoses in this group include Female Orgasmic Disorder, Male Orgasmic Disorder, and Premature Ejaculation. The orgasmic disorders related to a delay or absence of orgasm following normal sexual excitement. Premature Ejaculation relates to a male orgasm before it is desired (see pp. 547–554 in the *DSM* for more detail).

Sexual Pain Disorders

Dyspareunia is genital pain associated with sexual intercourse, by either a man or a woman. Vaginismus is recurrent or persistent involuntary contraction of the perineal muscles surrounding the outer third of the vagina when vaginal penetration with penis, finger, tampon, or speculum is attempted (see pp. 554–558 in the *DSM* for more detail).

Sexual Dysfunction Due to General Medical Condition, Substance Induced

Sexual dysfunction in this category can involve pain, hypoactive sexual desire, erectile dysfunction, or orgasmic disorders that causes marked distress or interpersonal difficulty. The difficulty is fully explained by the direct physiological effects of a general medical condition or substance induced. Seven subtypes are indicated on p. 559 in the *DSM* (see pp. 558–565 in the *DSM* for details regarding these two diagnostic categories).

Paraphilias

Paraphilias are recurrent, intense sexually arousing fantasies, sexual urges, or behaviors associated with unusual stimuli (nonhuman objects; the suffering or humiliation of oneself or one's partner, children, or other nonconsenting persons). These phenomena occur over a period of at least 6 months.

For Sexual Sadism, the diagnosis is appropriate if the person has acted on these urges with a nonconsenting person or the urges, sexual fantasies, or behaviors cause marked distress or interpersonal difficulty. For Pedophilia, Voyeurism, Exhibitionism, and Frotteurism, a diagnosis is made if the person has acted on the paraphilia or urges or sexual fantasies cause marked distress or interpersonal difficulty. For Fetishism, Sexual Sadomasochism, and Transvestic Fetishism, the behavior, sexual urge, or fantasy must cause clinically significant distress or impairment in social, occupational, or other important areas of functioning. The eight subtypes of Paraphilias are described briefly next.

Exhibitionism

This disorder involves recurrent, intense sexually arousing fantasies, sexual urges, or behaviors involving the exposure of one's genitals to an unsuspecting stranger, occurring for at least 6 months (see page 569 of the DSM for details).

Fetishism

This disorder involves the use of nonliving objects for sexual pleasure. Examples may include articles of clothing (bras, stockings). In the absence of the fetish, males may experience erectile dysfunction. Devices designed for sexual pleasure do not apply here (e.g., a vibrator). Female articles of clothing used for cross-dressing (as in Transvestic Fetishism) do not apply either. Once established, fetishism tends to be chronic (see pages 569–570 of the DSM for details).

Frotteurism

This disorder involves touching and rubbing against a nonconsenting person. The behavior typically occurs in crowded places from which the individual can more easily escape arrest. Most acts of frottage occur when the person is aged 15–25, after which there is a gradual decline in frequency (see page 579 of the DSM for details).

Pedophilia

This disorder involves sexual attraction toward prepubescent children. The culprit must be 16 years or older and at least 5 years older than the child. The course is usually chronic, especially in those attracted to males; recidivism rate involving a preference for males is roughly twice that for those preferring females (see pp. 571–572 in the *DSM* for a detailed discussion of male diagnostic features).

Sexual Masochism

This disorder involves recurrent, intense sexually arousing fantasies, sexual urges, or behaviors involving being subject to humiliation or suffering (real, not simulated acts). Masochistic acts may include restraint, blindfolding, paddling, spanking, whipping, beating, electrical shocks, cutting, infibulation (pinning and piercing), hypoxyphilia (sexual arousal by oxygen deprivation), and humiliation. Sexual masochism is usually chronic; increasing the severity of such acts over time during periods of stress may result in injury or even death (see pp. 572–573 in the *DSM* for details).

Sexual Sadism

This disorder involves recurrent, over a period of at least 6 months, intense sexually arousing fantasies, sexual urges, or behaviors involving inflicting humiliation or suffering on the victim (real, not simulated acts) (see pp. 573–574 in the *DSM* for details).

Transvestic Fetishism

This disorder involves a heterosexual male who for at least 6 months has recurrent, intense sexually arousing fantasies, sexual urges, or behaviors involving cross-dressing. The qualifier with Gender Dysphoria is used when a person has persistent discomfort with gender role or identity (see pp. 574–575 in the *DSM* for details).

Voyeurism

This disorder involves recurrent, over a period of at least 6 months, intense sexually arousing fantasies, sexual urges, or behaviors involving observing an unsuspecting person who is naked, in the process of disrobing, or engaging in sexual activity (see pp. 575–576 in the *DSM* for details).

Gender Identity Disorder

This diagnosis is appropriate when someone experiences a strong and persistent cross-gender identification and a persistent discomfort with his or her sex or sense of inappropriateness in the gender role of that sex. This condition cannot be concurrent with a physical intersex condition. The diagnosis is coded according to age range (in Children vs. in Adolescents or Adults). For sexually mature individuals, gender attraction is also specified (see pp. 576–582 in the *DSM*).

Sexual Disorder NOS

This category provides a diagnosis for a sexual disturbance that is neither a Sexual Dysfunction nor a Paraphilia. For example, feelings of inadequacy concerning sexual performance, distress about quality of relationships, or persistent and marked distress about sexual orientation.

EATING DISORDERS

This diagnostic group focuses on severe disturbances in eating behavior. There are only two disorders in this category, Anorexia Nervosa and Bulimia Nervosa. Both diagnoses involve a disturbance in perception of body shape and weight. The *DSM* makes a special note in this category regarding obesity; if it is determined that psychological factors are involved in weight control difficulty, this can be diagnosed as Psychological Factors Affecting Medical Condition (see p. 731 in the *DSM*).

Anorexia Nervosa

Anorexia Nervosa is diagnosed when an individual refuses to maintain a minimally normal body weight and is intensely afraid of gaining weight. If an individual weighs less than 85% of expected body weight or has a body mass index at or below 17.5 kg/squared meters, he or she meets one criterion for Anorexia Nervosa. Postmenarcheal females have amenorrhea (absence of at least three consecutive menstrual cycles). Two subtypes can be used to establish whether weight loss is accomplished by a Restricting Type (reducing calories or increasing activity) or whether the individual has engaged in Binge-Eating/Purging Type (see pp. 583–589 in the *DSM*).

Bulimia Nervosa

Bulimia Nervosa is characterized by repeated episodes of binge eating (eating a quantity of food within a 2-hour period that is larger than most people would eat and feeling a lack of control over this behavior) followed by inappropriate purging behaviors such as self-induced vomiting; misuse of laxatives, diuretics, or other medications; fasting; or excessive exercise. These behaviors must occur at least twice weekly on average, for 3 months. In this disorder, self-evaluation is overly influenced by body shape and weight. This behavior must not occur exclusively during episodes of Anorexia Nervosa. Two specifiers indicate Purging Type or Nonpurging Type (see pp. 589–594 in the *DSM*).

Eating Disorder NOS

This NOS category applies if all symptoms for Anorexia Nervosa are met except for amenorrhea or if weight is still within acceptable limits. It also applies if all criteria for Bulimia Nervosa are met except for the durational criteria. Eating Disorder NOS is appropriate if there is regular use of inappropriate purging after eating small amounts of food; repeated chewing and spitting out large amounts of food; and with binge-eating disorder, where binge eating exists without any purging behavior (see pages 594–595 of the *DSM* for details).

SLEEP DISORDERS

Sleep Disorders occupy 65 pages of the *DSM* (pp. 597–661), where a good deal about the sleep cycle (pp. 597–598), how it is measured using polysomnography (p. 598), and potential problems are carefully reviewed in great detail. Corresponding disorders in the 1990 edition of the American Sleep Disorder Association's *International Classification of Sleep Disorders (ICSD): Diagnostic and Coding Manual* are referenced within relevant sections as they correspond with the *DSM* diagnoses.

The *DSM* organizes Sleep Disorders into four major sections according to presumed etiology: Primary Sleep Disorders and Sleep Disorders related to a Mental Disorder, General Medical Condition, or Substance Induced.

Primary Sleep Disorders

Primary Sleep Disorders are those not due to mental disorder, general medical condition, or a substance (the remaining three categories in the grouping). They are presumed to result from endogenous abnormalities in the sleep–wake cycle, often complicated by conditioning factors. They are divided into two subtypes:

Dyssomnias

Dyssomnias are abnormalities in the amount, quality, or timing of sleep. *Primary Insomnia* involves difficulty in initiating and maintaining sleep, or nonrestorative sleep, for at least 1 month. *Primary Hypersomnia* is excessive sleepiness for at least 1 month, evidenced by either prolonged sleep or daytime sleep episodes that occur almost daily.

Narcolepsy is irresistible attacks of refreshing sleep that occur daily over a period of at least 3 months, with the existence of cataplexy (brief episodes of sudden bilateral loss of muscle tone, most often in association with intense emotion) and recurrent intrusions of elements of rapid eye movement sleep into the transition between sleep and wakefulness, manifested by either hypnopompic or hypnagogic hallucinations or sleep paralysis at the beginning or end of sleep episodes (see pp. 609–615 in the *DSM* for definition of terms).

Breathing-Related Sleep Disorders are abnormalities in ventilation during sleep that cause sleep disruption, excessive sleepiness, or less commonly insomnia. Conditions that cause breathing difficulty during sleep include obstructive or central sleep apnea syndrome or central alveolar hypoventilation syndrome.

Circadian Rhythm Sleep Disorder is a persistent or recurrent pattern of sleep disruption leading to excessive sleepiness or insomnia that is due to a mismatch between the sleep–wake schedule required by the environment and circadian sleep–wake pattern. Four specifiers indicate the details of the cause of sleep disruption. Delayed Sleep Phase Type relates to late sleep onset and late waking times, with an inability to fall asleep and awaken at a desired earlier time. Jet Lag Type occurs after traveling across more than one time zone, resulting in sleepiness at inappropriate times for that time zone. Shift Work Type relates to night shift work or frequently changing shift work. An Unspecified specifier is available when cause is not known.

If sleep difficulties result from environmental factors (noise, light, and interruptions), sleep deprivation, restless leg syndrome, or periodic limb movements or if it is difficult to tell the cause for sleep difficulty, Dyssomnia NOS is available (see pp. 598–630 in the *DSM*).

Parasomnias

Parasomnias are abnormalities in behavior or physiological events that occur in association with sleep, specific sleep stages, or sleep–wake cycle. Unlike

Dyssomnias, Parasomnias do not involve problems with the mechanisms generating sleep–wake states nor of their timing. Parasomnias involve the activation of physiological systems (autonomic nervous system, motor system, or cognitive processing) at inappropriate times during the sleep–wake cycle. There are four subtypes within this category.

Nightmare Disorder is the repeated occurrence of frightening dreams that lead to awakenings from sleep, usually during the second half of the sleep period. The person rapidly becomes oriented and alert on awaking, and it is often difficult to fall back asleep afterward. Frequent waking or the avoidance of sleep for fear of nightmares may cause excessive sleepiness, poor concentration, depression, anxiety, or irritability during the waking hours.

Sleep Terror Disorder involves abrupt awakenings from sleep usually beginning with a panicky scream or cry, resulting in autonomic arousal (tachycardia, rapid breathing, and sweating). In contrast with Nightmare Disorder, Sleep Terrors usually begin during the first third of the major sleep episode and last 1–10 minutes. During such an episode, it might be difficult to wake or comfort the individual. Upon awakening the following morning, the individual has amnesia for the event.

Sleepwalking Disorder is repeated episodes of complex motor behavior initiated during sleep, including rising from bed and walking about. These episodes typically occur during the first third of the night. During episodes, the individual may have reduced alertness and responsiveness, a blank stare, and is unresponsive to communication with others or efforts to be awakened. Upon awakening, the person has amnesia for the episode.

Parasomnias NOS is available for disturbances characterized by abnormal behavior or physiological events during sleep or sleep–wake transitions that do not meet criteria for the specific Parasomnias or its etiology is unclear (see pages 630–644 of the *DSM* for the diagnostic criteria for the various parasomnias).

Sleep Disorder Related to Another Mental Disorder

This disorder involves sleep disturbance that results from a diagnosable mental disorder, often a Mood or Anxiety Disorder, sufficiently severe to warrant independent clinical attention. It is presumed that the mental disorder somehow affects sleep–wake regulation. There are two subtypes for this category, Insomnia and Hypersomnia, both Related to Another Mental Disorder, and described symptomatically in a similar fashion to their Dyssomnia counterparts. Both difficulties must exist for at least 1 month (see pages 645–650 of the *DSM* for complete diagnostic criteria).

Sleep Disorder Due to a General Medical Condition

This disorder involves a prominent complaint of sleep disturbance that results from the direct physiological effects of a general medical condition on the sleep–wake system. Four different subtypes for this disorder include Insomnia, Hypersomnia, Parasomnia, and Mixed Types, which manifest similar to their Dyssomnia and Parasomnia counterparts (see pages 651–654 of the *DSM* for details).

Substance-Induced Sleep Disorder

This disorder involves prominent complaints of sleep disturbance that result from the concurrent use, or recent discontinuation of use, of a substance (including prescribed or over-the-counter medications). Examples of common substances involved include alcohol, amphetamines or other stimulants, caffeine, cocaine, opioids, sedatives, hypnotics, and anxiolytics. The same four subtypes noted for Sleep Disorder Due to a General Medical Condition also apply here. The disorder can be further specified via With Onset During Intoxication versus With Onset During Withdrawal (see pages 655–661 of the *DSM* for details).

IMPULSE CONTROL DISORDERS NOT ELSEWHERE CLASSIFIED

A number of diagnostic categories may list as a criterion difficulty with impulse control, including Substance-Related Disorders, Paraphilias, Antisocial Personality Disorder, Conduct Disorder, Schizophrenia, and Mood Disorders. This section covers diagnoses related to impulse control not covered in these other categories.

Impulse Control Disorders feature a failure to resist an impulse, drive, or temptation to perform an act that is harmful to self or to others. The individual may feel an increasing sense of tension or arousal before committing the act and then experience pleasure, gratification, or relief while committing the act. Afterward, there may or may not be regret, self-reproach, or guilt. There are six disorders in this section of the *DSM*.

Intermittent Explosive Disorder

This disorder involves several discrete episodes of failure to resist aggressive impulses resulting in serious assaults or destruction of property. The degree of aggressiveness expressed during such incidents is grossly out of proportion to any precipitating psychosocial stressors (see pp. 663–667 in the *DSM*).

Kleptomania

Kleptomania involves recurrent failure to resist impulses to steal objects not needed for personal use or monetary value. There may be a subjective sense of rising tension prior to committing theft and then a sense of pleasure, gratification, or relief when committing the act. For this diagnosis, the act is not committed out of anger or vengeance and is not done in response to an hallucination or delusion. Important diagnoses to consider as better accounting for this behavior are Conduct Disorder, Antisocial Personality Disorder, or a Manic Episode (see pp. 667–669 in the *DSM*).

Pyromania

Pyromania is a pattern of deliberate and purposeful fire setting for pleasure, gratification, or relief of tension. Prior to setting a fire, there may be tension or affective arousal. In general, there exists a fascination with fire in all its contexts. As with Kleptomania and stealing, fire setting or involvement with its correlates provides pleasure, gratification, or a release from tension. Fascination with fire is neither related to monetary gain, an expression of sociopolitical ideology, nor used to express anger or vengeance. It is employed neither to improve one's living circumstances nor to conceal criminal activity (see pp. 669–671 in the *DSM*).

Pathological Gambling

Pathological Gambling is defined as recurrent and persistent maladaptive gambling behavior. The diagnosis is not made if the behavior is better accounted for by a manic episode. Individuals with Pathological Gambling are preoccupied with gambling, seek the excitement they feel related to the gambling experience, and may continue to gamble despite attempts to cut back or stop the behavior. They may lie to conceal ongoing gambling activity. They may even resort to antisocial behavior (forgery, fraud, theft, or embezzlement) if resources become limited. Five of ten diagnostic criteria must be met to satisfy this diagnosis (see pp. 671–674 in the *DSM*).

Trichotillomania

Trichotillomania involves recurrent pulling out of one's hair for pleasure, gratification, or relief of tension that results in noticeable hair loss (see pp. 674–677 in the *DSM* for diagnostic features and associated features and disorders).

Impulse-Control Disorder NOS

This NOS category allows classification of other impulse control-related problems not classified elsewhere in the *DSM*, for example, skin picking.

ADJUSTMENT DISORDERS

If after an identifiable stressor or stressors, within 3 months of the event or events, a person develops emotional or behavioral symptoms that create marked distress in excess of what would be expected from such an event or events, Adjustment Disorder is an appropriate diagnosis. Symptoms cannot be related to the diagnosis of bereavement. Two specifiers indicate whether the disturbance lasts less than 6 months (Acute) or longer (Chronic). Six subtypes exist: with Depressed Mood, Anxiety, Mixed Anxiety and Depressed Mood, Disturbance of Conduct, Mixed Disturbance of Emotions and Conduct, and Unspecified (see pp. 679–683 in the *DSM* for diagnostic details).

PERSONALITY DISORDERS

Personality traits are defined in the *DSM* as "enduring patterns of perceiving, relating to, and thinking about the environment and oneself that are exhibited in a wide range of social and personal contexts" (APA, 2000, p. 686). Personality traits become problematic when they are inflexible and maladaptive. A Personality Disorder requires that two or more of the following areas are negatively impacted: (1) Cognition, or ways of perceiving and interpreting self, other people, and events; (2) Affectivity, or the range, intensity, lability, and appropriateness of emotional response; (3) Interpersonal functioning; and (4) Impulse control (APA, 2000, p. 689).

A Personality Disorder is an enduring pattern of inner experience and behavior that deviates markedly from the expectations of the individual's culture. It is pervasive across a broad range of circumstances, inflexible, has an onset in adolescence or early adulthood, is stable over time, and leads to distress or impairment (APA, 2000, p. 685).

Clusters of Personality Disorders

There are 10 specific disorders that relate to three broad categories or clusters of Personality Disorders labeled A–C, based on descriptive similarities. Cluster A relates to diagnoses characterized by odd or eccentric behavior and relates to the diagnoses Paranoid, Schizoid, and Schizotypal Personality

Disorders. Cluster B disorders present as dramatic, emotional, and erratic and relate to the diagnoses Antisocial, Borderline, Histrionic, and Narcissistic Personality Disorders. Cluster C relates to anxious or fearful enduring personality characteristics and is associated with the diagnoses Avoidant, Dependent, and Obsessive-Compulsive Personality Disorders. It is important to note that persons frequently present with co-occurring Personality Disorders from different clusters; the clustering system itself has serious limitations and has not been consistently validated (see pages 685–686 of the *DSM*).

Dimensional Models of Personality Disorders

Similar to efforts to explore a noncategorical model of diagnosis for Schizophrenia, the dimensional perspective for Personality Disorders described in the *DSM* conceptualizes Personality Disorders as maladaptive variants of personality traits that merge imperceptibly into normality and into one another. The literature associated with normal personality suggests many efforts to identify the most fundamental dimensions that underlie normal and pathological personality functioning.

There exists a robust, internationally validated, Five-Factor Model (FFM) of personality, also known as the "Big Five" model of personality functioning, that has shown promise to this end (see also Peterson, 2000). Dimensions of the Big Five model are represented by the acronym NEOAC: N for Neuroticism, an indication of coping style with emotionally difficult situations; E for Extraversion versus introversion, as classically defined; O for Openness to experience versus closedness, a construct shown to have a high correlation with intellectual functioning; A for Agreeableness versus antagonism, and; C for Conscientiousness. Efforts have been made to associate these measures of "normal" personality with evidences of psychopathology. This remains an active area of research that will likely manifest in some manner in the *DSM*-5 revision process.

Next, we turn to a review of the 10 categories of Personality Disorders as they are diagnosed currently within the *DSM*. We begin with the Cluster A Personality Disorders, characterized by odd or eccentric behavior.

Paranoid Personality Disorder

Paranoid Personality Disorder is a pattern of distrust and suspiciousness such that others' motives are interpreted as malevolent. Individuals with this disorder consistently manifest four or more of the seven criteria listed for the disorder. They may perceive malicious intent regardless of a lack of evidences or even evidence to the contrary. They may be preoccupied with unjustified doubts about the fidelity of associates, overscrutinizing their actions for evidence of hostile intentions. Individuals with this disorder may be hesitant to confide in others for fear of betrayal and persistently bear grudges for perceived wrongs of others. They may read derogatory meanings into benign events and may perceive attacks on their character that are not apparent to others (see pp. 690–694 in the *DSM* for more detail).

Schizoid Personality Disorder

Schizoid Personality Disorder is a pattern of detachment from social relationships and a restricted range of emotional expression. The diagnosis is met if four of seven possible criteria are met, including almost always choosing solitary activities, having little interest in sex with another, taking pleasure in few if any activities, lacking close relationships, appearing indifferent to praise or criticism, and may be perceived as emotionally cold, detached, or affectively flattened (see pp. 694–697 in the *DSM*).

Schizotypal Personality Disorder

Schizotypal Personality Disorder is a pattern of acute discomfort in close relationships, cognitive or perceptual distortions, and eccentricities of behavior. This diagnosis requires five of nine possible criteria to be present. A person with this disorder may experience ideas of reference (incorrect interpretations of casual incidents and external events as having a particular and unusual meaning specifically for the person). People with this disorder may be superstitious, possess odd beliefs or magical thinking, or have paranoid ideations. They may appear odd, eccentric, or peculiar (see pp. 697–701 in the *DSM*).

We continue our review of 10 Personality Disorders with Cluster B disorders, those characterized by dramatic, emotional, and erratic features.

Antisocial Personality Disorder

Antisocial Personality Disorder is a pattern of disregard for, and violation of, the rights of others that begins in childhood or early adolescence and continues into adulthood, indicated by three or more of seven possible criteria. It may be important for the identification of this disorder to incorporate information from collateral sources, as deceit and manipulation are central features of the disorder.

A person diagnosed with this disorder will have a history of some symptoms of Conduct Disorder before age 15 (see p. 93 of the *DSM* for a review of this disorder) and must be at least 18 years old. During adulthood, people with this disorder tend not to conform to social norms and may have difficulty with the legal system for repeatedly performing acts that are grounds for arrest. There may be a history of repeated aggressiveness and irritability or reckless regard for the safety of others. There may be a pattern of repeated failure to sustain consistent work behavior or to honor financial obligations. There may also be a lack of remorse for wrongs done to others (see pp. 701–706 in the *DSM*).

Borderline Personality Disorder

Borderline Personality Disorder is a pattern of instability in interpersonal relationships, self-image, and affects, and marked impulsivity. The disorder is indicated when at least five of nine criteria are met (p. 710 in the *DSM*).

People with Borderline Personality Disorder make frantic efforts to avoid real or imagined abandonment, related to an intolerance of being alone. They have a pattern of unstable and intense relationships, switching quickly between idealizing others to devaluing them. There is also an instability in self-image or sense of self. Impulsivity in at least two areas of life is potentially self-damaging. This may include suicidal or self-injurious behaviors; the *DSM* suggests that the rate of completed suicides for people with this diagnosis is as high as 10%. There may be marked reactivity of mood, chronic feelings of emptiness, and transient, stress-related paranoia or even severe dissociative symptoms (see pp. 706–710 in the *DSM*).

Histrionic Personality Disorder

Histrionic Personality Disorder is a pattern of excessive emotionality and attention seeking. Five or more of eight possible criteria must be met for this diagnosis, including discomfort when not the center of attention; inappropriate, sexually seductive or provocative behavior; rapidly shifting, shallow, or exaggerated expressions of emotion; and easily influenced by circumstances. A person with this disorder may consider relationships to be more intimate than they actually are (see pp. 711–714 in the *DSM*).

Narcissistic Personality Disorder

Narcissistic Personality Disorder is a pattern of grandiosity (in fantasy or actual behavior), need for admiration, and lack of empathy. Five or more of nine possible criteria must be met for this diagnosis, which may include exaggeration of achievements, inflated self-importance requiring excessive admiration, a sense of entitlement, interpersonal exploitation, lacking empathy, envious of others, and showing arrogant, haughty behaviors or attitudes (see pp. 714–717 of the *DSM*).

We complete our review of 10 Personality Disorders with Cluster C disorders, those characterized by anxious or fearful enduring personality characteristics.

Avoidant Personality Disorder

Avoidant Personality Disorder is a pattern of social inhibition, feelings of inadequacy, and hypersensitivity to negative evaluation. A person is diagnosed when at least four of seven possible criteria are met, including fear of criticism, disapproval, or rejection; avoiding intimate relationships for fear of being shamed or ridiculed; viewing self as socially inept, personally unappealing, or inferior to others, and; unusually reluctant to take personal risks or engage in new activity (see pp. 718–721 in the *DSM*).

Dependent Personality Disorder

Dependent Personality Disorder is a pattern of submissive and clinging behavior related to an excessive need to be taken care of. People with this disorder meet at least five of possible eight criteria, including needing excessive advice and assurance from others; needing others to assume responsibility for most major areas of their lives; fearing disagreement for loss of support; lacking self-confidence in judgment or abilities and; exaggerated fears of being left alone to fend for self (see pp. 721–725 in the *DSM*).

Obsessive-Compulsive Personality Disorder

Obsessive-Compulsive Personality Disorder is a pattern of preoccupation with orderliness, perfectionism, and control, at the expense of openness, flexibility, and efficiency. Persons with this disorder manifest four of eight possible criteria, including losing the major point of activities by focusing too intently on minutia; inability to complete tasks due to perfectionism; devoted to work to the exclusion of leisure activities; overly conscientious; reluctant to delegate tasks; miserly spending style, and; rigidity and stubbornness (see pp. 725–729 in the *DSM*).

Personality Disorder NOS

Personality Disorder NOS is a category provided for two situations: (1) the individual's personality pattern meets the general criteria for a Personality Disorder and traits of several different Personality Disorders are present, but the criteria for any specific Personality Disorder are not me; or (2) the individual's personality pattern meets the general criteria for a Personality Disorder, but the individual is considered to have a Personality Disorder that is not included in the *DSM* (e.g., passive–aggressive personality disorder, pp. 789–791 in Appendix B of the *DSM*; see page 79 of the *DSM*).

Other Conditions That May Be a Focus of Clinical Attention: Revision to the *DSM-5*

PREVIEW QUESTIONS

1. On what axis do clinicians place "Other Conditions"?
2. What types of relational problems can be coded for this diagnostic group?
3. When is Malingering considered an adaptive coping mechanism?
4. How is Borderline Intellectual Functioning defined?
5. When does Bereavement become a Mood Disorder?
6. After carefully reviewing diagnostic summaries provided in this text, go directly to the page intervals indicated and carefully review the diagnosis in its entirety.
7. What are some of the controversies associated with the Task Force and Work Group membership in the *DSM-5* revision process?
8. What are some of the proposed changes to the *DSM* for its fifth revision?
9. Describe the critical feedback the revision process has received from its stakeholders.

The conditions or problems listed in this section of the *DSM* are included in the multiaxial framework on Axis I, when they are important enough to warrant clinical attention. It may be that these conditions exist alone with no other diagnoses. They may coexist with other diagnoses that are related to problems or conditions in this section. Alternatively, these problems or conditions exist independent of other diagnoses.

PSYCHOLOGICAL FACTORS AFFECTING
MEDICAL CONDITIONS

This diagnosis is appropriate when one or more specific psychological or behavioral factors adversely affect a general medical condition. These factors may derive from Axis I or Axis II disorders or other psychological symptoms, personality traits, maladaptive health behaviors, or physiological reactions to life stressors. Psychological Factor Affecting Medical Condition is coded on Axis I, and the associated General Medical Condition is coded on Axis III (Appendix G of the *DSM* contains general medical condition codes common to mental disorders).

Psychological and behavioral factors have the potential to impact almost every presentation of general medical conditions; this diagnosis is made when they present as a clear focus of clinical attention. If such factors occur in proximity to an exacerbation of or delayed recovery from a medical condition, it may be inferred that psychological factors affect the course of a general medical condition. Such factors may interfere with effective treatment of medical conditions or create additional risk for the individual (e.g., smoking, when diagnosed with chronic obstructive pulmonary disorder). Psychological or behavioral factors may elicit a stress-related physiological response that precipitates or exacerbates a general medical condition (interpersonal conflict causing an increase in chest pain in someone with coronary artery disease).

Specificity of the Psychological Factor

The *DSM* offers a list of possible psychological factors to make the diagnosis more specific. *Mental Disorder Affecting . . .* is used when a clear Axis I or II diagnosis is affecting the course or treatment of a general medical condition. *Psychological Symptoms Affecting . . .* is used when Axis I-related symptoms are present, but the full diagnostic criteria are not present. *Personality Traits or Coping Style Affecting . . .* is appropriate to use when Axis II-related symptoms are present, but the full criteria are not sufficient for a diagnosis of a personality disorder.

Maladaptive Health Behaviors Affecting . . . can reflect the negative impact of health-related behaviors on a general medical condition (sedentary lifestyle, unsafe sex, overeating, alcohol and drug use). *Stress-Related Physiological Response Affecting . . .* is appropriate when the body's stress response is responsible for adversely affecting the course or treatment of a general medical condition (e.g., arrhythmia under great emotional distress). If another factor, or unidentified psychological or behavioral factor, is believed to significantly affect the course or treatment of a medical condition, *Other or Unspecified Factors Affecting . . .* is appropriate (see pp. 731–734 in the *DSM*).

Differential Diagnosis

A discussion of the differential diagnostic process is important for this particular diagnosis. *Psychological Factor Affecting Medical Condition* is appropriate when the direction of influence is the psychological factor toward or affecting the treatment or course of a medical condition. The diagnosis noted earlier, *Mental Disorder Due to General Medical Condition*, also involves a temporal relationship between psychological factors and medical condition, but it is in the opposite direction; the medical condition is believed to influence or cause the psychological difficulties through a direct physiological mechanism (see pp. 733–734 in the *DSM* for a comparative discussion of the impact of substance use, somatoform disorders, and pain disorders on the differential diagnostic process).

MEDICATION-INDUCED MOVEMENT DISORDERS

There are six subtypes of Medication-Induced Movement Disorders within the *DSM*. These disorders are frequently important in pharmacotherapy for mental and some physical disorders, and they are coded on Axis I.

Neuroleptic-Induced Parkinsonism is the first subtype and relates to a Parkinsonian tremor, muscular rigidity, or akinesia (absence or poverty of movement) developing within a few weeks of taking neuroleptic medication or discontinuing medication used to treat extrapyramidal symptoms. Neuroleptic medication refers to those with dopamine-antagonist properties, such as typical antipsychotic medication (chlorpromazine, haloperidol, and fluphenazine) and atypical antipsychotic agents (clozapine, risperidone, olanzapine, and quetiapine). Although the newer, atypical medications cause fewer and less intense side effects, Medication-Induced Movement Disorders still occur. *Neuroleptic Malignant Syndrome* is associated with severe muscle rigidity, elevated temperature, and other symptoms associated with neuroleptic medication.

Neuroleptic-Induced Acute Dystonia relates to abnormal positioning or spasm of the muscles of the head, neck, limbs, or trunk, developing within a few days of starting or raising the dose of neuroleptic medication (or reducing medication used to treat extrapyramidal symptoms). *Neuroleptic-Induced Acute Akathisia* relates to complaints of restlessness, fidgety movements of the legs, rocking from foot to foot, pacing, or inability to sit or stand still, within a few weeks after starting or raising the dose of neuroleptic medication, or reducing medication used to treat extrapyramidal symptoms.

Neuroleptic-Induced Tardive Dyskinesia may develop after a few months using neuroleptic medication (maybe a shorter time period for people who are elderly). Tardive dyskinesia is characterized by involuntary choreiform (rapid, jerky dyskinetic, involuntary movements associated with chorea), athetoid (involuntary, purposeless weaving motions of the body or extremities), or rhythmic movements of the tongue, jaw, or extremities, lasting at least a few weeks. *Medication-Induced Postural Tremor* manifests when one is trying to maintain a posture and a fine tremor occurs, in association with the use of medications like lithium, valproate, or some antidepressants. Finally, *Medication-Induced Movement Disorder NOS* is used when none of the subtypes in this group apply (see pp. 734–736 in the *DSM* for greater detail).

OTHER MEDICATION-INDUCED DISORDERS

This very focused category contains one diagnosis, *Adverse Effects of Medication Not Otherwise Specified*, to code side effects of medications, other than the movement disorders coded above. Examples include hypotension, cardiac arrhythmias, or priapism.

RELATIONAL PROBLEMS

The focus of this diagnostic group is on the interactions among members of a relational unit (e.g., family). If patterns of interaction are associated with clinically significant impairment in functioning or symptoms among one or more members of the relational unit, a diagnosis from this grouping may be appropriate. These diagnoses are commonly seen by health professionals and are a focus of clinical attention because they exacerbate or complicate the management of a disorder.

Within this section of the *DSM* begins the so-called "V-codes" all of which have codes that begin with the capital letter V. If related symptoms are the primary focus of clinical attention, V-codes can be listed on Axis I. If associated symptoms are present but not the primary focus of clinical attention, they can be noted on Axis IV. This category also includes Relational Problem NOS, to indicate relational problems not specified in the group, such as difficulty with a coworker. The following V-codes are described on pages 736–737 of the *DSM*.

Relational Problem Related to a Mental Disorder or General Medical Condition

Relational Problem Related to a Mental Disorder or General Medical Condition is used when a member of a relational unit has a mental disorder or general medical condition. The focus of clinical attention in this case is a pattern of impaired interaction that is associated with a mental disorder or general medical condition.

Parent–Child Relational Problem

Parent–Child Relational Problem is a useful diagnosis to make the focus of clinical attention a pattern of interaction between parent and child. Difficulties could manifest in communication, overprotection, or inadequate discipline. Clinically significant impairment exists in individual or family functioning, or the parent or child may develop clinically significant symptoms as a result of the relational problem.

Partner Relational Problem

This category of Relational Problems is appropriate when the focus of clinical attention is a pattern of negative communication, criticism, distortion, unrealistic expectations, or withdrawal between spouses or partners. The difficulties cause significant impairment in individual or family functioning or perhaps symptoms in one or both partners.

Sibling Relational Problem

Sibling Relational Problem is used when the focus of clinical attention is a significant impairment in individual or family functioning due to interaction among siblings or the development of symptoms in one or more siblings.

PROBLEMS RELATED TO ABUSE OR NEGLECT

Severe mistreatment of one individual by another through physical abuse, sexual abuse, or neglect are significant foci of clinical attention and can be identified in the multiaxial framework as five different *DSM* diagnostic V-codes. Physical Abuse of Child, Sexual Abuse of Child, Neglect of Child, Physical Abuse of Adult, and Sexual Abuse of Adult are the five codes for this grouping. For children, there is a specific coding if the focus of clinical attention is the victim. The same holds for the adult diagnoses, with the addition of focus of clinical attention on the perpetrator and whether abuse is by a partner or by someone other than partner (see pp. 738–739 in the *DSM*).

ADDITIONAL CONDITIONS THAT MAY BE A FOCUS OF CLINICAL ATTENTION

This collection of clinical concerns completes the listing of diagnoses officially accepted into the *DSM-IV-TR* as well as the V-codes begun in this section. *Additional Conditions That May Be A Focus Of Clinical Attention* are not combined for any thematic reason, but they address significant issues in mental health services (see pp. 739–742 in the *DSM* for details).

Noncompliance With Treatment

Failure to comply with treatment recommendations is an important data point for assessment and treatment planning as well as evaluating the efficacy of treatments employed. When the focus of clinical attention is noncompliance with treatment, this diagnosis may be important to note on Axis I.

People with mental disorders may be noncompliant with treatment because of medication risks or side effects, expense, religious beliefs, maladaptive coping style, or complications from a mental disorder itself (e.g., Schizophrenia, Schizoaffective Disorder, Bipolar Disorder, and Avoidant Personality Disorder).

Malingering

Malingering is the intentional production of false or grossly exaggerated physical or psychological symptoms, motivated by external incentives like avoiding responsibilities or obtaining something of value. In some instances, Malingering may be considered an adaptive behavior, such as feigning illness when captured by an enemy during wartime.

The *DSM* states that Malingering should be strongly suspected if any combination of four dynamics are present: a medicolegal context of assessment; discrepancies between objective assessments and self-report; lack of cooperation in assessment or treatment, and; the presence of Antisocial Personality Disorder.

Adult Antisocial Behavior

When adult antisocial behavior is present, and the criteria for Conduct Disorder, Impulse-Control Disorder, or an Impulse-Control Disorder are not met,

Adult Antisocial Behavior is an appropriate diagnosis on Axis I. Behavior of thieves, racketeers, or dealers in illegal substances, who do not meet the criteria for the aforementioned three disorders, may receive this diagnosis.

Child or Adolescent Antisocial Behavior

When child or adolescent antisocial behavior is present, and the criteria for Conduct Disorder and Impulse-Control Disorder are not met, Child or Adolescent Antisocial Behavior may be an appropriate diagnosis. An example of behavior associated with this diagnosis includes isolated antisocial acts (as opposed to a pattern of antisocial behavior).

Borderline Intellectual Functioning

Borderline Intellectual Functioning is coded on Axis II, along with the Mental Retardation diagnoses. Borderline Intellectual Functioning is defined as an IQ in the range of 71–84. Diagnosis of Mental Retardation begins with an IQ of 70 or lower. The *DSM* warns that distinguishing the difference between Borderline Intellectual Functioning and Mental Retardation may be difficult when other mental disorders coexist (e.g., Schizophrenia).

Age-Related Cognitive Decline

When a cognitive impairment is not attributable to a specific mental disorder or neurological condition, and there is objectively identified decline in cognitive functioning (but within normal limits for the aging process), Age-Related Cognitive Decline may be diagnosed. Those with this diagnosis may indicate difficulty with memory or complex problem solving.

Bereavement

This diagnosis addresses a reaction to the death of a loved one. Symptoms of Bereavement may resemble those of a Major Depressive Episode, for which one may or may not seek treatment. A diagnosis of Major Depressive Disorder is not given until Bereavement symptoms have been present for 2 months after the loss. However, the duration of "normal" Bereavement varies considerably across cultures.

Academic Problem

Academic Problem is diagnosed when such a problem warrants clinical attention, either by itself or due to a mental disorder. In addition to failing grades, this diagnosis may also be appropriate for someone significantly underachieving in the absence of a Learning or Communication Disorder or any other mental disorder that would account for the problem.

Occupational Problem

Occupational Problem is diagnosed when such a problem warrants clinical attention, either by itself or due to a mental disorder. Difficulties encountered with this diagnosis may include job dissatisfaction or uncertainty about career choice.

Identity Problem

This diagnosis is appropriate when someone has difficulty with identity development across a wide range of life areas, including long-term goals, career choice, friendship patterns, sexual orientation, moral values, or group loyalties.

Religious or Spiritual Problem

Religious or Spiritual Problem may be diagnosed when there are distressing experiences related to questioning of faith, conversion to new faith, questioning spiritual values, and the like. These conflicts may or may not be related to organized religion and associated institutions.

Acculturation Problem

This category relates to difficulty adjusting to a different culture, such as that experienced in immigration, or with navigating multiple generations of immigrants.

Phase of Life Problem

Phase of Life Problem relates to difficulty with a particular phase of life or other life circumstance that is not due to a mental disorder, or if it is due to a mental disorder, it is sufficiently severe to warrant independent clinical attention. Such problems may arise while entering school, leaving parental control, starting a new career, marriage, divorce, or retirement.

REVISION TO THE *DSM-5*

The revision process of the *DSM-IV-TR* began back in 1999 when the *DSM-5* planning sessions were first held through National Institute of Mental Health (NIMH) supported international research conferences as well as the publication of a series of monographs with research reviews assembled during these conferences. More than 400 scientists, clinicians, and others with psychological expertise from around the world participated in an effort to expand the scientific basis for mental disorder classification (Regier, Narrow, Kuhl, & Kupfer, 2009). To encourage thinking beyond the *DSM-IV* framework, many former participants in the development of the *DSM-IV-TR* were not involved in this planning process.

As the revision process evolves, recent developments in research and practice will inevitably influence aspects of the *DSM-5*. For example, brain imaging and other technologies (Peterson, VanVleet, & Goldman, 2009) and emerging knowledge on biological and genetic factors in mental disorders will likely impact *DSM-5* content. Early in 2010, the American Psychiatric Association posted the proposed changes for the *DSM-5* on the Internet for public review and comment.

WORK GROUP AND TASK FORCE MEMBERSHIP

The *DSM-5* work group members were assembled in 2007, including over 120 world-renowned scientific researchers and clinicians with expertise in neuroscience, biology, genetics, statistics, epidemiology, public health, nursing, pediatrics, and social work. The *DSM-5* Task Force members are a smaller group, numbering 27 in all, who collectively represent research scientists from psychiatry and other disciplines, clinical care providers, and consumer and family advocates.

Work group membership has not gone unchallenged. For example, one work group member was protested to by transgender and gay rights activists for his position on discouraging transgender children and adolescents from changing their biological gender. These protests were assuaged by a member of the gay advisory committee who stated that the group member's views were not as extreme as some believed them to be.

Another controversy was generated by Integrity in Science, a project for the Center for Science in the Public Interest, revealing that the American Psychiatric Association (APA) allowed task force members to have financial relationships with drug companies, as long as their annual income from it did not exceed $10,000. The task force described the task force member's involvement as ranging from small to extensive. Several other stakeholders have expressed their concern regarding the potential conflicts of interest, even with the monetary limitation in place.

On another money-related matter, Senator Charles Grassley from the state of Iowa wrote a letter to the president of APA, concerned about a New York Times article that suggested drug companies provide about 30% of APA's operating budget. APA has gone on record in a press release to suggest that every effort has been made to eliminate conflicts of interest in the *DSM*'s revision process.

AREAS OF POTENTIAL DEVELOPMENT FOR THE *DSM-5*

In general, new diagnoses, or those not already covered in the *DSM* or only covered by the NOS category, would only be considered for addition to the *DSM* if research had established that they should be included, rather than be included in order to stimulate more research. The NOS diagnostic categories were created for frequent instances that are at the boundary of specific categorical definitions.

This writer regularly saves listserv postings that address developments in the diagnosis and treatment of mental disorders. Coupled with recent peer-reviewed literature on the *DSM*, and the recent posting of the *DSM-5* Web site requesting feedback on recommended changes for the *DSM-5*, these sources of information inform the following review of potential changes in the *DSM-5*. It is important to note that these are areas of suggested change posted for public comment, so they may change or evolve over time.

Conceptual Framework

The conceptual framework that has guided the *DSM* since its third revision remains in place for the fifth revision of the *DSM* (Regier et al., 2009). Specifically, diagnoses are validated by their separation from other disorders, common clinical course, and genetic aggregation in families and are further differentiated by future laboratory tests. Advances in science since the third edition make the latter criteria more salient, with the emergence of anatomical and functional imaging (Peterson et al., 2009), molecular genetics, pathophysiological variations, and neuropsychological testing (Lezak, Howieson, & Loring, 2004).

Dimensional Assessments

Current emphases for the fifth revision include refining mental disorders to reflect more useful diagnostic categories, with dimensional continuities between disorders and clear thresholds between pathology and normality. Regier and associates (2009) opined that the single most important task

moving forward will be the incorporation of simple dimensional measures for assessing syndromes within broad diagnostic categories as well as
supraordinate dimensions that cross current diagnostic boundaries. The
specific meaning of these terms remains to be seen, but in any case, we
should see more prominent use of dimensional measures in the *DSM-5*,
a major change from the fourth revision (Regier et al., 2009).

Overlap in Diagnoses

The *DSM* makes clear that its diagnostic categories are not mutually exclusive and that overlap is an issue in the differential diagnostic process. For
example, Hypochondriasis is characterized by symptoms not unlike those
in Anxiety Disorders. Olatunji, Deacon, and Abramowitz (2009) suggest
that it is in fact an anxiety disorder and recommend considering this for
future *DSM* revisions.

In another example of a change addressing diagnostic overlap, stakeholders in the *DSM* revision process are considering a new, dimensional,
single diagnostic category called Autism Spectrum Disorders, which will
subsume Autistic Disorder, Asperger's Disorder, Childhood Disintegrative
Disorder, and Pervasive Developmental Disorder NOS. There are also recommendations to add new categories of learning disorders and to change
the term *mental retardation* to *intellectual disability*.

Binge Eating

Population estimates suggest that 1 in 30 Americans engage in binge-
eating behavior. There has not been consensus within psychiatry regarding
whether binge eating belongs aside anorexia nervosa and bulimia nervosa
as a separate mental disorder. The associated work group and *DSM-5* task
force will have to decide whether there are a distinct set of symptoms, a
recognizable pattern of progression, and a predictable response to treatment (Wilson, Wilfley, Agras, & Bryson, 2010).

Embitterment

During a summer 2009 meeting of the APA in San Francisco, there appeared
to be receptivity toward developing a *DSM* diagnosis to address people who
feel they have been wronged by someone and are so bitter that they cannot
stop ruminating about their circumstances. Posttraumatic embitterment is a
proposed diagnosis, akin to Posttraumatic Stress Disorder as it is a response
to trauma that endures; people are left seething for revenge.

Obesity

Although it will likely cause some conflict with other medical specialties, obesity is now being considered a diagnosable factor in mental health. There is no doubt that it has an impact on mental health. The argument to be made for inclusion in the *DSM-5* is whether it presents sufficient impairment or distress to warrant a diagnosis.

Parental Alienation

Some experts believe that children become alienated from a loving parent in many cases of divorce with little or no justification and that the associated distress and/or resulting impairment in functioning warrants diagnostic consideration. Bernet (2008) is making the case for inclusion of Parental Alienation in the *DSM-5*. The concept of a parental alienation syndrome dates back to 1985, when a Colombia University Professor of Psychiatry, Richard Gardner, first coined the term.

Temper Dysregulation Disorder With Dysphoria (TDD)

This newly proposed diagnosis for the Mood Disorder section of the *DSM* is recommended out of the recent finding that many wildly aggressive, irritable children have been misdiagnosed with Bipolar Disorder or Oppositional Defiant Disorder when they do not have it. Medication is prescribed for conditions like Bipolar Disorder that can have harmful side effects, raising greater concern for the harm caused by misdiagnosis. A behavioral disorder on the other hand argues for behavioral treatment appropriate for children with anger management problems.

Addiction and Related Disorders

A proposed change that will surely have ripple effects throughout the addictions treatment community is eliminating the terms *substance abuse* and *dependence* and replacing them with *Addiction-Related Disorders*. The proposal maintains Substance Use Disorders and proposes to list each drug in its own category. The rationale for eliminating the old term dependence is to better distinguish between compulsive drug-seeking behavior in addiction and the normal response of tolerance and withdrawal from some prescribed medications.

There is also proposed the creation of a new category Behavioral Addictions, in which Gambling Disorder will be the sole diagnosis for now.

Internet addiction is another phenomenon addressed, but at present it is recommended as a condition for further study.

Suicide and Risk

There are newly proposed suicide scales for adolescents and adults that are intended to identify individuals most at risk. The scales explore dynamics like impulsive behavior and heavy drinking. The *DSM-5* Task Force has also recommended the establishment of a new Risk Syndromes category, to help clinicians identify early stages of some chronic and severe mental disorders.

CRITICS OF THE REVISION PROCESS

This writer printed off all missives from cyberspace on the revision efforts for the *DSM-5*. The following bits of information are not formally connected with personal communications, and names not associated with a publication are withheld to avoid any particular controversy. The issues are reviewed here because they were released for public consumption by *DSM* stakeholders concerned about the revision process.

Controversy

Efforts to revise the *DSM-IV-TR* have been chronicled on the Internet through postings to various listservs, and controversy lurks at every turn. There are former *DSM* contributors who are not pleased with the degree of open access to the revision process. Still others may prefer a radical departure from old traditions and prefer the paradigm shift away from diagnostic lists informed by the medical model to dimensional models of mental disorders, particularly for personality disorders given the latest research on general personality structure (Widiger & Trull, 2007).

Secrecy

Some have accused the *DSM-5* revision process of being conducted "in secret" when the minutes of the revision meetings were not released to maintain *DSM-5* confidentiality. Opponents to this method of managing the revision process point to the *ICD-11* revision efforts where minutes of revision meetings are posted with no restrictions (http://www.who.int/mental_health/evidence/en/; these postings appear to stop at the end of 2008). As a result of these protests, these communications were made available to interested parties, and the proposed changes for the *DSM* are available for public review and comment at the time of this writing (February 2010, http://www.dsm5.org).

Lack of Psychologist Involvement

Two former task force members from the *DSM-IV* revision, Peter Nathan, PhD and Thomas Widiger, PhD, shared some of their concerns about the revision process with *The National Psychologist* (Vol. 18: #3). Although the *DSM-IV* revision task force included four psychologists, only one psychologist is on the *DSM-5* task force, the same psychologist who was criticized for his perspectives on treating people dealing with transgender issues. Nathan saw the participation of psychologists as a positive development in the *DSM-IV*, reducing criticism over the historic *DSM* emphasis on psychopharmacological treatment over psychosocial treatment. Widiger stated that he feared the lack of psychologist involvement in the *DSM-5* will result in a "medicalization" of many *DSM* diagnoses in the fifth edition.

APA REVISION EFFORTS

The APA has made an effort to recruit input from wider research and consumer communities by creating a Web site (noted above). An options book will be disseminated in summer 2010 to facilitate field testing to evaluate the utility of alternative diagnoses in various settings. The Chair of the *DSM-5* Task Force, David J. Kupfer, MD, stated in a press release that "Our ultimate goal is to have a manual that is based on the best available science and that is useful in a clinical setting." The original release date of 2012 has been postponed to 2013.

CONCLUSION TO PART II

After a thorough review of the *ICF* in Part I of this text, Part II focused on the *DSM-IV-TR*. Part II of this text was meant to be used alongside the *DSM-IV-TR* itself. Relevant page numbers of the *DSM* were listed for each diagnostic aspect summarized.

In Part I, the intention of our review was to highlight the *ICF* as a new development in health care classification. In Part II, we reviewed the historical legacy of the *DSM*, up to and including its recent revision process for the *DSM-5*. Parts I and II of this text come together in a meaningful way in Part III, where we will explore the *ICF-DSM* nexus and prospects for further development of both classification systems, one informing the other.

PART III

Cross-Walking the *DSM* to *ICF*

BRINGING IT ALL TOGETHER

Goals Achieved in This Text

Part I. Writing this text accomplished several important goals. We have established the ubiquity of disability and in particular mental illness. We have reviewed a most important international development in the conceptualization of disability and the classification of health and functioning in the *ICF* and its relationship to the *ICD* as part of the WHO Family of Classifications. We've reviewed the historical context of the development of the *ICF* to have a better understanding how conceptions of disability have developed over time.

A careful review of the *ICF* and related literature presented the *ICF* conceptual framework, its two parts, each with two components. The components of the *ICF* were defined and their relationships described. We concluded with a review of ethical tenets of the *ICF* that inform a collaborative assessment enterprise, clinical implementation of the *ICF*, and future research. It was recommended that the *ICF* itself be read as a companion text to Part I of this text.

Part II. With the *ICF* as our conceptual basis, we embarked on an ambitious review of the nearly 1,000 pages of the *DSM-IV-TR*. Its historical context was explored, and its conceptual framework was discussed in relation to the *ICF*. The framework of the mental disorders section of the *ICD*-10 system was presented as a basis of comparison in the Appendix.

The differential diagnostic process was presented with an overview of the 17 diagnostic categories of the *DSM*. Various critiques of the *DSM* were offered in the context of recent revision efforts for the *DSM-5*. It was recommended that the *DSM-IV-TR* be read as a companion text to the overview in Part II. Relevant page numbers of the *DSM-IV-TR* were provided to help coordinate reading Part II along with the *DSM-IV-TR* itself.

Part III. As we conclude with Part III, we bring together the complex review of the *ICF* and *DSM* into a meaningful whole, with practical applications for current and aspiring mental health practitioners. We will explore how mental disorders have been conceptualized in recent times and how the *ICF* can make these conceptualizations more complete. We will describe how the conceptual framework of the *ICF* is complementary to the *DSM* multiaxial framework and outline what major diagnostic categories of the *DSM* match well with components from the *ICF*.

Many Different Professions, One System of Describing Mental Health and Functioning

There is quite a variety of professionals involved in mental health care. Acute care psychiatric hospitals may employ technicians, like psychiatric technicians or mental health workers, to provide direct care of essential mental health and safety needs. Psychiatric nurses, psychiatrists, and now prescribing psychologists may provide pharmacotherapy intervention and oversight. Clinical psychologists and neuropsychologists may provide expertise in assessment of brain–behavior relationships, and speech language pathologists often provide expertise on evaluation of communication functioning. Psychologists, licensed mental health counselors, marriage and family therapists, and social workers plan and administer psychotherapeutic interventions as well as provide feedback about medication trials. Occupational therapists may provide daily living skills training. Physical therapists may become involved if there are also physical impairments in rehabilitation.

Outpatient treatment of mental health also involves a broad array of service providers. Often the first line of treatment is one's primary care provider (medical doctor, doctor of osteopathy, or nurse practitioner). Patients may be referred to physiatrists, psychiatrists, prescribing psychologists, or psychiatric nurse practitioners for chronic and severe conditions for specialized medication management. Psychologists and speech language pathologists may provide ongoing assessment and therapy for certain mental health issues. Psychotherapists may provide short- or longer-term psychotherapy. Rehabilitation services professionals, or rehabilitation counselors, may provide expertise in adjusting to work and independent living-related activities.

Given the many different professions involved in mental health care, in order to deliver effective and coordinated services there is a need for collaboration across very different professional contexts. Each profession has its own developmental history, origin of knowledge and skill base, and developing body of knowledge and research. Each has its own scope of practice, standards of care, and clinical procedures. It is easy to imagine how terminologies that develop around these different disciplines may vary greatly across contexts.

The *ICF* can serve as the bridge between professions by creating a common language that addresses what Body Structures are involved in mental disorders, how these changes impair Body Functioning (Activity and Activity Limitations), and how these impairments affect one's ability to participate (Participation and Participation Restrictions) in one's environmental context (Environmental and Personal Factors). As these professions work together in various clinical settings, it makes good sense to have a common language of functioning, disability, and health across professions using a transdisciplinary approach to treating mental disorders.

Facilitating communication during treatment planning and treatment administration will optimize the effectiveness of overall mental health treatment within inpatient and outpatient settings. Having a common language in assessment of functioning will allow ongoing assessment of treatment progress to be seamless and transdisciplinary. Using common functional terminology in the evaluation of treatment outcomes in mental health will facilitate the construction of knowledge bases that can be shared across disciplines. Having a classification system like the *ICF* that is the product of a collaboration across nations will facilitate the international sharing of treatment planning and outcome data, greatly enhancing our knowledge base and encouraging international collaboration in addressing mental health and functioning.

Regardless of the diagnostic system employed, the *DSM* or the *ICD*, or others in current use and development internationally (e.g., *Schedules for Clinical Assessment in Neuropsychiatry, Chinese Classification of Mental Disorders, Research Diagnostic Criteria, Schedule for Affective Disorders and Schizophrenia, Feighner Criteria*), the *ICF* can serve as the functional complement that completes the overall mental health and functioning picture, within international contexts.

CHAPTER 10

Conceptualizing and Classifying Psychological Functioning, Disability, and Health

PREVIEW QUESTIONS

1. How have mental disorders been conceptualized in recent times?
2. How does the *ICF* make the *DSM* more complete?
3. Describe how the conceptual framework of the *ICF* is complementary to the *DSM* multiaxial framework.
4. Which major diagnostic categories of the *DSM* match well with which components of the *ICF*?

Mental disorders that have a great impact on the manifestation of psychological disability include Schizophrenia, Schizoaffective Disorder, Bipolar Disorder, Major Depressive Disorder, Borderline Personality Disorder, and Posttraumatic Stress Disorder (Bond, 1995; Hong, 2009). These diagnoses are often considered severe and are associated with high treatment costs. Episodic and unpredictable fluctuations in symptoms of these mental disorders have historically contributed to variability in functioning, including sporadic work histories (Ahrens, Frey, & Senn Burke, 1999; Baron & Linden, 2009; Baron & Salzer, 2000; Cook & Razzano, 2000; Garske, 1999; Strauss, Hafez, Lieberman, & Harding, 1985).

Historically, people disabled by a mental disorder accounted for one-third of working-age adults who received Supplemental Security Income from the Social Security Administration and for 27% who received Social Security Disability Insurance (Burt & Aron, 2003). At the start of this century, psychiatric disability was the primary disabling condition for 20% of the people who receive services from the State-Federal Vocational Rehabilitation (VR) system (Hayward & Schmidt-Davis, 2003). Taken with the prevalence data presented in Part I of this text, the need to work effectively in diagnosing and treating psychological disability is paramount in contemporary health care.

We begin Part III of this text with a discussion of how mental disorders have been conceptualized historically and how the diagnosis of psychological disability relates to the conceptual framework of the *ICF*. We then compare and contrast the conceptual frameworks of the *DSM* and the *ICF* and explore their complementarity at the component level of the *ICF* as they relate to the *DSM* major diagnostic categories. We complete Part III with a discussion of the development of *ICF* core sets for mental disorders, with specifics provided for the depression core set, and prospects for future development.

DIAGNOSIS AND TREATMENT OF PSYCHOLOGICAL DISABILITY

Historically, efforts in mental health practice and research have been focused on diagnosing a mental disorder that interferes with a person's personal, social, or occupational functioning (Anthony, Cohen, Farkas, & Gagne, 2002; Pratt, Gill, Barrett, & Roberts, 2007). However, relatively little has surfaced in the literature to date on methods to systematically define psychological health and functioning. The *ICF* can contribute significantly to the mental health profession's ability to talk about health and health-related states in association with mental disorders.

Diagnosis of Psychological Disability

Psychological disability has been described in the literature through diagnostic methodologies (e.g., Stengel's work referenced in Part II of this text), where symptoms are identified, objective testing may be conducted, diagnostic criteria are considered, and these data applied to some system or taxonomy to determine an appropriate diagnosis. Systems or taxonomies are constructed by mental health professionals based on clinical experience in working with people with mental disorders and related research. To construct these systems, symptoms manifested in mental disorders are formulated into algorithms to categorize or classify various diagnoses. Diagnoses are based on particular patterns of symptoms and signs, illness course, and history and consequences of impairment (Baron & Linden, 2008; Hong, 2009).

As we have just reviewed in the first two parts of this text, in the United States, the diagnostic system that is most prominent in diagnosing psychological impairment is the *Diagnostic and Statistical Manual of Mental Disorders, Fourth Edition—Text Revision (DSM-IV-TR*; APA, 2000; hereafter the *DSM*). Nearly all professionally delivered mental health services and health insurance systems in the United States require information from the *DSM*. If not the *DSM*, third-party payers may require information from the *ICD-9-CM* in order for individuals to receive services. The section of the *ICD-9-CM* relevant to psychological disability is the fifth chapter, Classification of Mental and Behavioral Disorders (see Appendix for a listing of the major diagnostic categories for the latest revision, the *ICD-10*). Investing time to learn and understand these systems is very important for all aspiring mental health professionals (MacDonald-Wilson & Nemec, 2005).

Diagnoses Are Not Enough

The diagnoses in the *DSM* are useful for communicating presentations of mental disorders, but as discussed in Part I of this text, diagnoses alone are poor predictors of health outcomes. Diagnoses alone are not sufficient to fully inform intervention targeting and evaluation of the effectiveness of treatment. Diagnostic information alone does not predict well actual functioning in various contexts (Baron & Linden, 2009). Classification systems informed by the medical model like the *DSM* and the *ICD* are of limited utility in describing the impact of a health condition on the person and his or her functioning (Anthony et al., 2002; Baron & Linden, 2009; MacDonald-Wilson & Nemec, 2005).

Importance of Context

A comprehensive review of the literature in 2002 suggested that serious mental disorders affect most areas of functioning, and improvements in functioning were not achieved through "traditional" treatment approaches (Anthony et al., 2002; McReynolds, 2002). The review indicates that techniques that derive from the psychiatric rehabilitation literature (e.g., increasing community integration and independence through strengthening both client skills and environmental supports) are effective in working with people with chronic mental disorders. One reason for the success of this specialized approach may be its sensitivity to the person–environment interaction (Anthony et al., 2002; Baron & Linden, 2009; MacDonald-Wilson & Nemec, 2005; McReynolds, 2002).

Lazarus and Folkman (1984) provided a good deal of useful scholarship on stress and coping with disability, and it was their contention that psychological stress is produced when persons perceive their resources to cope with a specific context to be insufficient or overtaxed. The fact that our well-being is affected by our context dates back 2,000 years to the philosopher Hippocrates (Gallagher, 1993). The success of psychiatric rehabilitation treatment paradigms may be due in large part to treatment planning that is sensitive to the importance of context in mental health and functioning.

Contextual Factors in the ICF

Just as the *ICF* provides the biopsychosocial framework that is sensitive to the role of contextual factors in *ICD* diagnoses, the *ICF* can be used to create a more complete conceptualization of mental health and functioning using both the *DSM*'s mental disorders and the *ICF*'s classification of health, functioning, and disability to create a more complete mental health picture. The success experienced within the psychiatric rehabilitation specialization, given its contextual emphasis in treatment, may also be experienced in treatment planning informed by combining *DSM* diagnostic information with the *ICF* contextual framework and coding system.

ICF as the Missing Piece to the *DSM*

The introduction of the *DSM* notes, "It is precisely because impairments, abilities, and disabilities vary widely within each diagnostic category that assignment of a particular diagnosis does not imply a specific level of impairment or disability" (p. xxxiii). This statement written at the beginning of the *DSM* acknowledges the limitations of diagnoses alone and the need to keep in mind the functional data that were used to arrive at diagnoses to begin with. The *ICF* can provide, as it does with its sister classification the *ICD*, the functional information that complements the diagnostic information provided by the *DSM* (Baron & Linden, 2008, 2009).

The *ICF* and its conceptual framework extend beyond diagnostic information, such as impairments and symptoms, and presents a glossary of functioning that allows for a more complete description of current health and functioning. Further, consequences of impairments classified in the *ICF* are classified through performance of daily activities and of participation in life situations, while considering the environmental and personal factors that affect psychological health (Baron & Linden, 2008, 2009; Peterson, 2005). The comprehensive view of the *ICF* holds promise for understanding the complex issues that limit or facilitate success for people who have mental disorders (MacDonald-Wilson & Nemec, 2005).

The *DSM* also suggests that, like other conceptions in medicine and science, the concept of mental disorder cannot be consistently defined and operationalized to cover all situations. The *ICF*'s conceptual framework can be used to fill this gap by focusing our attention on consistently classified components of functioning influenced in various contexts.

According to the *DSM*, medical conditions are defined on various levels of abstraction; for example, structural pathology (e.g., pathology within the central nervous system) and etiology (memory loss caused by dementia). These abstractions can be associated with other abstract concepts like symptom presentation (memory difficulty caused by dementia) and deviance from a psychological norm (low scores on psychological tests of attention, concentration, and memory). Symptom presentation and deviation from the norm can be described by the *ICF* using Body Functions and Structures and their qualifiers to clarify the level of impairment. Pathology and etiology are also addressed by the *ICD* system and overlap somewhat with Body Functions and Body Structures within the *ICF*.

To address the complexity of mental disorder as it impacts functioning in a given context, the *ICF* components of Activity and Participation can be used along with their qualifiers, to capture how mental impairments manifest in limiting what a person is capable of doing as well as how the environment either facilitates or prevents functioning through activity limitations and participation restrictions. These components can be compared and contrasted, illustrating what a person with a given mental disorder is capable of doing, in contrast with what a person actually does do within his or her context (Environmental and Personal components of the *ICF*).

Treatment of Psychological Disability

Accurate diagnosis is the focus of mental health professionals working with mental disorders, followed by appropriate prescription of medications and therapies designed to reduce or eliminate symptoms and to improve overall psychological functioning (MacDonald-Wilson, Nemec, Anthony, & Cohen, 2001). Although there are ample data to support the fact that treatment from mental health professionals is clinically useful and effective (Nathan & Gorman, 2007), we also know that many areas of functioning remain affected despite treatment efforts, such as work functioning, school functioning, or community and social functioning (Anthony et al., 2002; MacDonald-Wilson & Nemec, 2005).

In its introduction, the *DSM* notes, "To formulate an adequate treatment plan, the clinician will invariably require considerable additional information about the person being evaluated beyond that required to make a *DSM*-IV diagnosis" (p. xxxv). In Part I of this text, we established the great value of the *ICF* as a complement to the *ICD*, in particular with intervention targeting and evaluation of treatment outcomes. This author believes the *ICF* can provide "considerable additional information" to the *DSM* as described in Part II of this text.

When mental disorders are addressed not only by diagnosis but also with clear descriptions of related Impairments, Activity Limitations, Participation Restrictions, and Contextual Factors (Environmental and Personal), the overall picture of health becomes more complete. Mental Disorder can be described more clearly using impairments in Body Functions, and the manifestation of disability in context can be illustrated using the concepts of Activity Limitations and Participation Restrictions.

With a more complete conceptualization of health and functioning, more precise intervention targeting can occur through accurate identification of activity limitations and participation restrictions. Appropriate treatments can be selected with the understanding of the treatment context (Environmental and Personal Factors). In addition, given that the *ICF* was created to describe functioning and health as well as disability, strengths in functioning and health will also inform the selection of treatments that build on strengths as well as address difficulties.

COMPARING *DSM* AND *ICF* CONCEPTUAL FRAMEWORKS

In our discussion of diagnosing and treating psychological disability, we noted the utility of diagnostic information as provided by the *DSM* and the *ICD* systems and also how diagnoses alone fall short of presenting the entire mental health and functioning picture. We then highlighted the importance of contextual factors in disability, health, and functioning and how the *ICF* provides a biopsychosocial approach that is sensitive to contextual factors and complementary to diagnostic systems. Using diagnosis and functioning data together facilitates accurate diagnosis, treatment, and evaluation of related outcomes in the treatment of mental disorders. Within this context, we now turn to a direct comparison of the *DSM* and *ICF* conceptual frameworks.

Shared Biopsychosocial Perspectives

Returning to our discussion of models of disability, although the early versions of the *DSM* grew out of the medical model of disability, early in its development Stengel's influence impacted the multiaxial framework by considering both biological and psychological factors simultaneously as they affect a given mental disorder. Although ultimately the *DSM* is a diagnostic system that provides data akin to the *ICD*, the *DSM* eventually grew into a system that in some ways embraces the biopsychosocial model of disability.

The *DSM* focuses on Psychosocial and Environmental Problems in Axis IV and general medical factors in Axis III (meaning conditions and disorders that are listed outside the "Mental and Behavioral Disorders" chapter of the *ICD*). The Global Assessment of Functioning Scale on Axis V can consider either level of symptom severity or demonstrated functional impairment, a remarkable complement to our earlier *ICF*-based discussion on how disability manifests differently across individuals. The mental disorders themselves as classified in Axes I and II are in kind with the *ICD* taxonomy and in fact cross-classified. Taken together, the multiaxial diagnostic system is consistent with a biopsychosocial conceptualization of disability.

DSM stakeholders do not endorse the mind/body duality that separates the physical from mental aspects of disorders and health. They recognize the broad literature base that supports their reciprocal relationship in manifestations of functioning, disability, and health. This is quite consistent with the biopsychosocial approach that informs the *ICF*'s conceptual framework and the reciprocal interactions among the components of the *ICF* conceptual framework (see Figure 3.1).

The *DSM* instructs users to classify disorders that people have, not the people themselves. This is similar to the ethical guidelines provided for the *ICF* as to its purpose, to classify functioning, disability, and health but not people. In keeping with the exhortation from Beatrice Wright to use person-first, disability-sensitive language (Wright, 1983), the *DSM* instructs users to avoid substituting the individual with a diagnostic label ending with -ic (e.g., schizophrenic).

An Important Difference

The *ICF* conceptual framework differs from the *DSM* in one important way. Codes within the *ICF* are considered nonoverlapping and mutually exclusive, with more detailed codes being subsumed by higher level ones. Although the *DSM* uses a categorical system, it is with the admission that each category of mental disorder may overlap with others in some way. Within the *DSM*, because of the nature of mental disorders and the contexts in which they occur, categories of mental disorders are neither discrete nor mutually exclusive.

ICF MODEL OF DISABILITY AND *DSM* MENTAL DISORDERS

Let us present specific components of the *ICF* as they would apply to describing mental health functioning. As you may recall from Part I of the text, the *ICF* is made up of two parts, each with two components. The first part relates to the individual and has two components, Body Functions and Structures and Activities and Participation. The second part of the *ICF* addresses Contextual Factors, consisting two components, Environmental Factors, and an as yet unclassified Personal Factors component.

The following discussion will address the One-Level Classification of the *ICF*, which is the most basic level comprising chapter numbers only across the two parts and related four components of the *ICF* (less Personal Factors, as yet unclassified). Body Functions and Structures have eight chapters each, Activities and Participation have no chapters, and Environmental Factors have five chapters in the One-Level Classification.

Body Functions and Structures

Within the Body Functions and Structures component of the *ICF*, the chapters most relevant to psychological function are the first chapters in each section, Mental Functions and Structures of the Nervous System; these chapters will be addressed at the end of this section. Given the biopsychosocial nature of mental disorders and the *ICF*, *DSM* diagnostic criteria may be informed in some way by data from all *ICF* chapters. The Body Functions and Body Structures components form a parallel list, one dealing with anatomical structures the other with related functions (refer to Figure 3.4 for a complete listing of chapters within the *ICF* and Table 5.1 that lists the major diagnostic categories of the *DSM-IV-TR*).

ICF *Chapters 2 and 3*

The parallel second chapters in the Body Functions and Structures component, Sensory Functions and Pain and the Eye, Ear and Related Structures, have obvious association with *DSM* Pain Disorders and with a number of disorders involving psychotic symptomatology. The parallel third chapters addressing Voice and Speech Function and Structures Involved in Voice and Speech relate closely to *DSM* Communication Disorders as well as the impact of some disorders on speech (e.g., slowed speech with depression, pressured speech with mania).

ICF *Chapters 4 and 5*

The fourth parallel chapters addressing Functions of the Cardiovascular, Hematological, Immunological and Respiratory Systems, and Structures of the Cardiovascular, Immunological and Respiratory Systems would relate to diagnoses involving Substance-Related Disorders, Anxiety Disorders, or Somatoform Disorders in the *DSM*. The fifth parallel chapters addressing Functions of the Digestive, Metabolic, and Endocrine Systems and Structures related to the Digestive, Metabolic, and Endocrine Systems would relate to Somatoform Disorders, Feeding and Eating Disorders of Infancy or Early Childhood, Eating Disorders, Sleep Disorders, and complications from depression within the *DSM*.

ICF *Chapters 6, 7, and 8*

The sixth parallel chapters, Genitourinary and Reproductive Functions and Structures Related to the Genitourinary and Reproductive Systems, relate closely with Elimination Disorders and Sexual Dysfunctions of the *DSM*. The seventh parallel chapters, Neuromusculoskeletal and Movement-Related Functions, and Structures Related to Movement would inform diagnoses like Motor Skills Disorder, Tic Disorders, Somatoform Disorders (note how the *ICF* would not make a distinction between inability to move an arm due to spinal cord injury vs. a Conversion Disorder) or Medication-Induced Movement Disorders within the *DSM*. Finally, the eighth parallel chapter, Functions of the Skin and Related Structures and Skin-Related Structures relate well to factors considered in Problems Related to Abuse or Neglect, Trichotillomania, and Impulse Control Disorder–Skin Picking.

ICF *Chapter 1: Mental Functions*

Chapter 1 of the Body Structures chapter is called Structures of the Nervous System, which of course includes the central and peripheral nervous systems. The parallel Chapter 1 for Body Functions is called Mental Functions. This section includes subcomponents of *Global Mental Functions*, such as the functions of consciousness, orientation, intellect, temperament and personality, energy and drive, and sleep; and *Specific Mental Functions* such as attention, memory, psychomotor, emotional, perceptual, thought, higher-level cognitive functions, mental functions of language, calculation, the mental function of sequencing complex movements, and experience of self and time. Quite an array could be constructed to compare all Two-Level Classification Codes with the major diagnostic categories of the *DSM*.

It is this level of analysis that informs the ongoing work in code set development, which is presented in Chapter 10.

A Clear Relationship

It is clear from our review of the One-Level Classification of Body Functions and Structures within the *ICF* as it relates to the *DSM* that the Body Functions and Structures component of the *ICF* consistently related in a meaningful way with the major diagnostic classifications within the *DSM*. If we were to explore the first level of branching in the Two-Level Classification of the *ICF* for this component, greater classificatory precision could be achieved as we look at specific diagnoses within each major diagnostic group along with their diagnostic criteria as listed in the *DSM*. The Detailed Classification of the *ICF*, which includes up to five levels of detail in some instances, brings a broad palette of functioning classification from which to draw to document the functioning associated with specific *DSM* diagnoses and associated subtypes.

Activities and Participation

The manifestation of function and impairment in an individual's context is classified in the component Activities and Participation. As we reviewed in Part I of this text, Body Functions and Structures were designed to be used with the Activities and Participation component of the *ICF*, and all are qualified in some way to establish levels of functioning in a given context.

ICF *Chapter 1*

Chapter 1 of Activities and Participation, *Learning and Applying Knowledge,* includes such codes as listening, acquiring skills, focusing attention, solving problems, and making decisions. This component chapter would be quite useful in documenting functioning that informed diagnoses like Mental Retardation, Learning Disorders, Pervasive Developmental Disorders, Delirium, Dementia Amnestic Disorders, and Schizophrenia and Other Psychotic Disorders.

ICF *Chapter 2*

Chapter 2 of the Activities and Participation component, *General Tasks and Demands,* contains functional codes related to undertaking multiple tasks, carrying out a daily routine, and handling multiple stresses and psychological demands. This component chapter could relate to the diagnosis already listed for Chapter 1 but also include all of the Personality Disorders listed for Axis II of the *DSM*.

ICF *Chapter 3*

Chapter 3, Communication, codes behaviors like receiving spoken messages, producing nonverbal messages, conversation, and discussion. The major diagnostic areas already indicated for the Body Functions and Structures, Chapter 3, of that *ICF* component.

ICF *Chapters 4, 5, and 6*

Chapter 4, Mobility, addresses movement from the immediate to the public environment and relates well to *ICF* codes associated with Chapter 7 of Body Functions and Structures. Chapter 5, Self-Care, addresses functioning that maintains personal hygiene. Any *DSM* diagnosis that results in disorganized behavior (e.g., Schizophrenia, Manic Episode, Substance Abuse) may compromise personal hygiene and be informed by this *ICF* chapter. Chapter 6, Domestic Life, focuses on activities of daily living associated with maintaining a household. The Activities and Participation chapter might relate to diagnoses already associated with Chapter 7 of Body Functions and Structures as well as those diagnoses associated with poor personal hygiene.

ICF *Chapter 7*

Chapter 7, Interpersonal Interactions and Relationships, relates basic interpersonal interactions such as showing warmth or responding to basic cues, complex interpersonal interactions such as initiating and terminating relationships, maintaining social space, and family or intimate relationships. Nearly every mental disorder, especially those with severe and chronic impairments, has the potential to complicate interpersonal interactions and relationships, so this chapter of the *ICF* relates to the *DSM* as a whole.

ICF *Chapters 8 and 9*

Chapter 8 of the Activities and Participation component of the *ICF* is Major Life Areas. The life areas classified include Educational, Work and Employment, and Economic Life. As with Chapter 7 of this component, there are few if any *DSM* diagnoses that would not relate to functioning in this area.

Chapter 9, Community, Social and Civic Life, is a social extension of Chapter 7 of this component, and the related *DSM* diagnoses are relevant here as well.

Environmental Factors

In the context of Mental Disorders, the environment can be a facilitator or a barrier to the ability to be active and participate in one's context. Environmental factors in the *ICF* are addressed through the Environmental Factors component.

ICF *Chapters 1 and 2*

The first two chapters of this component of the *ICF* are most relevant to people with physical disabilities. Chapter 1 classifies Products and Technology in the environment. Chapter 2 addresses Natural Environment and Human-Made Changes to the Environment.

ICF *Chapters 3 and 4*

Chapter 3, Support and Relationships, lists interpersonal contact that begins in the immediate family and extends to strangers in public. Chapter 4, Attitudes, involves attitudes that parallel this spectrum of interpersonal contact and some additional health-related interpersonal contact. As with Chapter 7 of Activities and Participation, all *DSM* mental disorders can potentially impact Chapter 4, especially given the stigma that has been so well documented in the psychiatric rehabilitation literature (Pratt et al., 2007).

ICF *Chapter 5*

Chapter 5, Services, Systems, and Policies, lists 20 categories of social service entities that are quite relevant to community mental health resources. This is another example of an *ICF* component chapter that could apply to nearly any *DSM* diagnosis. Social system supports in the environment can be critical to success in independent living or the work arena for people with mental disorders (see also Cook & Razzano, 2000; Dellario, 1985; Fabian, Waterworth, & Ripke, 1993; Granger, Baron, & Robinson, 1997; MacDonald-Wilson, Rogers, Ellison, & Lyass, 2003; MacDonald-Wilson, Rogers, Massaro, Lyass, & Crean, 2002; Noble, 1998; Rogers, Anthony, & Danley, 1989). Detailed *ICF* coding may greatly enhance how current social supports are monitored and evaluated for success.

CHAPTER 11

ICF Core Sets for
Mental Disorders

PREVIEW QUESTIONS

1. What are *ICF* Core Sets?
2. What methods were used to construct the Core Set for Depression?
3. Describe what aspects of the *ICF* code are part of the Core Set for Depression.
4. What has the Core Set for Depression taught us about future work with the *ICF*?

We discussed in Part I of this text the *ICF*-related efforts to construct subsets of the *ICF* codes used to describe patient functioning, in particular, clinical, research, and health-related settings. Called core sets, in clinical practice, they can be used in clinical assessment, intervention targeting, and evaluation of treatment outcomes (Grill et al., 2005; Stucki et al., 2005). Work began with 12 core sets selected as "most burdensome chronic conditions" in acute hospital and postacute rehabilitation facilities (Stucki et al., 2005, p. 350). More recently, researchers in Italy evaluated the use of *ICF* Core Sets for implementation in rehabilitation settings. *ICF* Core Sets or simplified instruments derived from the *ICF* show promise for more targeted classification efforts.

International research in the development of core sets is ongoing, including general neurological conditions (Stier-Jarmer et al., 2005), dementia, pain management, spinal cord injury, traumatic brain injury, and stroke (see http://www.icf-research-branch.org). It is important to note that these efforts are based on international consensus building efforts, and the experts involved are likely influenced by systems other than the *DSM*, such as the *ICD-10*.

ICF Core Sets have been constructed for depression (Cieza et al., 2004), both a comprehensive version and a brief version (Ayuso-Mateos,

2009; Stucki et al., 2005). A core set is being developed at the Universidad Autonoma de Madrid, Spain, for bipolar disorder (Ayuso-Mateos, 2009). Data available from Core Set for Depression are reviewed next.

CORE SET FOR DEPRESSION

The first *ICF* Core Set generated for a mental disorder was for depression (Cieza et al., 2004). It stands to reason that the first coding effort focused on depression; the Global Burden of Disease analysis showed that unipolar depressive disorders were ranked as the fourth leading cause of burden among all diseases (WHO, 2001b). Depression accounted for 4.4% of the total Disability Adjusted Years (DALYs) and was the leading cause of Years Lived with Disability (YLD), accounting for 11.9% of total YLDs.

By the year 2020, depression is expected to increase to 5.7% of the total burden of disease, becoming the second leading cause of DALYs lost. Worldwide, it will be second only to ischemic heart disease for DALYs lost. If recent trends continue, depression will be the highest ranked cause of burden of disease in countries reporting data to WHO (WHO, 2001b).

This overview of how the code set for depression was constructed is based on the 2004 publication by Cieza and associates.

Need for Effective Assessment and Treatment

Developing an *ICF* Core Set for Depression made sense due to the international prevalence of the mental disorder, and the associated need for effective treatment was also a compelling rationale. Depression has been associated with significant loss of quality of life (Kennedy, Eisfeld, & Cooke, 2001; Whalley & McKenna, 1995), increased morbidity and mortality (Everson, Roberts, Goldberg, & Kaplan, 1998; Murphy, Monson, Olivier, et al., 1987; Vaccarino, Kaal, Abramson, & Krumholz, 2001), and economic burden largely due to lost work productivity (Wang, Simon, & Kessler, 2003).

When Cieza and associates (2004) began work on the *ICF* Core Set for Depression, they reviewed current assessment modalities and found that depressive disorders are most often reported to and managed by primary-care physicians (Wittchen, Holsboer, & Jacobi, 2001). In light of increasing patient demands and the limited time and resources available to primary-care doctors, the use of complex and detailed measures to evaluate depressive symptoms was thought almost impossible. They surmised that it would be useful application of the *ICF* to identify relevant code sets that can result in an efficient and practical tool covering the spectrum of symptoms and limitations in functioning of patients dealing with depression.

Based on the *ICF*, a consensus building process was conducted with rehabilitation health professionals to identify a list of *ICF* categories relevant to depression. They set out to construct a *Brief ICF Core Set* to be rated in all patients included in a clinical study with depression and a *Comprehensive ICF Core Set* to guide multidisciplinary assessments in patients with depression.

Method of Core Set Development

Our earlier discussion relating *ICF* codes to the *DSM* addressed only One- and Two-Level Classification Codes within the *ICF* structure. This core set initiative focused on the Detailed Level of *ICF* Classification. Core set development involved a formal decision-making and consensus process, which integrated evidence gathered from preliminary studies, including a Delphi exercise (Weigl et al., 2004), a systematic review (Brockow et al., 2004), and empirical data collection using the *ICF* checklist (Ewert et al., 2004). After training in the *ICF* and based on review of preliminary studies, relevant *ICF* categories were identified in a formal consensus process by international experts from different backgrounds.

Twenty experts (including six psychiatrists, six physicians specializing in physical and rehabilitation medicine, four psychologists, two physical therapists, one nurse, and one occupational therapist) from eight countries participated. The decision-making process involved three working groups, two groups of five and one group of six. The process was facilitated by a coordinator and three working group leaders.

Results

The 121 categories of the *Comprehensive ICF Core Set for Depression* are made up of 45 (37%) categories from the component *Body Functions*, 48 (40%) from the component *Activities and Participation*, and 28 (23%) from the component *Environmental Factors*. No categories from the component *Body Structures* are included. Tables for the Comprehensive Core Set for Depression include one for Body Functions (Table 11.1), one for Activities and Participation (Table 11.2), and one table for Environmental Factors (Table 11.3).

TABLE 11.1 *ICF* **Categories for Body Functions, Comprehensive Core Set for Depression**

ICF Code 2nd Level	ICF Code 3rd Level	ICF Category Title
b117		Intellectual functions
b126		Temperament and personality functions
	b1260	Extraversion
	b1261	Agreeableness
	b1262	Conscientiousness
	b1263	Psychic stability
	b1265	Optimism
	b1266	Confidence
b130		Energy and drive functions
	b1300	Energy level
	b1301	Motivation
	b1302	Appetite
	b1304	Impulse control
b134		Sleep functions
	b1340	Amount of sleep
	b1341	Onset of sleep
	b1342	Maintenance of sleep
	b1343	Quality of sleep
	b1344	Functions involving the sleep cycle
b140		Attention functions
b144		Memory functions
b147		Psychomotor functions
b152		Emotional functions
	b1520	Appropriateness of emotion
	b1521	Regulation of emotion
	b1522	Range of emotion
b160		Thought functions
	b1600	Pace of thought
	b1601	Form of thought
	b1602	Content of thought
	b1603	Control of thought

b164		Higher-level cognitive functions
	b1641	Organization and planning
	b1642	Time management
	b1644	Insight
	b1645	Judgment
b180		Experience of self and time functions
	b1800	Experience of self
	b1801	Body image
b280		Sensation of pain
b460		Sensations associated with cardiovascular and respiratory functions
b530		Weight maintenance functions
b535		Sensations associated with the digestive system
b640		Sexual functions
b780		Sensations related to muscles and movement functions

Cieza et al. (2004).

TABLE 11.2 *ICF* Categories for Activities Participation, Comprehensive Core Set for Depression

ICF Code 2nd Level	*ICF* Code 3rd Level	*ICF* Category Title
d110		Watching
d115		Listening
d163		Thinking
d166		Reading
d175		Solving problems
d177		Making decisions
d210		Undertaking a single task
d220		Undertaking multiple tasks
d230		Carrying out daily routine
	d2301	Managing daily routine
	d2302	Completing the daily routine
	d2303	Managing one's own activity level

(*Continued*)

TABLE 11.2 (Continued)

ICF Code 2nd Level	ICF Code 3rd Level	ICF Category Title
d240		Handling stress and other psychological demands
d310		Communicating with—receiving spoken messages
d315		Communicating with—receiving nonverbal messages
d330		Speaking
d335		Producing nonverbal messages
d350		Conversation
d355		Discussion
d470		Using transportation (car, bus, train, plane, etc.)
d475		Driving (riding bicycle and motorbike, driving car, riding animals, etc.)
d510		Washing oneself
d520		Caring for body parts
d540		Dressing
d550		Eating
d560		Drinking
d570		Looking after one's health
d620		Acquisition of goods and services
d630		Preparing meals
d640		Doing housework
d650		Caring for household objects
d660		Assisting others
d710		Basic interpersonal interactions
d720		Complex interpersonal interactions
d730		Relating with strangers
d750		Informal social relationships
d760		Family relationships
d770		Intimate relationships
d830		Higher education

d845	Acquiring, keeping, and terminating a job
d850	Remunerative employment
d860	Basic economic transactions
d865	Complex economic transactions
d870	Economic self-sufficiency
d910	Community life
d920	Recreation and leisure
d930	Religion and spirituality
d950	Political life and citizenship

Cieza et al. (2004).

TABLE 11.3 *ICF* Categories for Environmental Factors, Comprehensive Core Set for Depression

ICF Code 2nd Level	*ICF* Code 3rd Level	*ICF* Category Title
	e1101	Drugs
e165		Assets
e225		Climate
e240		Light
e245		Time-related changes
e250		Sound
e310		Immediate family
e320		Friends
e325		Acquaintances, peers, colleagues, neighbors, and community members
e330		People in positions of authority
e340		Personal care providers and personal assistants
e355		Health professionals
e360		Health-related professionals
e410		Individual attitudes of immediate family members
e415		Individual attitudes of extended family members

(*Continued*)

TABLE 11.3 (Continued)

ICF Code 2nd Level	*ICF* Code 3rd Level	*ICF* Category Title
e420		Individual attitudes of friends
e425		Individual attitudes of acquaintances, peers, colleagues, neighbors, and community members
e430		Individual attitudes of people in positions of authority
e440		Individual attitudes of personal care providers and personal assistants
e450		Individual attitudes of health professionals
e455		Individual attitudes of health-related professionals
e460		Societal attitudes
e465		Social norms, practices, and ideologies
e525		Housing services, systems, and policies
e570		Social security services, systems, and policies
e575		General social support services, systems, and policies
e580		Health services, systems and policies
e590		Labor and employment services, systems, and policies

Cieza et al. (2004).

Some specifics about the development of the Depression Core Set are worth noting.

Body Functions

It was not surprising that most of the functions selected within the component *Body Functions* were mental functions. Many of them are at the detailed level of the *ICF* classification, suggesting that an in-depth understanding is required to fully classify functioning associated with depression.

A number of somatic items were included by the consensus panel, including pain, sensations associated with cardiovascular, respiratory, digestive, and muscular and movement functions. Weight maintenance and sexual functions were also thought relevant to the core set.

Activities and Participation

A total of 48 categories and all nine chapters of the Activities and Participation component of the *ICF* were endorsed by the consensus panel. Activity limitations and participation restrictions appeared particularly relevant for the diagnosis of depression. The high importance of the support and relationships from "significant others" for patients with depression is also reflected in the number of selected categories within this chapter, suggesting the need to involve the family or "significant others" in the treatment process.

Environmental Factors

All chapters of the component Environmental Factors are represented in the Depression Core Set. The 28 Environmental Factors categories, or 23% of the categories of the core set, represent aspects of the physical, social, and attitudinal environment of patients with depression.

The chapter Attitudes represents more than one-third of the total number of Environmental Factors included in the core set, perhaps reflecting the impact that attitudes of "significant others" and society in general can have on people with depression. People suffering from mental and behavioral disorders face stigma and discrimination in all parts of the world, influencing their individual behavior, social life, and general functioning and recovery (WHO, 2001b).

The relevance of mental health policy and service provision was discussed and recognized in the Depression Core Set group. Five categories of the chapter Services, Systems and Policies were included in the core set. As with Activities and Participation, the importance of Support and Relationships was endorsed here as well.

Discussion of the Results

The *Comprehensive ICF Core Set* for Depression was one of 12 such code sets constructed in the initial effort to create seminal core sets for the most burdensome of chronic health conditions. As it turned out, the Depression Core Set is the second largest of the 12 seminal core sets, with the largest being that for cerebral vascular accidents (stroke). The fact that

121 categories were included reflects the complexity of health and functioning in patients with depression.

Body Structures

No category from the component *Body Structures* was selected. The inclusion of the category s110 *structure of the brain* was discussed among the different experts. At the end of a long discussion, they decided that the brain is a relevant body structure but not an indispensable body structure to comprehensively describe the functioning and health of patients with depression. The *structure of the brain* was, therefore, not included in the *ICF Core Sets*.

Issue of Suicide

The panel of experts wanted to include an *ICF* category to address suicide, but this is not currently addressed within the *ICF*. Since Mood Disorders like depression are found in as many as 90% of completed suicides (Goldsmith, Pellmar, Kleinman, & Bunney, 2002), such a category needs to be addressed in clinical studies and multidisciplinary assessments of patients with depression. Thus, the inclusion of a category addressing suicide should be considered in possible future revisions of the *ICF*.

Brief ICF Core Set for Depression

The Brief *ICF* Core Set for Depression represents a far narrower view, focusing on the most important chapters and categories for the different components. There were some procedural difficulties with the consensus exercise to select the brief items, and therefore extensive validation and testing of the comprehensive set is necessary in order to inform the selection of a definitive Brief *ICF* Core Set for Depression.

Problems notwithstanding, the Brief Core Set contains 21 Second-Level classifications and 10 Detailed-Level classifications or 26% of the Comprehensive Core Set. Nine *ICF* categories were chosen from the Body Functions component, 12 from Activities and Participation, and 10 from Environmental Factors. The fourth table included here from the study reveals the results of the second ranking exercise to create the *Brief ICF Core Set for Depression* (see Table 11.4).

Critique

The Comprehensive Core Set with 121 items may still be too long for some clinical settings. Therefore, it will be important to test and validate this first

TABLE 11.4 *ICF* Categories, Brief Core Set for Depression, Rank Order

ICF Component	Rank Order	*ICF* Code	*ICF* Category Title
Body Functions	1	b1263	Psychic stability
	2	b1300	Energy level
	3	b1301	Motivation
	4	b1522	Range of emotion
	5	b1265	Optimism
	6	b140	Attention functions
	7	b1521	Regulation of emotion
	8	b1302	Appetite
	9	b147	Psychomotor functions
Activities and Participation	1	d2301	Managing daily routine
	2	d177	Making decisions
	3	d175	Solving problems
	4	d770	Intimate relationships
	5	d240	Handling stress and other psychological demands
	6	d760	Family relationships
	7	d350	Conversation
	8	d570	Looking after one's health
	8.5	d163	Thinking
	9	d510	Washing oneself
	10	d2303	Managing one's own activity level
	10	d845	Acquiring, keeping, and terminating a job
Environmental Factors	1	e310	Immediate family
	2	e320	Friends
	3	e355	Health professionals
	4	e1101	Drugs
	5	e410	Individual attitudes of immediate family members

(*Continued*)

TABLE 11.4 (Continued)

ICF Component	Rank Order	*ICF* Code	*ICF* Category Title
	6	e325	Acquaintances, peers, colleagues, neighbors, and community members
	7	e420	Individual attitudes of friends
	8	e580	Health services, systems, and policies
	9	e450	Individual attitudes of health professionals
	10	e415	Individual attitudes of extended family members

Cieza et al. (2004).

version from the perspectives of different professions, in different clinical settings and in different countries.

One clear limitation of an effort like this one is that irrespective of the quality of experts with different professional backgrounds from eight different countries, the results of any consensus process will likely differ with different groups of experts. For all the above-mentioned reasons, the first version of the *ICF Core Sets* is only recommended for validation or pilot studies.

CORE SET FOR MOOD DISORDERS

Given the *ICF*'s sheer depth and breadth of classificatory precision, having 1,464 categorical codes from which to choose, as an entire code it is unwieldy for clinical practice and research. The utility of developing *ICF* Core Sets for other mental disorders is clear. Within the Department of Psychiatry at the Universidad Autonoma de Madrid, Spain, work is underway to develop a new Core Set for Bipolar Disorder (Ayuso-Mateos, 2009). Just as the Core Set for Depression was among the more complex core sets constructed to date, the complex limitations in functioning and various interactions with environmental factors associated with Bipolar Disorder will encourage a complex and complete core set of *ICF* codes. Further, associated research will reveal areas where the *ICF* is currently insufficient and needs further development (e.g., no current way to address suicidality in the current iteration of the *ICF*).

CHAPTER 12

The Promise of the *ICF-2* and the *DSM-5*

PREVIEW QUESTIONS

1. What is the immediate utility of the *ICF* as it exists now?
2. What are some of the important new directions for development of the *ICF*?
3. What are some of the concerns expressed regarding the *DSM-5* revision process?
4. How can the *DSM-5* revision efforts move forward most effectively?

We conclude this text with a discussion of future directions for the *ICF* and *DSM* classification systems and related recommendations for mental-health professionals.

FUTURE DIRECTIONS FOR THE *ICF*

In Part I of this text, we supported the significance of the historical development of the *ICF* for health care in general and for mental health care specifically. We reviewed the prevalence of disability and described the WHO Family Classification System as it is currently constructed. We also described ongoing core set and cross-walking efforts, clinical implementation initiatives, including the development of *ICF*-based assessment tools. We conclude our discussion of the *ICF* by highlighting critical future directions for the nascent coding system.

Immediate Utility and Activity

Although the *ICF* is in its first iteration of its current conceptual framework, and the implementation manual for the United States is still in preparation, the *ICF* as it exists has immediate utility for both clinical research and educational endeavors. First, the conceptual framework is useful in conceptualizing disability in various contexts (Peterson & Paul, 2009). One can use the components of the *ICF* to organize case information, target interventions, and evaluate the effectiveness of treatment.

For example, Body Functions and Structures inform biological bases of behavior and impairment as well as potential in functioning. Activities and Participation bring to focus functioning within a given context or what a person is able to do in the real world. The difference between what one can ideally do and what one does may become the focus of intervention targeting. Consideration of facilitators and barriers in the environment directly inform the differences between Activity and Participation or between one's capacity in function and ultimate performance in a given context. *ICF* constructs within its rich conceptual framework, can be used to organize information into a meaningful picture of health and functioning, inform treatment and research, and ultimately provide foci for evaluating the efficacy of an intervention.

Further, while core set research is in the very early stages of its development, individuals working with the *ICF* can create their own core sets and contribute to the peer-reviewed literature with proposed core set revisions, new code sets, and related assessment tools. It seems very important at this time in the *ICF*'s development for its stakeholders to realize the potential impact their work can have on the future development of the *ICF*, to be concerned with what the *ICF* can be used for at this point rather than what it cannot, and use information about its shortcomings to create solutions that better the *ICF*.

Clinical Implementation Manual for the *ICF*

From 2001–2002, the author participated in the alpha drafting effort for the WHO-APA collaboration, *The Procedural Manual and Guide for the Standardized Application of the ICF.* The alpha drafting team's work laid the foundation for ongoing manual development efforts that continue as this book goes to press. According to the APA practice directorate (personal communication, February 12, 2010) the *Manual* (see Reed et al., 2005) is in the final editing process, and should be ready for release sometime during 2010.

Once the alpha drafting team's work was done, similarly constructed multidisciplinary teams continued work on different aspects of the *ICF*. Current professional associations involved with developing the manual include the American Occupational Therapy Association, the American

Physical Therapy Association, the American Speech-Language-Hearing Association, the American Therapeutic Recreation Association, and the National Association of Social Workers. These associations are committed to raising the level of awareness about the *ICF* within their respective memberships, and recognize the utility of the *ICF* for informing care provided by their members.

The Body Functions section of the manual was available online during 2007 with invitation to a broad range of stakeholders to comment on its utility in classifying functioning, disability, and health. The plan was to continue posting sections of the manual for public review and feedback. At the present time, the complete manual is in the final editing stage and will hopefully be distributed in tandem with the next meeting of the North American Collaborating Center's annual meeting in 2010.

As stakeholders learn the value of the *ICF*'s biopsychosocial approach, it will be clear how it can improve intervention targeting, facilitate the evaluation of treatment outcomes in a systematic way that can be shared internationally with other research efforts. The release of the Clinical Implementation Manual will greatly assist consistent application of the *ICF* in the United States, and hopefully enhance its utility in mental health practice. Readers interested in ongoing international development efforts for the *ICF* can point their browsers to http://www.who.int/classifications/icf/en for the English version of the *ICF*-based Web site. Readers are also encouraged to explore the *ICF* through *ICF* Browser, the online version of the *ICF*, at http://apps.who.int/classifications/icfbrowser/.

Future Core Sets

We reviewed the literature that suggested the need for *ICF* Core Sets of codes in order for the *ICF* to be practically useful, especially in clinical settings. A review of the literature revealed little progress in mental disorder core set development beyond the work done for depression. There is a core set development underway, specifically the development of a core set for Bipolar Disorder (Ayuso-Mateos, 2009). The *ICF* Research Branch of the WHO Family of International Classifications Collaborating Center suggested on their Web site that several other core set development efforts underway relevant to mental health, including core sets for dementia, sleep, and traumatic brain injury. These ongoing initiatives are critical to successful clinical implementation and related research for the *ICF* in working with people who have mental disorders.

Eventually, a compendium of available core sets for mental disorders can be included in a text such as this one, in parallel with the presentation of the *DSM* and *ICD*. Given the upcoming revision of the *DSM* to its fifth edition (estimated 2013), developing an *ICF* Core Set specific to *DSM-IV-TR* criteria may not be the most auspicious use of one's time, which is the most compelling reason why our current level of cross-walking analysis remained at the one- and two-level of classification. A subsequent edition of this text may expand to include core sets for the most frequently occurring mental disorders as defined in the *DSM-5*, and as informed by core set research.

Refinement of *ICF* Components

Baron and Linden (2008) recommended that future work on the *ICF* focus on convergence in terminology between the *ICF* and *ICD* systems. Specifically, they recommend making the distinctions between Body Functions and Activities and Participation more clear. Jones and Sinclair (2008) concur with Baron and Linden's recommendation, suggesting that Activities and Participation codes need greater specificity.

It is also clear that the Personal factor component of the *ICF* needs to be part of the actual classification system. Consumers of mental health services will play a critical role in the development of codes in this category, trying to capture the complexity of demographic variables and the contextual nuances of an individual's health and functioning. Having Personal factor codes will vastly improve the ability of the *ICF* to convey standardized disability and health information across disciplines and nationalities.

ICF and the *ICD*

Baron and Linden (2008) also used the *ICF* conceptual framework to make the distinction between "disorders of function" and "disorders of capacity." Disorders of function relate directly to impairments associated with mental disorders that can be coded under Body Functions. Disorders of capacity are those coded under Activities and Participation. They propose that there is no one-to-one relationship between functions and capacity, and that both have direct and indirect influence on adaptive functioning (2009), supporting the utility of the distinction between these *ICF* components.

Related to this conceptual discussion, Baron and Linden (2005) created an instrument to specifically measure "disorders of capacity" through the *Mini-ICF-P*, measuring disorders of capacity in the context of mental disorders. They rated 13 capacity domains that can be impaired by psychopathology: (1) adherence to regulations, (2) structuring of tasks,

(3) flexibility, (4) competency, (5) endurance, (6) assertiveness, (7) contact with others, (8) public exposure, (9) intimacy, (10) nonwork activities, (11) self-maintenance, (12) mobility, and (13) judgment. Each item in the *Mini-ICF-P* is rated on a Likert Scale: 0 = no disability; 1 = mild disability; 2 = moderate disability; 3 = severe disability; and 4 = total disability.

They applied the *Mini-ICF-P* instrument to explore sick leave as it relates to impairment from mental disorders. They found support for their contention that severity of symptoms does not consistently predict social and occupational consequences of mental disorders. The importance of disorders of capacity and disorders of participation (activity limitations and participation restrictions based on the social context) was emphasized in the results of their study.

The United States is a member of the World Health Organization (WHO), and as such is required to report mortality and morbidity data to WHO using the *ICD*, and as mentioned in Part I of this text, is encouraged to use the *ICF* where appropriate in health-related initiatives such as those that use the *ICD*. Because of the *ICD*'s salience in mental health care, and its sister-relationship with the *ICF*, a list of the mental and behavioral disorders section of the *ICD* is included in the Appendix as a comparative reference to both the *ICF* and *DSM-IV-TR*. The reader is encouraged to follow the URL link listed at the end of the appendix to explore the complete clinical descriptions and diagnostic guidelines associated with these codes.

ICF-DSM Nexus

The author believes that the *ICF* in its current iteration shows promise for enriching the utility of the well-established *DSM*. Axes III, IV, and V of the *DSM* have long called attention to the functional impact of biopsychosocial factors on mental health and functioning. The *ICF* provides a broader field from which to draw detailed classification of specific mental functions, related impairments, activity limitations, and participation restrictions, all sensitive to personal and environmental factors for a given person's circumstance of health and functioning.

As clinical implementation efforts continue for the *ICF*, and revision efforts progress for the *ICD-11* and the *DSM-5*, the time is right for clinicians and researchers to explore the nexus between diagnosis and function. Cross-walking efforts between the *ICF* and *DSM* will bring the many benefits of using functional data to enhancing diagnostic information. As *ICF* Core Sets are constructed and developed in association with specific *DSM* and *ICD* diagnoses, the core sets can be used to create assessment tools that are informed by both diagnosis and function, creating a more comprehensive picture of mental health and function.

Conclusion: *ICF*

In today's economic climate where most are being asked to do more with less, the prospects of clinicians embracing something that does not have a readymade instrument that saves time or money, or the promise of researchers pursuing vigorous scholarship in an area not associated with significant external funding, are remote at best. Notwithstanding these factors, I believe the *ICF* holds great promise for affecting how all of health care thinks about functioning, disability, and health.

While a limited number of instruments exist at present or are currently in development, the conceptual framework of the *ICF* is ready for application to any clinical scenario, can inform assessment and treatment of people with psychological difficulties, and has been and can be used effectively to educate students in the health professions. Instruments are being constructed using the *ICF* framework. Core sets have been and will continue to be established to inform future use of the *ICF* with specific disability presentations. Other applications will include applying the *ICF* for use in specific contexts (e.g., Peterson & Paul, 2009; see also the special issue on using the *ICF* in different treatment settings, published in *Disability and Rehabilitation*, 2008).

FUTURE DIRECTIONS FOR THE *DSM*

Our review of the *DSM-IV-TR* in Part II of this text was ambitious and cursory, and relied on simultaneous consumption of the *DSM-IV-TR* itself. Important companion materials were suggested, and the importance of appropriate training was emphasized in this review. *DSM*'s historical context was presented as a parallel to the history presented in Part I of the text. The *DSM*'s organization, conceptual framework, and qualifiers were systematically presented. The *DSM*'s diagnoses were reviewed from front to back, and we ended with a brief discussion of the *DSM-5* revision process. We will expand that discussion here as we conclude Part III of our text.

Hopefully, Part II's level of detail, in tandem with the presentation of the *ICF* in Part I, and the integrative discussion that began Part III of this text, were sufficient to highlight the synergy created by combining these conceptual frameworks into an integrated picture of health, functioning, and disability. Here we close with the author's suggestions for the *DSM* revision process, and some encouragement to aspiring mental health professionals.

DSM-5

Given the wide range of professional stakeholders involved historically with the assessment, diagnosis, and treatment of mental disorders based on the *DSM*, including the recent emergence of many master's terminal mental health professionals (e.g., Licensed Mental Health Counselors, Licensed Clinical Professional Counselors, Licensed Professional Clinical Counselors and the like) who are receiving third-party payment for their mental health-related services, it will be important for the *DSM* to be inclusive of the professions that use it in clinical practice and research. Unfortunately, the current key stakeholders in the *DSM-5* Task Force and associated diagnostic work groups have been largely only psychiatrists.

Psychologists have played an important role in the *DSM*'s development historically, bringing assessment and treatment expertise to working with people who have mental disorders. There is only one psychologist currently involved with the *DSM-5* Task Force, a departure from more inclusive revision processes. In contrast, the *ICD-11* revision process is multidisciplinary by design, and its revision process includes psychologists as key stakeholders to the chapter on mental and behavioral disorders. The International Union of Psychological Science is officially represented on the *ICD* revision steering committee (Martin, 2009).

It is my humble opinion that the APA's apparent efforts to strengthen psychiatrists' role and diminish others' role in the *DSM-5* revision process is unwise. The controversies surrounding conflicts of interest and lack of transparency in the *DSM* revision process are of great concern, and could place a strain on the perceptions stakeholders have about the *DSM*. The APA administrative decision to limit the institutional memory around the table at early planning meetings, while probably a good idea creatively, caused considerable political turmoil in cyberspace and added to concerns of credibility for the revision process. The APA could do damage to the *DSM* by becoming too exclusive with the revision efforts for its taxonomy of mental disorders. All of these developments raise the question whether a single mental health association should have solitary control of the official diagnostic system for so many other mental health professionals.

The *ICD-11* is moving forward with international revision efforts in harmony with the *DSM*, and has the potential to become the dominant taxonomy in international mental health. The Health Insurance Portability and

Accountability Act (HIPAA), a massive piece of legislation that governs how medical information is shared electronically (see Peterson, Hautamaki, & Walton, 2007) requires the use of *ICD* codes rather than *DSM* codes in all electronic transactions. Eventually, *ICD-11* data will be integrated into health informatics systems that are accessible worldwide. The *ICD-11* will impact reporting and billing practices internationally for years to come (Martin, 2009). I believe the utility of the *DSM* will be optimized by including all of its stakeholders in the revision process, and to do otherwise, given the zeitgeist surrounding the *ICD* and the *ICF*, could be to the *DSM's* detriment.

Conclusion: *DSM-5*

It will be interesting to see how many of the current recommendations for additions and modifications to the *DSM-5* actually result in lasting change. There are some who believe that the course of the *DSM-5* revision process has been too secretive, and too revolutionary for the state of our knowledge base. Some believe that the effort to identify sub-threshold disorders as a primary prevention to the development of more severe mental disorders is premature relative to the science needed to identify such subtle differences; the assessment technology may simply not be available. Open and vigorous debate around these issues, involving all *DSM* stakeholders in the process, will help to resolve these issues.

Several examples are worth noting here. The proposal to include a Psychosis Risk Syndrome presents a potential risk of a good many false positives, overtreatment, and the associated psychological distress, as our assessment resources are quite limited in this area. Another proposed diagnosis, Mixed Anxiety Depressive Disorder, has been perceived as tapping vague enough symptoms that a large segment of the population would become diagnosable, quickly becoming one of the most common of all mental disorders in the *DSM*. A third potential problem exists in the proposed Minor Neurocognitive Disorder, the proposed cutoff for which could include up to 13.5% of the population (see prevalence discussion in Part I of this text as a basis of comparison of prevalence of other mental disorders). The proposed Temper Dysfunctional Disorder with Dysphoria could be conceived as a misguided medicalization of temper outbursts. They are also proposing that depressive symptoms manifested during bereavement may be diagnosed as Major Depressive Disorder, potentially making grief resulting from the loss of a loved one a mental disorder. There are other examples of proposed diagnoses that have the potential for creating great complexity in the forensic arena, simply because they relate to behavior that is present in large portions of the population. These proposed changes as this text goes to press could result in a dramatic increase in the rates of mental disorders, and change the nature of what defines a mental disorder. Again, open vigorous debate among all stakeholders needs to occur, informed by our best scholarship, to resolve concerns around these proposed revisions.

The proposed revisions also suggest changes to the *DSM* multiaxial system itself. The proposal to remove the axes all together would eliminate the distinction of diagnoses as states (Axis I) versus traits (Axis II), the contribution of medical conditions to functioning (Axis III), contextual stressors (Axis IV), as well as the loss of a convenient and familiar rating for overall severity of symptoms or degree of resulting impairment (Axis V). In this writer's opinion, such a change would move the *DSM* more toward the medical model, and away from the biopsychosocial approach to which the multiaxial system currently aspires. This stands in stark contrast with the international movement to embrace the biopsychosocial model, as manifest in the *ICD-11* and *ICF*-related efforts.

One thing is clear from the *DSM-5* revision efforts to date; they have not been collaborative with other key stakeholders in mental health care. The degree to which *DSM* stakeholders are willing to be inclusive of other mental health professions will be telling for the future of the *DSM*. It will also be interesting to see whether the use of the *DSM* is impacted by the increasing presence of the *ICD* codes in the international management of medical information.

On the bright side of all things *DSM* and *ICF*, as these systems evolve, revision efforts can be coordinated to obtain maximum benefit for both systems. Just as efforts are underway to harmonize the *ICD-11* and *DSM-5*, similar efforts can be made with the next version of the *ICF*, including the ongoing development of mental disorder core sets, cross walking the *ICF* to existing seminal assessment tools, and perhaps even the development of instruments uniquely based on the *ICF-DSM* nexus explored in this text.

FUTURE DIRECTIONS FOR MENTAL-HEALTH PROFESSIONALS AND THE *ICF*

One thing seems clear from our review of the psychological aspects of functioning, disability, and health; there exists an ongoing theme of change. Revisions of the *ICD* and *DSM* systems have reflected the changes of the times in which they were revised. Movement away from the medical model toward a more inclusive model of disability, and embracing the dignity and worth of all people through the civil rights movement, effected lasting change in these classification systems, including the *ICF*. There is no doubt that more change will come; it may be difficult to know what mental health care will look like 5, 10, or even 20 years from now.

Treatments That Work

One bit of good news for the future of mental health care is that there are treatments that work, plain and simple. "There is a substantial evidence base underlying psychopharmacological and psychosocial treatments" (Nathan & Gorman, 2007, p. viii). The degree to which they work depends on the accurate conceptualization of the problem being treated, the skilled application of the requisite treatment that has evidence of effectiveness, and appropriate follow-up in assessing treatment outcomes. Recent research suggests that there are important differences (that can be shown empirically) in efficacy among treatments, and those consuming this new research are responding by basing their treatment efforts in kind (Nathan & Gorman, 2007). We have shown in this text how the *ICF* can assist with case conceptualization, how it can inform the treatment of mental disorders and evaluation of related outcomes, and promote mental health.

It was mentioned earlier in Part II of this text that there exists a detailed evaluative review of current research on treatments for mental disorders that are effective, edited by Nathan and Gorman, and currently in its third edition (2007). The chapters of their text were written by psychologists and psychiatrists, all who contributed in significant ways to the scholarship in their respective areas of practice. The intent of their text was to

> . . . present the most rigorous, scientifically based evidence for the efficacy of treatments that is available. At the same time, it is clear that for some disorders there are treatments widely recognized by experienced clinicians to be useful that may not have been subjected to rigorous investigation for a variety of reasons. Our aim is to be clear with the readers what treatments are felt by a large number of experts to be valuable but have never been properly, scientifically examined, and what treatments are known to be of little value. (p. vii)

At the beginning of Nathan & Gorman's text, there is a Summary of Treatments that work according to "syndrome" or diagnosis. For each syndrome they list a specific treatment type, and present standard of proof that support the treatment's efficacy. Related seminal references are provided. Twenty syndromes are reviewed in the summary, and the pharmacological and psychosocial treatments associated with each syndrome range in number from two to five treatments for each syndrome.

Managing such a body of knowledge requires advanced, graduate-level coursework in diagnosis and treatment of mental disorders, psychopharmacology, and theories of counseling and psychotherapy, which is outside the scope of this text. However, the reader is encouraged to keep current with the peer reviewed literature related to pharmacological and psychosocial treatment of mental disorders, and the Nathan and Gorman text is a great way to become familiar with contemporary practice. It is also an exemplar for the *DSM-5* Revision task force, how psychologists and psychiatrists can work collaboratively to promote best practices in both professions, for the good of the mental health care enterprise.

Psychotherapy and Behavior Change

Another resource that has become a standard reference for psychotherapy citation and practice is Bergin and Garfield's *Handbook of Psychotherapy and Behavior Change*, currently in its fifth edition under new editorship (Lambert, 2004). The text is over 800 pages in length and quite dense in content, and has been a seminal reference for understanding psychotherapy since 1971. In addition to focusing on thorough overviews of empirical studies supporting different therapies, the text also addresses the limitations of traditional science for working in some contexts in mental health, and the philosophical struggle between empiricists and theorists in psychotherapeutic endeavors. Qualitative methods are embraced as a way to provide evidence for the validity and reliability of psychotherapy.

Bergin and Garfield's Handbook provides an overview of the research on constructs essential to the psychotherapeutic process. Client, therapist, process, and outcome variables research is reviewed in great detail in sections one and two of the text. The reader learns how these variables impact the efficacy and effectiveness of psychotherapy. The text provides an overview of the major approaches to psychotherapy, including behavioral, cognitive, cognitive-behavioral, and experiential therapies. The text concludes with an overview of the research addressing application of psychotherapy in special groups and settings, including working with children and adolescents, couples and families, small groups, and culturally diverse populations. There is also a chapter focusing on pharmacotherapy, or the use of psychopharmacology with psychotherapy.

There has been much debate among experts in psychology and psychiatry about what treatments work and why they are effective. Historically, some have been inclined to conclude that all psychosocial therapies work due to a set of common therapeutic factors, and that our efforts should focus on those common factors to successful treatment. Others in competing fields and managed care have argued that none of the talk therapies work better than a placebo. A careful review of the peer-reviewed literature supports the effectiveness of pharmacological and psychosocial treatments for mental disorders. The two seminal reference texts just reviewed are recommended reading to inform diagnosis and treatment of mental disorders. In this author's opinion, it is particularly exciting that we are just beginning to tap into the utility of using functional information (*ICF*) in addition to diagnostic information (*DSM*, *ICD*) to enhance this body of work.

You Can Make a Difference

One way to remain current with ongoing change is through your professional associations, both locally and nationally. Maintaining effective professional networks can be much easier when being active within your organization in some capacity. Consuming peer-reviewed publications that address mental health issues is critical to remaining current in a science (i.e., psychology) that is relatively young and ever-expanding in its depth and breadth of knowledge. It was through professional association and publication activity that the author became involved in *ICF*-related initiatives that contributed to the content of this text.

The reader is encouraged not to underestimate the role that you can play within your own profession in contributing to the development of something like the *ICF*. Being willing to collaborate with local universities in research, and remaining current in the literature associated with it provides you with the opportunity to make a real contribution to your discipline. The *ICF* is relatively new in its development, so prospects for your involvement in seminal work are promising.

An Invitation for Your Feedback

The reader is encouraged to provide any feedback about the contents of this book directly to the author's e-mail address, at dpeters3@exchange.calstatela.edu. Because it is the author's first text and the first iteration of this enterprise, there are no doubt errors to correct, major points overlooked, and possibilities unexplored. Your critical feedback or complements are equally welcomed and appreciated.

ICD-10 Chapter 5: Mental and Behavioral Disorders

Major categories for this section of the *ICD-10*, F00–F99, Mental and Behavioral Disorders:

1.1 (F00–F09) Organic, including symptomatic, mental disorders
1.2 (F10–F19) Mental and behavioral disorders due to psychoactive substance use
1.3 (F20–F29) Schizophrenia, schizotypal and delusional disorders
1.4 (F30–F39) Mood (affective) disorders
1.5 (F40–F48) Neurotic, stress-related and somatoform disorders
1.6 (F50–F59) Behavioral syndromes associated with physiological disturbances and physical factors
1.7 (F60–F69) Disorders of adult personality and behavior
1.8 (F70–F79) Mental retardation
1.9 (F80–F89) Disorders of psychological development
1.10 (F90–F98) Behavioral and emotional disorders with onset usually occurring in childhood and adolescence
1.11 (F99) Unspecified mental disorder

Major categories with their subcategories for F00–F99—Mental and behavioral disorders (the actual *ICD-10* for this section, 267 pages in all, contains clinical descriptions and diagnostic guidelines, which are not included here).

Source: Adapted from *International Statistical Classification of Diseases and Related Health Problems, Tenth Revision (ICD-10)* by the World Health Organization, 1992, Geneva, Switzerland: Author.

(F00–F09) Organic, including symptomatic, mental disorders

(F00.) Dementia in Alzheimer's disease

(F01.) Vascular dementia

(F01.1) Multi-infarct dementia

(F02.) Dementia in other diseases classified elsewhere

(F02.0) Dementia in Pick's disease

(F02.1) Dementia in Creutzfeldt-Jakob disease

(F02.2) Dementia in Huntington's disease

(F02.3) Dementia in Parkinson's disease

(F02.4) Dementia in human immunodeficiency virus (HIV) disease

(F03.) Unspecified dementia

(F04.) Organic amnesic syndrome, not induced by alcohol and other psychoactive substances

(F05.) Delirium, not induced by alcohol and other psychoactive substances

(F06.) Other mental disorders due to brain damage and dysfunction and to physical disease

(F06.0) Organic hallucinosis

(F06.1) Organic catatonic disorder

(F06.2) Organic delusional (schizophrenia-like) disorder

(F06.3) Organic mood (affective) disorders

(F06.4) Organic anxiety disorder

(F06.5) Organic dissociative disorder

(F06.6) Organic emotionally labile (asthenic) disorder

(F06.7) Mild cognitive disorder

(F06.8) Other specified mental disorders due to brain damage and dysfunction and to physical disease

(F06.9) Unspecified mental disorder due to brain damage and dysfunction and to physical disease

• Organic brain syndrome NOS

(F07.) Personality and behavioral disorders due to brain disease, damage, and dysfunction

(F07.0) Organic personality disorder

(F07.1) Postencephalitic syndrome

(F07.2) Postconcussional syndrome

(F07.8) Other organic personality and behavioral disorders due to brain disease, damage, and dysfunction

(F07.9) Unspecified organic personality and behavioral disorder due to brain disease, damage, and dysfunction

(F09.) Unspecified organic or symptomatic mental disorder

(F10–F19) Mental and behavioral disorders due to psychoactive substance use

Subtypes of each code from F10–F19:

(F1x.0) Acute intoxication

(F1x.1) Harmful use

(F1x.2) Dependence syndrome

(F1x.3) Withdrawal state

(F1x.4) Withdrawal state with delirium

(F1x.5) Psychotic disorder

(F1x.6) Amnesic syndrome

(F1x.7) Residual and late-onset psychotic disorder

(F1x.8) Other mental and behavioral disorder

(F1x.9) Unspecified mental and behavioral disorder

(F20–F29) Schizophrenia, schizotypal and delusional disorders

(F20.) Schizophrenia

(F20.0) Paranoid schizophrenia

(F20.1) Hebephrenic schizophrenia (Disorganized schizophrenia)

(F20.2) Catatonic schizophrenia

(F20.3) Undifferentiated schizophrenia

(F20.4) Postschizophrenic depression

(F20.5) Residual schizophrenia

(F20.6) Simple schizophrenia

(F20.8) Other schizophrenia

- Cenesthopathic schizophrenia
- Schizophreniform disorder NOS
- Schizophreniform psychosis NOS

(F20.9) Schizophrenia, unspecified

(F21.) Schizotypal disorder

(F22.) Persistent delusional disorders

(F22.0) Delusional disorder

(F22.8) Other persistent delusional disorders

- Delusional dysmorphophobia
- Involutional paranoid state
- Paranoia querulans

(F22.9) Persistent delusional disorder, unspecified

(F23.) Acute and transient psychotic disorders

(F23.0) Acute polymorphic psychotic disorder without symptoms of schizophrenia

(F23.1) Acute polymorphic psychotic disorder with symptoms of schizophrenia

(F23.2) Acute schizophrenia-like psychotic disorder

(F23.3) Other acute predominantly delusional psychotic disorders

(F23.8) Other acute and transient psychotic disorders

(F23.9) Acute and transient psychotic disorder, unspecified

(F24.) Induced delusional disorder

- Folie à deux
- Induced paranoid disorder
- Induced psychotic disorder

(F25.) Schizoaffective disorders

(F25.0) Schizoaffective disorder, manic type

(F25.1) Schizoaffective disorder, depressive type

(F25.2) Schizoaffective disorder, mixed type

(F25.8) Other schizoaffective disorders

(F25.9) Schizoaffective disorder, unspecified

(F28.) Other nonorganic psychotic disorders

- Chronic hallucinatory psychosis

(F29.) Unspecified nonorganic psychosis

(F30–F39) Mood (affective) disorders

(F30.) Manic episode

(F30.0) Hypomania

(F30.1) Mania without psychotic symptoms

(F30.2) Mania with psychotic symptoms

(F30.8) Other manic episodes

(F30.9) Manic episode, unspecified

(F31.) Bipolar affective disorder

(F31.0) Bipolar affective disorder, current episode hypomanic

(F31.1) Bipolar affective disorder, current episode manic without psychotic symptoms

(F31.2) Bipolar affective disorder, current episode manic with psychotic symptoms

(F31.3) Bipolar affective disorder, current episode mild or moderate depression

(F31.4) Bipolar affective disorder, current episode severe depression without psychotic symptoms

(F31.5) Bipolar affective disorder, current episode severe depression with psychotic symptoms

(F31.6) Bipolar affective disorder, current episode mixed

(F31.7) Bipolar affective disorder, currently in remission

(F31.8) Other bipolar affective disorders
- Bipolar II disorder
- Recurrent manic episodes NOS

(F31.9) Bipolar affective disorder, unspecified

(F32.) Depressive episode

(F32.0) Mild depressive episode

(F32.1) Moderate depressive episode

(F32.2) Severe depressive episode without psychotic symptoms

(F32.3) Severe depressive episode with psychotic symptoms

(F32.8) Other depressive episodes
- Atypical depression
- Single episodes of "masked" depression NOS

(F32.9) Depressive episode, unspecified

(F33.) Recurrent depressive disorder

(F33.0) Recurrent depressive disorder, current episode mild

(F33.1) Recurrent depressive disorder, current episode moderate

(F33.2) Recurrent depressive disorder, current episode severe without psychotic symptoms

(F33.3) Recurrent depressive disorder, current episode severe with psychotic symptoms

(F33.4) Recurrent depressive disorder, currently in remission

(F33.8) Other recurrent depressive disorders

(F33.9) Recurrent depressive disorder, unspecified

(F34.) Persistent mood (affective) disorders

(F34.0) Cyclothymia

(F34.1) Dysthymia

(F34.8) Other persistent mood (affective) disorders

(F34.9) Persistent mood (affective) disorder, unspecified

(F38.) Other mood (affective) disorders

(F38.0) Other single mood (affective) disorders
- Mixed affective episode

(F38.1) Other recurrent mood (affective) disorders
Recurrent brief depressive episodes

(F38.8) Other specified mood (affective) disorders

(F39.) Unspecified mood (affective) disorder

(F40–F48) Neurotic, stress-related, and somatoform disorders
(F40.) Phobic anxiety disorders

(F40.0) Agoraphobia

(F40.1) Social phobias
- Anthropophobia
- Social neurosis

(F40.2) Specific (isolated) phobias
- Acrophobia
- Animal phobias
- Claustrophobia
- Simple phobia

(F40.8) Other phobic anxiety disorders

(F40.9) Phobic anxiety disorder, unspecified
- Phobia NOS
- Phobic state NOS

(F41.) Other anxiety disorders

(F41.0) Panic disorder (episodic paroxysmal anxiety)

(F41.1) Generalized anxiety disorder

(F42.) Obsessive-compulsive disorder

(F43.) Reaction to severe stress and adjustment disorders

(F43.0) Acute stress reaction

(F43.1) Posttraumatic stress disorder

(F43.2) Adjustment disorder

(F44.) Dissociative (conversion) disorders

(F44.0) Dissociative amnesia

(F44.1) Dissociative fugue

(F44.2) Dissociative stupor

(F44.3) Trance and possession disorders

(F44.4) Dissociative motor disorders

(F44.5) Dissociative convulsions

(F44.6) Dissociative anaesthesia and sensory loss

(F44.7) Mixed dissociative (conversion) disorders

(F44.8) Other dissociative (conversion) disorders
- Ganser's syndrome
- Multiple personality

(F44.9) Dissociative (conversion) disorder, unspecified

(F45.) Somatoform disorders

(F45.0) Somatization disorder
- Briquet's disorder
- Multiple psychosomatic disorder

(F45.1) Undifferentiated somatoform disorder

(F45.2) Hypochondriacal disorder
- Body dysmorphic disorder
- Dysmorphophobia (nondelusional)

- Hypochondriacal neurosis
- Hypochondriasis
- Nosophobia

(F45.3) Somatoform autonomic dysfunction
- Cardiac neurosis
- Da Costa's syndrome
- Gastric neurosis
- Neurocirculatory asthenia

(F45.4) Persistent somatoform pain disorder
- Psychalgia

(F45.8) Other somatoform disorders

(F45.9) Somatoform disorder, unspecified

(F48.) Other neurotic disorders

(F48.0) Neurasthenia

(F48.1) Depersonalization-derealization syndrome

(F48.8) Other specified neurotic disorders
- Dhat syndrome
- Occupational neurosis, including writer's cramp
- Psychasthenia
- Psychasthenic neurosis
- Psychogenic syncope

(F48.9) Neurotic disorder, unspecified
- Neurosis NOS

(F50–F59) Behavioral syndromes associated with physiological disturbances and physical factors

(F50.) Eating disorders

(F50.0) Anorexia nervosa

(F50.1) Atypical anorexia nervosa

(F50.2) Bulimia nervosa

(F50.3) Atypical bulimia nervosa

(F50.4) Overeating associated with other psychological disturbances

(F50.5) Vomiting associated with other psychological disturbances

(F50.8) Other eating disorders
- Pica in adults

(F50.9) Eating disorder, unspecified

(F51.) Nonorganic sleep disorders

(F51.0) Nonorganic insomnia

(F51.1) Nonorganic hypersomnia

(F51.2) Nonorganic disorder of the sleep–wake schedule

(F51.3) Sleepwalking (somnambulism)

(F51.4) Sleep terrors (night terrors)

(F51.5) Nightmares

(F52.) Sexual dysfunction, not caused by organic disorder or disease

(F52.0) Lack or loss of sexual desire
- Frigidity
- Hypoactive sexual desire disorder

(F52.1) Sexual aversion and lack of sexual enjoyment
- Anhedonia (sexual)

(F52.2) Failure of genital response
- Female sexual arousal disorder
- Male erectile disorder
- Psychogenic impotence

(F52.3) Orgasmic dysfunction
- Inhibited orgasm (male)(female)
- Psychogenic anorgasmy

(F52.4) Premature ejaculation

(F52.5) Nonorganic vaginismus

(F52.6) Nonorganic dyspareunia

(F52.7) Excessive sexual drive

(F52.8) Other sexual dysfunction, not caused by organic disorder or disease

(F52.9) Unspecified sexual dysfunction, not caused by organic disorder or disease

(F53.) Mental and behavioral disorders associated with the puerperium, not elsewhere classified

(F53.0) Mild mental and behavioral disorders associated with the puerperium, not elsewhere classified
- Postnatal depression NOS
- Postpartum depression NOS

(F53.1) Severe mental and behavioral disorders associated with the puerperium, not elsewhere classified
- Puerperal psychosis NOS

(F54.) Psychological and behavioral factors associated with disorders or diseases classified elsewhere

(F55.) Abuse of nondependence-producing substances

(F59.) Unspecified behavioral syndromes associated with physiological disturbances and physical factors

(F60–F69) Disorders of adult personality and behaviour

(F60.) Specific personality disorders

(F60.0) Paranoid personality disorder

(F60.1) Schizoid personality disorder

(F60.2) Dissocial personality disorder
- Antisocial personality disorder

(F60.3) Emotionally unstable personality disorder
- Borderline personality disorder

(F60.4) Histrionic personality disorder

(F60.5) Anankastic personality disorder
- Obsessive-compulsive personality disorder

(F60.6) Anxious (avoidant) personality disorder

(F60.7) Dependent personality disorder

(F60.8) Other specific personality disorders
- Eccentric personality disorder
- "Haltlose" type personality disorder
- Immature personality disorder
- Narcissistic personality disorder
- Passive–aggressive personality disorder
- Psychoneurotic personality disorder

(F60.9) Personality disorder unspecified

(F61.) Mixed and other personality disorders

(F62.) Enduring personality changes, not attributable to brain damage and disease

(F63.) Habit and impulse disorders

(F63.0) Pathological gambling

(F63.1) Pathological fire-setting (pyromania)

(F63.2) Pathological stealing (kleptomania)

(F63.3) Trichotillomania

(F64.) Gender identity disorders

(F64.0) Transsexualism

(F64.1) Dual-role transvestism

(F64.2) Gender identity disorder of childhood

(F65.) Disorders of sexual preference

(F65.0) Sexual fetishism

(F65.1) Fetishistic transvestism

(F65.2) Exhibitionism

(F65.3) Voyeurism

(F65.4) Paedophilia

(F65.5) Sadomasochism

(F65.6) Multiple disorders of sexual preference

(F65.8) Other disorders of sexual preference
- Frotteurism
- Necrophilia
- Zoophilia

(F66.) Psychological and behavioral disorders associated with sexual development and orientation

(F66.0) Sexual maturation disorder

(F66.1) Ego-dystonic sexual orientation

(F66.2) Sexual relationship disorder

(F66.8) Other psychosexual development disorders

(F66.9) Psychosexual development disorder, unspecified

(F68.) Other disorders of adult personality and behavior

(F68.0) Elaboration of physical symptoms for psychological reasons

(F68.1) Intentional production or feigning of symptoms or disabilities, either physical or psychological (factitious disorder)

  • Munchausen syndrome

(F68.8) Other specified disorders of adult personality and behavior

(F69.) Unspecified disorder of adult personality and behavior

(F70–F79) Mental retardation

(F70.) Mild mental retardation

(F71.) Moderate mental retardation

(F72.) Severe mental retardation

(F73.) Profound mental retardation

(F78.) Other mental retardation

(F79.) Unspecified mental retardation

(F80–F89) Disorders of psychological development

(F80.) Specific developmental disorders of speech and language

(F80.0) Specific speech articulation disorder

(F80.1) Expressive language disorder

(F80.2) Receptive language disorder

  • Wernicke's aphasia

(F80.3) Acquired aphasia with epilepsy (Landau-Kleffner)

(F80.8) Other developmental disorders of speech and language

  • Lisping

(F80.9) Developmental disorder of speech and language, unspecified

(F81.) Specific developmental disorders of scholastic skills

(F81.0) Specific reading disorder

  • Developmental dyslexia

(F81.1) Specific spelling disorder

(F81.2) Specific disorder of arithmetical skills

  • Developmental acalculia

  • Gerstmann syndrome

(F81.3) Mixed disorder of scholastic skills

(F81.8) Other developmental disorders of scholastic skills

(F81.9) Developmental disorder of scholastic skills, unspecified

(F82.) Specific developmental disorder of motor function

- Developmental dyspraxia

(F83.) Mixed specific developmental disorders

(F84.) Pervasive developmental disorders

(F84.0) Childhood autism

(F84.2) Rett's syndrome

(F84.4) Overactive disorder associated with mental retardation and stereotyped movements

(F84.5) Asperger syndrome

(F88.) Other disorders of psychological development

(F89.) Unspecified disorder of psychological development

(F90–F98) Behavioral and emotional disorders with onset usually occurring in childhood and adolescence

(F90.) Hyperkinetic disorders

(F90.0) Disturbance of activity and attention

- Attention-deficit hyperactivity disorder
- Attention deficit syndrome with hyperactivity

(F90.1) Hyperkinetic conduct disorder

(F90.8) Other hyperkinetic disorders

(F90.9) Hyperkinetic disorder, unspecified

(F91.) Conduct disorders

(F91.0) Conduct disorder confined to the family context

(F91.1) Unsocialized conduct disorder

(F91.2) Socialized conduct disorder

(F91.3) Oppositional defiant disorder

(F91.8) Other conduct disorders

(F91.9) Conduct disorder, unspecified

(F92.) Mixed disorders of conduct and emotions

(F92.0) Depressive conduct disorder

(F92.8) Other mixed disorders of conduct and emotions

(F92.9) Mixed disorder of conduct and emotions, unspecified

(F93.) Emotional disorders with onset specific to childhood

(F93.0) Separation anxiety disorder of childhood

(F93.1) Phobic anxiety disorder of childhood

(F93.2) Social anxiety disorder of childhood

(F93.3) Sibling rivalry disorder

(F93.8) Other childhood emotional disorders
- Identity disorder
- Overanxious disorder

(F93.9) Childhood emotional disorder, unspecified

(F94.) Disorders of social functioning with onset specific to childhood and adolescence

(F94.0) Elective mutism

(F94.1) Reactive attachment disorder of childhood

(F94.2) Disinhibited attachment disorder of childhood

(F94.8) Other childhood disorders of social functioning

(F94.9) Childhood disorder of social functioning, unspecified

(F95.) Tic disorders

(F95.0) Transient tic disorder

(F95.1) Chronic motor or vocal tic disorder

(F95.2) Combined vocal and multiple motor tic disorder (de la Tourette)

(F95.8) Other tic disorders

(F95.9) Tic disorder, unspecified

(F98.) Other behavioral and emotional disorders with onset usually occurring in childhood and adolescence

(F98.0) Nonorganic enuresis

(F98.1) Nonorganic encopresis

(F98.2) Feeding disorder of infancy and childhood

(F98.3) Pica of infancy and childhood

(F98.4) Stereotyped movement disorders

(F98.5) Stuttering (stammering)

(F98.6) Cluttering

(F98.8) Other specified behavioral and emotional disorders with onset usually occurring in childhood and adolescence
- Attention deficit disorder without hyperactivity
- Excessive masturbation
- Nail-biting
- Nose-picking
- Thumb-sucking

(F98.9) Unspecified behavioral and emotional disorders with onset usually occurring in childhood and adolescence

(F99) Unspecified mental disorder

(F99.) Mental disorder, not otherwise specified

The reader is referred directly to the *ICD-10 Classification of Mental and Behavioural Disorders* for complete clinical descriptions and diagnostic guidelines associated with these codes, http://www.who.int/classifications/apps/icd/icd10online/.

References

Ahrens, C. S., Frey, J. L., & Senn Burke, S. C. (1999). An individualized job engagement approach for persons with severe mental illness. *The Journal of Rehabilitation, 65,* 17–24.

American Medical Association. (2010). *Current procedural terminology.* Chicago: Author.

American Psychiatric Association. (1952). *Diagnostic and statistical manual of mental disorders.* Washington, DC: Author.

American Psychiatric Association. (1968). *Diagnostic and statistical manual of mental disorders* (2nd ed.). Washington, DC: Author.

American Psychiatric Association. (1973). *Diagnostic and statistical manual of mental disorders* (2nd ed., 6th printing change). Washington, DC: Author.

American Psychiatric Association. (1980). *Diagnostic and statistical manual of mental disorders* (3rd ed.). Washington, DC: Author.

American Psychiatric Association. (1987). *Diagnostic and statistical manual of mental disorders* (3rd ed., rev.). Washington, DC: Author.

American Psychiatric Association. (1994). *Diagnostic and statistical manual of mental disorders* (4th ed.). Washington, DC: Author.

American Psychiatric Association. (2000). *Diagnostic and statistical manual of mental disorders* (4th ed., text revision). Washington, DC: Author.

American Speech-Language-Hearing Association (ASHA). (2004). *Scope of practice in audiology* (ASHA Suppl. 24). Rockville, MD: Author.

Anthony, W. A., Cohen, M. R., Farkas, M., & Gagne, C. (2002). *Psychiatric rehabilitation* (2nd ed.). Boston: Boston University Center for Psychiatric Rehabilitation.

Ayuso-Mateos, J. L. (2009). Disability and ICF core sets in mood disorders. *European Psychiatry, 24,* S212.

Baron, R., & Salzer, M. C. (2000). The career patterns of persons with serious mental illness: Generating a new vision of lifetime careers for those in recovery. *Psychiatric Rehabilitation Skills, 4,* 136–156.

Baron, S., & Linden, M. (2005). Disorders of functions and disorders of capacity in relation to sick leave in mental disorders. *International Journal of Psychiatry, 55,* 57–63.

Baron, S., & Linden, M. (2008). The role of the "International Classification of Functioning, Disability and Health, ICF" in the description and classification of mental disorders. *European Archives of Psychiatry and Clinical Neuroscience, 258*(Suppl. 5), 81–85.

Baron, S., & Linden, M. (2009). Disorders of functions and disorders of capacity in relation to sick leave in mental disorders. *International Journal of Social Psychiatry, 55*, 57–63.

Bassett, S. S., Chase, G. A., Folstein, M. F., & Regier, D. A. (1998). Disability and psychiatric disorders in an urban community: Measurement, prevalence and outcomes. *Psychological Medicine, 28*, 509–517.

Beauchamp, T. L., & Childress, J. F. (1994). *Principles of biomedical ethics* (4th ed.). Oxford, England: Oxford University Press.

Bernet, W. (2008). Parental alienation disorder and DSM-V. *The American Journal of Family Therapy, 36*, 349–366.

Bhugra, D. (2005). The global prevalence of schizophrenia. *PLoS Medicine, 2*, 151. Published online 2005 May 31. doi:10.1271/journal.pmed.0020151

Bickenbach, J. E. (2003). Functional status and health information in Canada: Proposals and prospects. *Health Care Financing Review, 24*(3), 89–102.

Bickenbach, J. E., Chatterji, S., Badley, E. M., & Üstün, T. B. (1999). Models of disablement, universalism and the International Classification of Impairments, Disabilities and Handicaps. *Social Science and Medicine, 48*, 1173–1187.

Bodenreider, O. (2005, June). *Mapping new vocabularies to the UMLS: Experience with ICF.* Symposium conducted at the meeting of the World Health Organization's North American Collaborating Center, Mayo Clinic, Rochester, MN.

Boldt, C., Grill, E., Wildner, M., Portenier, L., Wilke, S., Stucki, G., et al. (2005). ICF Core Set for patients with cardiopulmonary conditions in the acute hospital. *Disability and Rehabilitation, 27*, 375–380.

Bond, G. R. (1995). Psychiatric rehabilitation. In A. E. Dell Orto & R. P. Marinelli (Eds.), *Encyclopedia of disability and rehabilitation.* New York: MacMillan.

Boonen, A., Braun, J., van der Horst Bruinsma, I. E., Huang, F., Maksymowych, W., Kostanjsek, N., et al. (2010). ASAS/WHO ICF Core Sets for ankylosing spondylitis (AS): How to classify the impact of AS on functioning and health. *Annals of the Rheumatic Diseases, 69*, 102–107.

Brandsma, J. W., Lakerveld-Heyl, K., & Van Ravensberg, C. D. (1995). Reflection on the definition of impairment and disability as defined by the World Health Organization [Special issue: The International Classification of Impairments, Disabilities, and Handicaps (ICDH): Perspectives and developments, 119–127]. *Disability & Rehabilitation: An International Multidisciplinary Journal, 17*(3–4).

Brandt, D. (2005, June). *Physical therapy and the ICF: Functional stepping stones to the future.* Symposium conducted at the meeting of the World Health Organization's North American Collaborating Center, Mayo Clinic, Rochester, MN.

Brault, M. (2005). *Current population reports* (pp. 70–117). Washington, DC: U.S. Census Bureau.

Brault, M. W. (2009). *Review of changes to the measurement of disability in the 2008 American Community Survey.* Washington, DC: U.S. Census Bureau.

Brockow, T., Wohlfahrt, K., Hillert, A., Geyh, S., Weigl, M., Franke, T., et al. (2004). Identifying the concepts contained in the outcome measures of clinical trials on depressive disorders using the International Classification of Functioning, Disability and Health as a reference. *Journal of Rehabilitation Medicine, 36*(Suppl. 44), 49–55.

Brown, S. C. (1993). Revitalizing "handicap" for disability research. *Journal of Disability Policy Studies, 4,* 55–73.

Brown, S., & Lent, R. (Eds.). (2008). *Handbook of counseling psychology* (4th ed.). Hoboken, NJ: John Wiley & Sons.

Bruyère, S. M., & Peterson, D. B. (2005). Introduction to the special section on the International Classification of Functioning, Disability and Health (ICF): Implications for rehabilitation psychology. *Rehabilitation Psychology, 50,* 103–104.

Bruyère, S. M., Van Looy, S. A., & Peterson, D. B. (2005). The International Classification of Functioning, Disability and Health (ICF): Contemporary literature review. *Rehabilitation Psychology, 50,* 113–121.

Burns, C. (1991). Parallels between research and diagnosis: The reliability and validity issues of clinical practice. *The Nurse Practitioner, 16*(10), 42–45, 49–50.

Burt, M. R., & Aron, L. Y. (2003). *Promoting work among SSI/DI beneficiaries with serious mental illness.* Retrieved January 22, 2005, from http://www.socialsecurity.gov

Chan, F., & Leahy, M. J. (Eds.). (1999). *Disability and health care: Case manager's desk reference.* Lake Zurich, IL: Vocational Consultants Press.

Chan, F., & Leahy, M. J. (Eds.). (2005). *Case management for rehabilitation health professionals* (2nd ed., Vol. 1). Osage Beach, MO: Aspen Professional Services.

Chute, C. G. (2005, June). *The spectrum of clinical data representation: A context for functional status.* Symposium conducted at the meeting of the World Health Organization's North American Collaborating Center, Mayo Clinic, Rochester, MN.

Cieza, A., Brockow, T., Ewert, T., Amman, E., Kollerits, B., Chatterji, S., et al. (2002). Linking health-status measurements to the International Classification of Functioning, Disability and Health. *Journal of Rehabilitation Medicine, 34,* 205–210.

Cieza, A., Chatterji, S., Andersen, C., Cantista, P., Herceg, M., Melvin, J., et al. (2004). ICF core sets for depression. *Journal of Rehabilitation Medicine, 44,* 128–134.

Coenen, A. (2005, June). *Mapping ICF to the International Classification for Nursing Practice (ICNP).* Symposium conducted at the meeting of the World Health Organization's North American Collaborating Center, Mayo Clinic, Rochester, MN.

Cook, J. A., & Razzano, L. (2000). Vocational rehabilitation for persons with schizophrenia: Recent research and implications for practice. *Schizophrenia Bulletin, 26,* 87–203.

Cottone, R. R., & Tarvydas, V. M. (2007). *Counseling ethics and decision making.* New York: Merrill/Prentice Hall.

De Kleijn-De Vrankrijker, M. W. (2003). The long way from the International Classification of Impairments, Disabilities and Handicaps (ICIDH) to the International Classification of Functioning, Disability and Health (ICF). *Disability and Rehabilitation, 25,* 561–564.

Dellario, D. (1985). The relationship between mental health, vocational rehabilitation, interagency functioning, and outcome of psychiatrically disabled persons. *Rehabilitation Counseling Bulletin, 28,* 167–170.

Dell Orto, A. E., & Power, P. W. (Eds.). (2007). *The psychological and social impact of illness and disability.* New York: Springer Publishing Company.

DiCowden, M. A. (2005, June). *The impact of ICF coding in practice.* Symposium conducted at the meeting of the World Health Organization's North American Collaborating Center, Mayo Clinic, Rochester, MN.

Dohrenwend, B. P., Turner, J. B., Turse, N. A., Adams, B. G., Koen, K. C., & Marshall, R. (2006). The psychological risk of Vietnam for U.S. veterans: A revisit with new data and methods. *Science, 313,* 979–982.

Duchan, J. F. (2004). Where is the person in the ICF? *Advances in Speech-Language Pathology, 6*(1), 63–65.

Duggan, C. H., Albright, K. J., & LeQuerica, A. (2008). Using the ICF to code and analyse women's disability narratives. *Disability and Rehabilitation, 30,* 978–990.

Elliott, T., Kurylo, M., & Rivera, P. (2002). Positive growth following an acquired physical disability. In C. R. Snyder & S. Lopez (Eds.), *Handbook of positive psychology* (pp. 687–699). New York: Oxford University Press.

Elliott, T., & Leung, P. (2005). Vocational rehabilitation: History and practice. In W. B. Walsh & M. Savickas (Eds.), *Handbook of vocational psychology* (3rd ed., pp. 319–343). New York: Erlbaum.

Engel, G. L. (1977). The need for a new medical model: A challenge for biomedicine. *Science, 196,* 129–136.

Everson, S. A., Roberts, R. E., Goldberg, D. E., & Kaplan, G. A. (1998). Depressive symptoms and increased risk of stroke mortality over a 29-year period. *Archives of Internal Medicine, 158,* 1133–1138.

Ewert, T., Fuessl, M., Cieza, A., Andersen, A., Chatterji, S., Kostanjsek, N., et al. (2004). Identification of the most common patient problems in patients: ICF Core Sets for depression. *Journal of Rehabilitation Medicine, 44,* 133–134.

Ewert, T., Grill, E., Bartholomeyczik, S., Finger, M., Mokrusch, T., Kostanjsek, N., et al. (2005). ICF Core Set for patients with neurological conditions in the acute hospital. *Disability and Rehabilitation, 27,* 367–373.

Fabian, E. S., Waterworth, A., & Ripke, B. (1993). Reasonable accommodations for workers with serious mental illness: Type, frequency, and associated outcomes. *Psychosocial Rehabilitation Journal, 17,* 163–172.

Frank, R. G., & Elliott, T. R. (2000). Rehabilitation psychology: Hope for a psychology of chronic conditions. In R. G. Frank & T. R. Elliott (Eds.), *Handbook of rehabilitation psychology* (pp. 1–9). Washington, DC: American Psychological Association.

Frank, R. G., Rosenthal, M., & Caplan, B. (Eds.). (2009). *Handbook of rehabilitation psychology* (2nd ed.). Washington, DC: American Psychological Association.

Gallagher, W. (1993). *The power of place.* New York: Poseidon Press.

Garske, G. G. (1999). The challenge of rehabilitation counselors: Working with people with psychiatric disabilities. *The Journal of Rehabilitation, 65,* 21–25.

Gatchel, R. J., Polatin, P. B., Mayer, T. G., & Garcy, P. D. (1994). Psychopathology and the rehabilitation of patients with chronic low back pain disability. *Archives of Physical Medicine and Rehabilitation, 75,* 666–670.

Goldsmith, K., Pellmar, T. C., Kleinman, A. M., & Bunney, W. E. (2002). *Reducing suicide: A national imperative*. Washington, DC: The National Academic Press.

Granger, B., Baron, R., & Robinson, S. (1997). Findings from a national survey of job coaches and job developers about job accommodations arranged between employers and people with psychiatric disabilities. *Journal of Vocational Rehabilitation, 9*, 235–251.

Grill, E., Ewert, T., Chatterji, S., Kostanjsek, N., & Stucki, G. (2005). ICF Core Sets development for acute hospital and early post-acute rehabilitation facilities. *Disability and Rehabilitation, 27*, 361–366.

Grill, E., Hermes, R., Swoboda, W., Uzarewicz, C., Kostanjsek, N., & Stucki, G. (2005b). ICF Core Set for geriatric patients in early post-acute rehabilitation facilities. *Disability and Rehabilitation, 27*, 411–417.

Hansen, M. S., Fink, P., Frydenberg, M., & Oxhoj, M. L. (2002). Use of health services, mental illness, and self-rated disability and health in medical inpatients. *Psychosomatic Medicine, 64*, 668–675.

Harris, M. R. (2005, June). *Clinical and administrative mappings to the ICF*. Symposium conducted at the meeting of the World Health Organization's North American Collaborating Center, Mayo Clinic, Rochester, MN.

Hayward, B., & Schmidt-Davis, H. (2003). *Longitudinal study of the Vocational Rehabilitation Services Program*. Retrieved February 2, 2004, from http://www.ed.gov/rschstat/eval/rehab/vr-final-report-2.pdf

Holloway, J. D. (2004). A new way of looking at health status. *Monitor on Psychology, 35*, 32.

Hong, G. K. (2009). Psychiatric disabilities. In M. G. Brodwin, F. W. Siu, J. Howard, & E. R. Brodwin (Eds.), *Medical, psychosocial, and vocational aspects of disability* (3rd ed., pp. 249–262). Athens, GA: Elliott & Fitzpatrick.

Howard, D., Nieuwenhuijsen, E. R., & Saleeby, P. (2008). Health promotion and education: Application of the ICF in the US and Canada using an ecological perspective. *Disability and Rehabilitation, 30*, 942–954.

Hurst, R. (2003). The international disability rights movement and the ICF. *Disability and Rehabilitation, 25*, 572–576.

Jones, G. C., & Sinclair, L. B. (2008). Multiple health disparities among minority adults with mobility limitations: An application of the ICF framework and codes. *Disability and Rehabilitation, 30*, 901–915.

Kennedy, C. (2003). Functioning and disability associated with mental disorders: The evolution since ICIDH. *Disability & Rehabilitation, 25*, 611–619.

Kennedy, S. H., Eisfeld, B. S., & Cooke, R. G. (2001). Quality of life: An important dimension in assessing the treatment of depression? *Journal of Psychiatry and Neuroscience, 26*(Suppl.), S23–S28.

Kessler, R. C., Bergland, P. A., Demler, O., Jin, R., Walters, E. E. (2005a). Lifetime prevalence and age-of-onset distributions of the DSM-IV disorders in National Comorbidity Survey Replication (NCS-R). *Archives of General Psychiatry, 62*, 593–602.

Kessler, R. C., Chiu, W. T., Demler, O., Walters, E. E. (2005b). Prevalence, severity, and comorbidity of twelve-month DSM-IV disorders in the National Comorbidity Survey Replication (NCS-R). *Archives of General Psychiatry, 62*, 617–627.

Kessler, R. C., Greenberg, P. E., Mickelson, K. D., Meneades, L. M., & Wang, P. S. (2001). The effects of chronic medical conditions on work loss and work cutback. *Journal of Occupational and Environmental Medicine, 43*, 218–225.

Kitchener, K. S. (2000). *Foundations of ethical practice, research, and teaching in psychology.* Mahwah, NJ: Lawrence Erlbaum Associates, Publishers.

Kohler, F., Cieza, A., Stucki, G., Geertzen, J., Burger, H., Dillon, M. P., et al. (2009). Developing core sets for persons following amputation based on the International Classification of Functioning, Disability and Health as a way to specify functioning. *Prosthetics and Orthotics International, 33*, 117–129.

Lambert, M. J. (Ed.). (2004). *Bergin and Garfield's handbook of psychotherapy and behavior change* (5th ed.). New York: John Wiley & Sons.

Lazarus, R. S., & Folkman, S. (1984). *Stress, appraisal, and coping.* New York: Springer Publishing Company.

Leonardi, M., Bickenbach, J., Üstün, T. B., Kostanjsek, N., & Chatterji, S. (2006). Comment: The definition of disability: What is in a name? *Lancet, 368*(9543), 1219–1221.

Lezak, M. D., Howieson, D. B., & Loring, D. W. (2004). *Neuropsychological assessment* (4th ed.). New York: Oxford University Press.

Lutz, B. J., & Bowers, B. J. (2007). Understanding how disability is defined and conceptualized in the literature. In A. E. Dell Orto & P. W. Power (Eds.), *The psychological and social impact of illness and disability* (5th ed., pp. 11–21). New York: Springer Publishing Company.

MacDonald-Wilson, K. L., & Nemec, P. B. (2005). The ICF in psychiatric rehabilitation. *Rehabilitation Education, 19*, 159–176.

MacDonald-Wilson, K. L., Nemec, P. B., Anthony, W. A., & Cohen, M. R. (2001). Assessment in psychiatric rehabilitation. In B. Bolton (Ed.), *Handbook of measurement and evaluation in rehabilitation* (3rd ed., pp. 423–448). Baltimore: Paul H Brookes.

MacDonald-Wilson, K. L., Rogers, E. S., Ellison, M. L., & Lyass, A. (2003). A study of the social security work incentives and their relation to perceived barriers to work among persons with serious mental illnesses. *Rehabilitation Psychology, 48*, 301–309.

MacDonald-Wilson, K. L, Rogers, E. S., Massaro, J. M., Lyass, A., & Crean, T. (2002). An investigation of reasonable workplace accommodations for people with psychiatric disabilities: Quantitative findings from a multisite study. *Community Mental Health Journal, 38*, 35–50.

Madden, R., Choi, C., & Sykes, C. (2003). The ICF as a framework for national data: The introduction of the ICF into Australian data dictionaries. *Disability and Rehabilitation, 25*, 676–682.

Maini, M., Nocentini, U., Prevedini, A., Giardini, A., & Muscolo, E. (2008). An Italian experience in the ICF implementation in rehabilitation: Preliminary theoretical and practical considerations. *Disability and Rehabilitation, 30*, 1146–1152.

Martin, S. (2009). Improving diagnosis worldwide. *Monitor on Psychology, 40*(9), 62–65.

Massel, H. K., Liberman, R. P., Mintz, J., & Jacobs, H. E. (1990). Evaluating the capacity to work of the mentally ill. *Psychiatry: Journal for the Study of Interpersonal Processes, 53*, 31–43.

Max, W., Rice, D. P., & Trupin, L. (1995). *Medical expenditures for people with disabilities* (Disability Statistics Abstract, No. 12). Washington, DC: U.S. Department of Education, National Institute on Disability and Rehabilitation Research (NIDDR).

Mayo, N. E., & McGill, J. (2005, June). *Standardizing clinical assessments to the ICF*. Symposium conducted at the meeting of the World Health Organization's North American Collaborating Center, Mayo Clinic, Rochester, MN.

McCrone, P., & Phelan, M. (1994). Diagnosis and length of psychiatric inpatient stay. *Psychological Medicine, 24*, 1025–1030.

McReynolds, C. J. (2002). Psychiatric rehabilitation: The need for a specialized approach. *The International Journal of Psychosocial Rehabilitation, 7*, 61–69.

Morita, E., Weigl, M., Schuh, A., & Stucki, G. (2006). Identification of relevant ICF categories for indication, intervention planning and evaluation of health resort programs: A Delphi exercise. *International Journal of Biometeorology, 50*, 183–191.

Murphy, J. M., Monson, R. R., Olivier, D. C., Sobol, A. M., & Leighton, A. H. (1987). Affective disorders and mortality: A general population study. *Archives of General Psychiatry, 44*, 473–480.

Murray, C. J. L., & Lopez, A. D. (1996). The global burden of disease: A comprehensive assessment of mortality and disability from diseases, injuries, and risk factors in 1990 and projected to 2020. In C. J. L. Murray & A. D. Lopez (Eds.), *The global burden of disease and injury series* (pp. 247–293). Cambridge, MA: Harvard University Press.

Nathan, P. E., & Gorman, J. M. (Eds.). (2007). *A guide to treatments that work* (3rd ed.). New York: Oxford University Press.

National Advisory Mental Health Council. (1993). Health care reform for Americans with severe mental illness: Report of the National Advisory Mental Health Council. *American Journal of Psychiatry, 150*, 1447–1465.

Nieuwenhuijsen, E. R. (1995). The ICIDH in the USA: Applications and relevance to ADA goals. *Disability and Rehabilitation, 17*(3–4), 154–158.

Noble, J. H. (1998). Policy reform dilemmas in promoting employment of persons with severe mental illness. *Psychiatric Services, 49*, 775–781.

Olatunji, B. O., Deacon, B. J., & Abramowitz, J. S. (2009). Is hypochondriasis an anxiety disorder? *British Journal of Psychiatry, 194*, 481–482.

Olkin, R. (1999). *What psychotherapists should know about disability?* New York: Guilford Press.

Olkin, R., & Pledger, C. (2003). Can disability studies and psychology join hands? *American Psychologist, 58*, 296–304.

Ong, L. Z., Peterson, D. B., Chronister, J. A., Chui, C., & Chan, F. (2009). Personality profiles of undergraduate and graduate students in rehabilitation counselling and services. *Australian Journal of Rehabilitation Counselling, 15*(2), 92–106.

Ormel, J., Oldehinkel, T., Brilman, E., & vanden Brink, W. (1993). Outcome of depression and anxiety in primary care: A three wave 3 1/2 year study of psychopathology and disability. *Archives of General Psychiatry, 50*, 759–766.

Peterson, D. B. (2000). Clinical problem-solving in micro-case management: Computer-assisted instruction for information gathering strategies in rehabilitation counseling. *Rehabilitation Counseling Bulletin, 43*(2), 84–96.

Peterson, D. B. (2005). International Classification of Functioning, Disability and Health (ICF): An introduction for rehabilitation psychologists. *Rehabilitation Psychology, 50,* 105–112.

Peterson, D. B. (2009). The International Classification of Functioning, Disability & Health: Applications for professional counseling. In M. A. Stebnicki & I. Marini (Eds.), *The professional counselor's desk reference* (pp. 529–542). New York: Springer Publishing Company.

Peterson, D. B., & Aguiar, L. (2004). History & systems: United States. In T. F. Riggar & D. R. Maki (Eds.), *The handbook of rehabilitation counseling* (pp. 50–75). New York: Springer Publishing Company.

Peterson, D. B., & Elliott, T. R. (2008). Advances in conceptualizing and studying disability. In S. Brown & R. W. Lent (Eds.), *Handbook of counseling psychology* (4th ed., pp. 212–230). Hoboken, NJ: John Wiley & Sons.

Peterson, D. B., Hautamaki, J. B., & Walton, J. L. (2007). Ethics and technology. In R. R. Cottone & V. M. Tarvydas (Eds.), *Counseling ethics and decision making* (3rd ed., pp. 184–211). New York: Merrill/Prentice Hall.

Peterson, D. B., Mpofu, E., & Oakland, T. D. (2010). Concepts and models in disability, functioning, and health. In E. Mpofu & T. Oakland (Eds.), *Rehabilitation and health assessment: Applying ICF guidelines* (pp. 3–26). New York: Springer Publishing Company.

Peterson, D. B., & Murray, G. C. (2006). Ethics and assistive technology service provision. *Disability and Rehabilitation: Assistive Technology, 1*(1–2), 59–67.

Peterson, D. B., & Paul, H. (2009). Using the International Classification of Functioning, Disability & Health (ICF) to conceptualize disability and functioning in psychological injury and law. *Psychological Injury and Law, 2*(3–4), 205–214.

Peterson, D. B., & Rosenthal, D. (2005a). The International Classification of Functioning, Disability and Health (ICF) as an historical allegory for history in rehabilitation education. *Rehabilitation Education, 19,* 95–104.

Peterson, D. B., & Rosenthal, D. (2005b). The International Classification of Functioning, Disability and Health (ICF): A primer for rehabilitation educators. *Rehabilitation Education, 19,* 81–94.

Peterson, D. B., & Threats, T. T. (2005). Ethical and clinical implications of the International Classification of Functioning, Disability and Health (ICF) in rehabilitation education. *Rehabilitation Education, 19,* 129–138.

Peterson, D. B., VanVleet, T., & Goldman, J. (2009). Neurological conditions. In M. G. Brodwin, F. W. Sui, J. Howard, & E. R. Brodwin (Eds.), *Medical, psychosocial, and vocational aspects of disability* (3rd ed., pp. 273–288). Athens, GA: Elliott & Fitzpatrick, Inc.

Pledger, C. (2003). Discourse on disability and rehabilitation issues: Opportunities for psychology. *American Psychologist, 58,* 279–284.

Pratt, C. W., Gill, K. J., Barrett, N. M., & Roberts, M. M. (2007). *Psychiatric rehabilitation* (2nd ed.). Oxford, UK: Elsevier, Inc.

Rabinowitz, J., Modai, I., & Inbar-Saban, N. (1994). Understanding who improves after psychiatric hospitalization. *Acta Psychiatrica Scandinavica, 89,* 152–158.

Reed, G. M., Dilfer, K., Bufka, L. F., Scherer, M. J., Kotzé, P., Tshivhase, M., et al. (2008). Three model curricula for teaching clinicians to use the ICF. *Disability and Rehabilitation, 30,* 927–941.

Reed, G. M., Lux, J. B., Jacobson, J. W., Stark, S., Threats, T. T., Peterson, D. B., et al. (2005). Operationalizing the International Classification of Functioning, Disability and Health (ICF) in clinical settings. *Rehabilitation Psychology, 50,* 122–131.

Regier, D. A., Narrow, W. E., Kuhl, E. A., & Kupfer, D. J. (2009). The conceptual development of the DSM-V. *American Journal of Psychiatry, 166,* 645–650.

Regier, D. A., Narrow, W. E., Rae, D. S., Manderscheid, R. W., Locke, B. Z., & Goodwin, F. K. (1993). The de facto mental and addictive disorders service system. Epidemiologic catchment area prospective 1-year prevalence rates of disorders and services. *Archives of General Psychiatry, 50,* 85–94.

Riggar, T. F., & Maki, D. R. (Eds.). (2004). *The handbook of rehabilitation counseling.* New York: Springer Publishing Company.

Robins, L. N., & Regier, D. A. (Eds.). (1991). *Psychiatric disorders in America: The epidemiologic catchment area study.* New York: The Free Press.

Rock, M. (2005, June). *Welcome WHO/ICF NACC to Mayo Clinic.* Symposium conducted at the meeting of the World Health Organization's North American Collaborating Center, Mayo Clinic, Rochester, MN.

Rogers, E. S., Anthony, W. A., & Danley, K. S. (1989). The impact of interagency collaboration on system and client outcomes. *Rehabilitation Counseling Bulletin, 33,* 100–109.

Rubin, S. E., & Roessler, R. T. (2008). *Foundations of the vocational rehabilitation process* (6th ed.). Austin, TX: PRO-ED.

Rusalem, H. (1976). A personalized recent history of vocational rehabilitation in America. In H. Rusalem & D. Malikin (Eds.), *Contemporary vocational rehabilitation* (pp. 29–45). New York: University Press.

Rusk, H. A. (1977). *Rehabilitation medicine* (4th ed.). St. Louis: Mosby.

Saha, S., Chant, D. Welham, J., & McGrath, J. (2005). A systematic review of the prevalence of schizophrenia. *PLoS Medicine, 2,* 141.

Savova, G., Harris, M., Pakhomov, S., & Chute, C. G. (2005, June). *Frame representation of ICF.* Symposium conducted at the meeting of the World Health Organization's North American Collaborating Center, Mayo Clinic, Rochester, MN.

Scherer, M. J., Blair, K. L., Banks, M. E., Brucker, B., Corrigan, J., & Wegener, J. H. (2004). Rehabilitation psychology. In W. E. Craighead & C. B. Nemeroff (Eds.), *The concise Corsini encyclopedia of psychology and behavioral science* (3rd ed., pp. 801–802). Hoboken, NJ: John Wiley & Sons.

Scheuringer, M., Stucki, G., Huber, E. O., Brach, M., Schwarzkopf, S. R., Kostanjsek, N., et al. (2005). ICF Core sets for patients with musculoskeletal conditions in early post-acute rehabilitation facilities. *Disability and Rehabilitation, 27,* 405–410.

Schneidert, M., Hurst, R., Miller, J., & Üstün, B. (2003). The role of environment in the International Classification of Functioning, Disability and Health (ICF). *Disability and Rehabilitation, 25,* 588–595.

Schraner, I., De Jonge, D., Layton, N., Bringolf, J., & Molenda, A. (2008). Using the ICF in economic analyses of assistive technology systems: Methodological implications of a user standpoint. *Disability and Rehabilitation, 30,* 916–926.

Schultz, I. Z., (2008). Disentangling the disability quagmire in psychological injury: Part 1—Disability and return to work: Theories, methods, and applications. *Psychological Injury and Law, 1,* 94–102.

Schultz, I. Z., & Stewart, A. M. (2008). Disentangling the disability quagmire in psychological injury and law, Part 2: Evolution of disability models: Conceptual, methodological and forensic practice issues. *Psychological Injury and Law, 1,* 103–121.

Seekins, T., Ipsen, C., & Arnold, N. L. (2007). Using ecological momentary assessment to measure participation: A preliminary study. *Rehabilitation Psychology, 52,* 319–330.

Segal, S. P., & Choi, N. G. (1991). Factors affecting SSI support for sheltered care residents with serious mental illness. *Hospital and Community Psychiatry, 42,* 1132–1137.

Simeonsson, R. J., Leonardi, M., Bjorck-Akesson, E., Hollenweger, J., Lollar, D., Martinuzzi, A., et al. (2006, November). *ICF-CY: A universal tool for practice policy and research*. Meeting of WHO Collaborating Centres for Familly of International Classifications, Tunis, Tunisia (Document P107).

Simeonsson, R. J., Leonardi, M., Lollar, D., Bjorck-Akesson, E., Hollenweger, J., & Martinuzzi, A. (2003). Applying the International Classification of Functioning, Disability and Health (ICF) to measure childhood disability. *Disability and Rehabilitation, 25*, 602–610.

Simeonsson, R. J., Scarborough, A. A., & Hebbeler, K. M. (2006). The ICF and ICD codes provide a standard language of disability in young children. *Journal of Clinical Epidemiology, 59*, 365–373.

Smart, J. (2005). The promise of the International Classification of Functioning, Disability & Health (ICF). *Rehabilitation Education, 19*, 191–199.

Spitzer, R. L., Gibbon, M., Skodol, A. E., Williams, J. B. W., & First, M. B. (2002). *DSM-IV-TR Case Book*. Washington, DC: American Psychiatric Publishing, Inc.

Stengel, E. (1957). *The scope and the methods of psychiatry: Inaugural lecture delivered 4th December, 1957*. Sheffield: University of Sheffield.

Stier-Jarmer M., Grill, E., Ewert, T., Bartholomeyczik, S., Finger, M., Mokrusch, T., et al. (2005). ICF core set for patients with neurological conditions in early post-acute rehabilitation facilities. *Disability and Rehabilitation, 27*, 389–396.

Stoll, T., Brach, M., Huber, E. O., Scheuringer, M., Schwarzkopf, S. R., Konstanjsek, N., et al. (2005). ICF Core Set for patients with musculoskeletal conditions in the acute hospital. *Disability and Rehabilitation, 27*, 381–387.

Stone, J. (2008). Guest editor's introduction and overview: Recent applications of the ICF. *Disability and Rehabilitation, 30*, 899–900.

Strauss, J., Hafez, H., Lieberman, R., & Harding, C. (1985). The course of psychiatric disorder: III. Longitudinal principles. *American Journal of Psychiatry, 142*, 289–296.

Stucki, G., Ewert, T., & Cieza, A. (2003). Value and application of the ICF in rehabilitation medicine. *Disability and Rehabilitation, 25*, 628–634.

Stucki, G., Üstün, T. B., & Melvin, J. (2005). Applying the ICF for the acute hospital and early post-acute rehabilitation facilities. *Disability and Rehabilitation, 27*, 349–352.

Sundar, V., Daumen, M., Conley, D., & Stone, J. (2008). The use of ICF codes for information retrieval in rehabilitation research: An empirical study. *Disability and Rehabilitation, 30*, 955–962.

Tarvydas, V. M., Peterson, D. B., & Michaelson, S. D. (2005). Ethical issues in case management. In F. Chan, M. Leahy, & J. Saunders (Eds.), *Case management for rehabilitation health professionals* (2nd ed., pp. 144–175).Osage Beach, MO: Aspen Professional Services.

Threats, T. (2002). Evidence based practice research using the WHO framework. *Journal of Medical Speech-Language Pathology, 10,* xvii–xxiv.

Threats, T. (2003). The framework for ASHA's revised scope of practice in speech-language pathology. *Speech Pathology Online.* Retrieved June 6, 2003, from www.speechpathology.com

Threats, T. T., & Worrall, L. (2004). Classifying communication disability using the ICF. *Advances in Speech-Language Pathology, 6,* 53–62.

Ueda, S., & Okawa, Y. (2003). The subjective dimension of functioning and disability: What is it and what is it for? *Disability and Rehabilitation, 25,* 596–601.

United Nations Department of Public Information [UNDPI] (1993). *The standard rules on the equalization of opportunities for persons with disabilities.* Adopted by the United Nations General Assembly, 48th session, resolution 48/96, annex, of 20 December 1993.

U.S. Department of Health and Human Services. (2000). *Healthy people 2010.* Washington, DC: U.S. Department of Health and Human Services.

Üstün, T. B., Ayuso-Mateos, J. L., Chatterji, S., Mathers, C., & Murray, C. J. L. (2004). Global burden of depressive disorders in the year 2000. *The British Journal of Psychiatry, 184,* 386–392.

Üstün, T. B., Chatterji, S., Bickenbach, J., Kostanjsek, N., & Schneider, M. (2003). International Classification of Functioning, Disability and Health: A new tool for understanding disability and health. *Disability and Rehabilitation, 25,* 565–571.

Vaccarino, V., Kaal, S. V., Abramson, J., & Krumholz, H. M. (2001). Depressive symptoms and risk of functional decline and death in patients with heart failure. *Journal of the American College of Cardiology, 38,* 199–205.

Vanleit, B. (2008). Using the ICF to address needs of people with disabilities in international development: Cambodian case study. *Disability and Rehabilitation, 30,* 991–998.

Velozo, C. A. (2005, June). *Tutorial: Developing measures based on the ICF.* Symposium conducted at the meeting of the World Health Organization's North American Collaborating Center, Mayo Clinic, Rochester, MN.

Wang, P. S., Simon, G., & Kessler, R. C. (2003). The economic burden of depression and the cost-effectiveness of treatment. *International Journal of Methods in Psychiatric Research, 12*, 22–33.

Weigl, M., Cieza, A., Andersen, A., Kollerits, B., Amann, E., Fussl, M., et al. (2004). Identification of the most relevant ICF categories in patients with chronic health conditions: A Delphi exercise. *Journal of Rehabilitation Medicine, 36*(Suppl. 44), 12–21.

Weigl, M., Cieza, A., Kostanjsek, N., Kirschneck, M., & Stucki, G. (2006). The ICF comprehensively covers the spectrum of health problems encountered by health professionals in patients with musculoskeletal conditions. *Rheumatology, 45*, 1247–1254.

Whalley, D., & McKenna, S. P. (1995). Measuring quality of life in patients with depression or anxiety. *Pharmacoeconomics, 8*, 305–315.

Widiger, T. A., & Trull, T. J. (2007). Plate tectonics in the classification of personality disorder. *American Psychologist, 62*, 71–83.

Wiggins, J. S. (Ed.). (1996). *The five-factor model of personality: Theoretical perspectives.* New York: Guilford Press.

Wildner, M., Quittan, M., Portenier, L., Wilke, S., Boldt, C., Stucki, G., et al. (2005). Core Set for patients with cardiopulmonary conditions in early post-acute rehabilitation facilities. *Disability and Rehabilitation, 27*, 397–404.

Wilson, G. T., Wilfley, D. E., Agras, W. S., & Bryson, S. W. (2010). Psychological treatments of binge eating disorder. *Archives of General Psychiatry, 67*, 94–101.

Winters, E. E., & Bowers, A. M. (Eds.). (1957). *Psychobiology: A science of man.* Springfield, IL: Charles C Thomas.

Wittchen, H. U., Holsboer, F., & Jacobi, F. (2001). Met and unmet needs in the management of depressive disorder in the community and primary care: The size and breadth of the problem. *Journal of Clinical Psychiatry, 62*(Suppl. 26), 23–28.

World Health Organization. (1980). *International Classification of Impairments, Disabilities, and Handicaps (ICIDH).* Geneva, Switzerland: Author.

World Health Organization. (1992). *International Statistical Classification of Diseases and Related Health Problems, tenth revision (ICD-10).* Geneva, Switzerland: Author.

World Health Organization. (1999). *ICIDH-2: International Classification System of Functioning and Disability; Beta-2 draft, Short Version.* Geneva, Switzerland: Author.

World Health Organization. (2001a). *International Classification of Functioning, Disability and Health: ICF.* Geneva, Switzerland: Author.

World Health Organization. (2001b). *World Health Report 2001. Mental health: New understanding, new hope.* Geneva, Switzerland: World Health Organization.

World Health Organization. (2002). *Innovative care for chronic conditions: Building blocks for action.* Geneva, Switzerland: Author.

World Health Organization. (2004). *The World Health Report 2004: Changing History, Annex Table 3: Burden of disease in DALYs by cause, sex, and mortality stratum in WHO regions, estimates for 2002.* Geneva, Switzerland: Author.

Wright, G. N. (1980). *Total rehabilitation.* Boston: Little, Brown and Company.

Wright, B. A. (1983). *Physical disability: A psychosocial approach* (2nd ed.). New York: Harper & Row.

Index